What Is She Like?

A new series of books from Cassell's Sexual Politics list, Women on Women *provides a forum for lesbian, bisexual and heterosexual women to explore and debate contemporary issues and to develop strategies for the advancement of feminist culture and politics into the next century.*

COMMISSIONING:
Roz Hopkins
Liz Gibbs
Christina Ruse

What Is She Like?

Lesbian Identities from the 1950s to the 1990s

Rosa Ainley

CASSELL

Cassell
Wellington House, 125 Strand, London WC2R 0BB

215 Park Avenue South, New York, NY 10003

First published 1995

**British Library Cataloguing-in-Publication
Data**
A catalogue record for this book is available from the
British Library.

ISBN   0–304–32898–7 (hardback)
       0–304–32900–2 (paperback)

Typeset by York House Typographic Ltd, London
Printed and bound in Great Britain by Biddles
Limited, Guildford and King's Lynn

contents

acknowledgements

big thank you to all interviewees and all those without whom, etc.

1 *introduction*

The lesbian is a very elusive creature – she burrows underground in her fear of identification. The Ladder, October 1956

Lesbian chic marries suffragette with supermodel and catches the zeitgeist. Joanna Briscoe, *Sunday Times*, 5 June 1994

From an era when the riotous demanded a whole new world with menaces, it's hard to downscale an epic fantasy to the level of a shopping and fucking novel. Paula Graham, *Diva*, no. 1, April 1994

I thought, 'I must be what they call a lesbian. ... I'm going to be tall and have crinkly hair.' Siobhan, *Daring Hearts*[1]

The popular image of the lesbian has moved from the manly, riding-crop-wielding Radclyffe Hall type, through the dungareed man-hating feminist to designer dykes and leather girls. Lesbianism has a new non-transgressive image in the media, and the lesbian world is doing its damnedest to fight off any smudges of feminism and aim for a sexuality as outlawish as that of gay men.

Queer identities, and the idea of developing and inclusive sexualities, have gained currency. What does this mean for lesbians, for whom fixed sexuality was the dominant philosophy until recently? Is there anything intrinsic to the notion of lesbianism, anything which has remained unchanged in the last forty years? What are the variables? Can there be any broad agreement about what it means to be a lesbian?

These are the questions, and *What Is She Like?* explores them broadly in the timespan from the 1950s to the 1990s, but gives no straight answers.

As Stuart Hall writes, 'Perhaps instead of thinking of identity as an already accomplished fact, ... we should think, instead of identity as a "production" which is never complete, as always in process, and always constituted within, not outside representation.'[2] I make no claim to any spurious notion of representativeness. Instead, my use of oral history interviews is a way of giving validity to personal experience in all its detail.

> Oral history widens the focus of history and narrows it ... allows many stories and versions to be heard and begins to question on a small scale how life was perceived and lived. It is a history which opposes the idea of the past as seamless 'heritage', one we can be nostalgic or romantic about. A lesbian oral history, especially, aims to deal with all that is ambiguous, troublesome, chaotic.[3]

In choosing this method to uncover the attitudes of lesbians to their own lives, I hoped not only to add to the important project of preserving the lesbian and gay history which the world prefers to hide. I also aimed to unravel some of the meanings behind the labels which have been stuck on lesbians, and the labels which we have chosen for ourselves.

Granted, some lesbians have no interest in the flurry of new-fangled labels – a dyke is a dyke is a dyke. But labels have always been used about us, from 'variants', 'inverts' and 'third sex' onwards. The words we ourselves use to describe our sexuality depend on where we come from and when we came out, but are part of a broader subcultural language. The importance of this – as seen in Polari, a language evolved and used mainly by gay men in the 1950s and 1960s – cannot be overemphasized. These uses of language fulfil a need to describe experience which would otherwise be ignored or distorted.

Since the purpose is to define our lives in our own terms, these terms are not always welcome when used by heterosexuals. Words which lesbians have reclaimed, such as 'dyke', are still used as insults. We may use some words amongst ourselves but not in conversation with others. Many of the women I interviewed, who had a variety of reasons why they preferred certain words to define their lesbianism, told me that it was not acceptable for straight people to use the same words.

Lesbians still suffer from popular use of terms coined by sexologists over fifty years ago, as they attempted to describe, define, categorize and contain. The current media labels are evidence of the mainstream's continuing need for lesbians to be easily defined. In rejecting such stereotypes, women may be forced to question those identities and so question whether they are inside or outside the 'community'.

It would seem, then, that leaping into a series of boxes, whether self-defined or imposed, is no progress. Certainly this book is not an attempt to match women to labels. But neither is there progress in an outlook which refuses to see difference. 'The social and psychological construction of identities is an ongoing process, one which defies any notion of essential or static determinants. Identities are never fixed, are complex, differentiated and are constantly repositioned.'[4]

The essentialist approach – which aims to define who lesbians are, how they are, why they are – is double-edged, as many interviewees commented. We need to know who and what we are for the sake of recognition, safety and solidarity, and yet we know how damaging that approach has been in our history, not only through sexology but also, in a very different way, through feminism.

I advertised for interviewees in the gay press, through youth groups, pensioners' groups, gay history groups, social groups, adult education centres, libraries, in newsletters, union journals, and reading groups. The ad read:

> What are you like?
> Looking for lesbians who'd be happy to be interviewed for a book on lesbian identity from the 1950s to 1990s. Old/young, scene, closets, queergirls, clubbers, designer dykes, lesbian feminists, romantic friends, sexual outlaws, politicos – I want to talk to you.

The response was enormous – far greater in numbers and wider in geography than I had resources to cover. Lesbian history has been hidden and ignored, as have the voices of individual lesbians. The exceptions have been a few women whose class background accommodated their lesbianism. Recording lesbians' lives and piecing together a lesbian history is an important project. There is a need for a national lesbian oral history project, but it is not the work of this book. We have assumed our validity, regardless of the gaps in our history, and are looking instead at the construction of our identity within its varied contexts. This is my focus.

I did not aim for the impossible: representing every shade of lesbian opinion. But I was concerned to interview women across the spectra of class, race and age, so that they could talk about a range of different experiences spread over the whole period covered by the book. Where I wished to include a particular experience or group, I took steps to find appropriate women. Nevertheless, this way of working will always leave 'gaps'.

Resources for research into the lives of contemporary lesbians are all around, given the media deluge of 1993/94. It is not so easy to find documentation of lesbian lives from earlier decades, or women who are prepared to come out on paper. Secrecy was part of the life and, for many women, still is. The following resources were extremely valuable: the Hall Carpenter Archive at the National Sound Archive (which houses the taped interview material), and at the LSE (which manages the print collection of magazines, leaflets and other ephemera); the Lesbian Archive; the Feminist Library.

Although my aim was to meet and interview women, some of my respondents did not want to be interviewed, or lived too far from me for this to be possible. In these cases I offered the option of communicating in writing. However, the difference in the resulting material was too evident, and I have chosen not to use it. Although the intrusion of the tape machine had some effect on the interviews, self-censorship and concerns about style and structure were more palpable in the written responses, and interfered in the telling. The advantages of the oral history interview are described in *Inventing Ourselves*:

> The interviews are now read, but they were spoken. The oral history interview encourages first-hand accounts, impressions, feelings, and the recording of experienced events over opinion and analysis. While the interviews are structured – and then further structured through editing – there is not an opportunity for the distance and reworking possible in written accounts.[5]

So that the interviewees did not lose all control of the material, I gave them the opportunity to veto passages which they did not want in print, and the option to use a pseudonym. I was generally impressed by the openness with which my tape machine and I were received.

There were some women who made contact with me and then did not return my messages, so that I was unable to interview them. I am interested in their reasons but can only guess that they changed their minds, got cold feet, were fickle or too busy, or did not like the sound of the project, or of me.

I interviewed some thirty women, for up to three hours each. In some cases I had met the woman beforehand. I produced a list of questions in order to ask women about the same areas of their lives, and also to give the interviewees an idea of the sort of information I wanted (see Appendix). The questions were based around some broad areas which have been central to lesbian existence. These included visibility, fashion, leisure, butch and femme, sex, and feminism. The questions were not intended as an end in themselves, but as springboards to women talking about various aspects of their lives. Some women made their own tapes, which proved very successful.

I was interested in why women felt motivated to answer my advert, give up time to meet me and spend a couple of hours being interviewed. When I asked, the reason given was always the importance of telling the story – each woman's own story and its part in the wider narrative of lesbian life, which they all felt was too seldom heard.

This book cannot only be about the ways in which lesbians see themselves. Although most of society might wish otherwise, and whatever our own positions on assimilation, we are part of society, reflecting and informing its mores. Stuart Hall says:

> [Identity is] a matter of 'becoming' as well as of 'being'. It belongs to the future as much as to the past. It is not something which already exists, transcending place, time, history and culture. Cultural identities come from somewhere, have histories. But like everything which is historical, they undergo constant transformation. Far from being eternally fixed in some essentialised past, they are subject to the continuous 'play' of history, culture and power.[6]

But not everyone is of the same opinion: commentators disagree about this as much as we do amongst ourselves. Dorothy Allison comments that even as part of a minority culture you are shaped by that hegemony of the majority or your resistance to it[7], while Elaine Axton asserts in *Shebang* that lesbians invent themselves, socially, sexually and sartorially[8]. What others think – as commentators of their own lives – follows.

Questions of identity have always defined and divided lesbians. Butch and femme, lesbian feminist and straight dyke, lifelong and more recent lesbians, SM and vanilla . . . these are a few well-documented divisions. Lillian Faderman identifies a major conundrum in her well-worn quote, that although 'Butch-and-fem were "politically incorrect" in the lesbian-feminist community, everyone looked butch.'[9]

Beyond the stereotypes are a host of other looks, and none. Many lesbians have congregated in major cities, where they can be both more visible in their lifestyles and more anonymous. Outside these cities, most lesbians probably look like the heterosexual women around them and pursue similar lives to theirs. Yet the majority of the population still views lesbianism with sheer horror. These people are often unaware of knowing any lesbians, and form their views from the media. Until recently, the media's interest in lesbians only involved warnings to lock up your wives and daughters, and occasional stories of violent relationships and other outrages. The horrified reactions of the wider population have serious effects on the lives of lesbians.

Although some lesbians living outside the major towns are cushioned by progressive workplaces and high salaries, the rest lead very different lives from the cool subcultural existence portrayed in the daily papers.

These women may live in heterosexual marriages, often isolated, closeted by necessity and habit. Their concerns are different from the subcultural urban lesbian. Whatever her circumstances, the urban lesbian has the comfort of knowing the scene is there, whether or not she chooses or is able to enter it. The meaning and interpretation of identity is shaped by cultural, social, political and historical events.

> Instead of a singular, universal essence, a true lesbian-ness, our lesbian identity is always differentiated, constituting a group of identities which only resemble one another. There is always this differentiation because the lesbian space, like any other space, is never purified of difference. For example, a lesbian-ness is not first a true lesbian-ness which later acquires a particular race or class externality. Like any other identity, the only lesbian identities which we can have are identities which have meaning in specific contexts, the specific configurations of multiple codes. (Con-)texts of lesbians: the meaning of lesbian-ness for the black DJ at a South London nightclub is not exactly the same as its meaning for the single mother in the dole queue in Belfast is not exactly the same as its meaning for the closeted Oxford graduate in the City is not exactly same as its meaning for the American sex trade worker in London's Soho, even if each of these individuals identifies as a lesbian.[10]

The lesbian and gay movement has had an effect on the identities which people adopt when they come out. They no longer need to position themselves in defiance to the mainstream, as many did in the past. The changes in family patterns and societal norms in western post-industrial society have also had an influence. The depoliticization of the Thatcher years, hailed by her in the famous quote 'There is no such thing as society', has caused many people to turn in on themselves, a reaction which has been used to explain the demise of feminism. Many now feel that the only changes they can make are to their own images.

For many women, coming out to family, friends, work colleagues and neighbours is still problematic or impossible. Lesbians with children risk being branded unfit mothers and losing the children in custody battles. For young women, information about sexuality which was available in schools has been curtailed and funding for youth groups cut. Older women and women with disabilities, who are often treated as asexual, may fear coming out to families and carers in case this affects the support they need. Several older women told me their lesbian identity was one of non-existence: 'What it is to be a lesbian is my unconscious doing terrible things and not letting me enter the real world.' (Alice, see Chapter 5.)

Meanwhile, after decades of legislative, social and media invisibility, lesbians have suddenly become news. This is partly due to the fact that various famous women have come out or are thought to be lesbians. It is doubtful whether the wider population has taken much note of models like Jenny Shimouzi, or music business figures like Me'Shell N'DegéOcello and Fem 2 Fem. It is only someone of the stature of kd lang who will have penetrated the public imagination sufficiently, and her wide attraction must be largely attributable to her androgynous looks. Seeing her may move people to a realization that not all lesbians are ugly and butch, but it may also reinforce ideas of lesbian androgyny. Those have been the choices: visible lesbians have to be either butch or androgynous.

Similarly, consider the inches of copy that were devoted to journalistic expressions of surprise that Judy Nelson, Martina Navratilova's ex-lover, looked like 'a Texan housewife', i.e. feminine, curly-haired, make-up-wearing and attractive. Martina herself is from eastern Europe, and a sportswoman as well as a lesbian. These constitute disadvantages so severe to make it a cruelty to assess her looks on the same scale as other women. Media stars, including Madonna and Shirley Conran, have been positively queuing to tell all about their lesbian experiences, as distinct from a lesbian life.

Questions about visibility, lesbian chic, assimilation, feminism and new lesbian images have been brought to the fore in comedy. Lea De Laria and Donna McPhail, two of the highlights of the growing lesbian comedy circuit, both appeared at the Edinburgh Festival in 1993. In the summer of 1994, McPhail appeared on *Have I Got News for You*? She has made coming out part of her act, and also wrote a column in *Shebang* about young lesbians in clubs wearing black lacy bras and enjoying themselves. 'How can we expect to be taken seriously when we all go around having fun? I distinctly saw women laughing. Don't they know that we're hideously oppressed?'[11] De Laria, whose whole show is about lesbian identity, thunders against lesbian chic: 'If being a lesbian is so chic, then why do they find the femmiest-looking girls and slap a little lipstick on them?' In this way she beats the mainstream to the backlash. Interestingly, the gay press was initially lukewarm about her. An article in the *Observer* attributed this to her outrageous behaviour.[12] Lea herself suggested it was to do with the assimilationist's fear of exposure, of someone blowing the carefully built-up fiction that lesbians and gays are no different from anyone else. 'But if we're just like everyone else, why have they been kicking us around for the last million years?' She pleads: 'Madonna is held up as the last word in lesbian chic: can't we please have a lesbian to be an example of lesbian chic?' De Laria enjoys presenting herself as the antithesis of lesbian chic, although she is a much fêted sign of the times.

During the summer of 1993 it seemed as though the legal invisibility of lesbians was about to be blown, with the assault on single mothers, the gay gene 'research', and changes in adoption rules and income support. Along with less recent events, such as the Warnock report, these developments seemed to augur an impending crackdown. The very fact that lesbians are mentioned in these reports is a major change. But there is nothing new behind the thinking that lesbians are unnatural, unfit to have or look after children at home or at work, and probably the result of an unfortunate slip of the DNA.

And yet, as far back as 1991, there were high-street posters of women kissing women (from Pop Against Homophobia) and even a Volvo billboard of women holding hands, which, at the very least, manifested an image of loving friendship. Between 1991 and 1993, the occasional article featuring lesbians, in women's magazines such as *Elle*, *Marie Claire* and *Cosmopolitan*, became a flood.

Articles have appeared in the *Evening Standard*, *Sunday Telegraph*, *Sunday Times*, *Sunday Mirror* and *Harpers and Queen*, as well as less surprisingly the *Independent*, *Company* and *New Woman*. The *Sun* has also cast its poisonous eye on lesbianism, shrieking that, now that lesbian chic has arrived, They're more dangerous than ever because you can't tell who They are. Fem 2 Fem appeared in *Playboy*. (Whether this is the ultimate entryist act or the ultimate sellout to male wank fantasies depends on where you are standing.) The *Sunday Mirror*[13] carried a sex survey which posed questions to women readers on fantasizing about sex with women, and assured them that attraction to women was natural. *Company*[14] concentrated on how good lesbian sex is, and stressed that the interviewees liked men. It also covered the difficulties of coming out – your straight friends dropping you, and your mother thinking it's a phase. The article was illustrated with a winsome photograph of a back view of a woman wearing a red lacy body, looking at herself in the mirror. This would not have looked out of place elsewhere in the magazine.

The right-wing London *Evening Standard* seemed in the summer of 1993 to have launched a series, all featuring new lesbian chic, one of which was advertised on the front page which must mean the paper saw it as a selling point. One wonders who had the groundbreaking revelation that lesbians are also commuters and newspaper buyers. In an interview with customers of the now defunct Dykes Delight lesbian sauna in Covent Garden, one woman was quoted as saying, 'Did you know that many of the strippers in Soho are lesbian? Lots of models are lesbian too'.[15] This is hardly news for lesbians, but may well be shockingly educational for the *Standard*'s readership, who are presumably more used to thinking of strippers and models as the acme of desirable femaleness, and, therefore, incontrovertibly straight and available.

In the same article, lesbians have apparently reached 'a whole new level of fashionable acceptability', and are 'just as likely to be wearing Nicole Farhi as Doctor Martens'. It is not only our fashion attitude which has improved, but also our sense of humour problem, 'in marked contrast to the sad belligerence that is still such a feature of male homosexuality'. It is not so long since gay men were witty, creative, fashionable, artistic funsters, while lesbians were belligerent, humourless, man-hating, hairy and ugly. What have lesbians done to deserve all this, apart from a small number discovering the joys of expensive clothes? And what have gay men done? Think politics, noise, AIDS, ACT UP and OutRage! Think also no more women's movement.

The Nicole Farhi comment is not just about a preference for a certain style. To shop there, a lesbian must acquire money from a job or a sugar mummy, and a certain age. Celia Kitzinger, quoted in the same article, to provide the voice of lesbianism past (and of reason), said, 'It's very glamorising, so it means that people don't have to deal with oppression.' The issue of *Vanity Fair* which featured k.d. lang and Cindy Crawford on the cover (pop star and supermodel, a photoshoot made in heaven) apparently leapt off the newsagents' racks. This provided another indication of the new fashionable acceptability. Lesbianism as an identity has become safe – even attractive – but on a superficial level. For lesbians who are not beautiful, talented, rich or famous, it is not so cool to be queer. Another view comes from Justine, the main character in Elizabeth Wilson's futuristic *The Lost Time Café*, as she sulkily fends off an attempt to define and label her: 'Isn't everyone just queer these days? Trying to redefine deviance, make it less predictable.'[16] Perhaps this will be the next stage.

While most UK commentators and lesbians agree that lesbian chic is a fairly empty marketing exercise, which does nothing to improve the lives of those outside the Lavender Lolly market, the situation is slightly different in the USA. It is quite a challenge to name a famous out dyke from the UK. In the States, they range from politicians to entertainers, editors to sportswomen. They have the limelight and they have power, not just good fashion sense.

Until the mid/late 1980s, the definition of 'lesbian' was usually con-flated with 'feminist'. For some women, the two continue to be inextricably linked. Other women saw the two as much more separate, or always saw feminism as an irrelevance, or as an embodiment of white middle-class values – which it largely was. It is fashionable in many lesbian circles to deride the notion of oppression, which was once central to feminist argument. Yet little has changed for most women, despite media claims to the contrary. Oppression is just called by different names. The advent of the designer dyke has been instrumental here – if dykes are fashionable and successful then, of course, they are not oppressed.

When the *Evening Standard* comes out with, 'Lesbian women [sic] have stopped fighting their battle to be treated like men, but have won the war to be accepted as women,'[17] the subtext is, 'Phew: non-threatening, lipstick-wearing, depilating lesbians.' Femmes and kikis are in the ascend-ant, media darlings at last. The *Pink Paper* suggested that this interest from the mainstream press, during the summer of 1993, was due to the media's silly season – an unusually negative attitude for the *Pink*.

This 1969 quote from *Titbits* shows how much movement there has been in press coverage: 'In the final part of our investigation into these misfits in the twilight of a hostile world we tell why women turn to lesbianism. And what can be done to help them.' In the same article the Albany Trust is described as 'a charitable foundation which aims to help women at odds with society'. Consider too the definition of purpose of the Daughters of Bilitis, a lesbian organization in the USA, in the first issue in October 1956 of its journal, *The Ladder*:

> Promoting the integration of the homosexual into society by:
> 1) education of the variant
> 2) education of the public

3) participation in research
4) investigation of the penal code.

There is certainly no reason to imagine that the change in press coverage is caused by a broadening of tolerance and understanding from the public at large.

Every time a survey of social attitudes appears, liberalization seems to have tempered every opinion except those relating to lesbians and gay men. Those responses still run along the lines of 'unnatural, plague carrying and dangerous to children'. One factor which could be influencing the tenor of press coverage is that some of the large number of women who came out during the 1970s and 1980s second wave of feminism are working in the media in positions of authority and influence.

This new visibility is not only evident in the print media. Late in 1993, two television soap operas took up lesbian story-lines, joined by another two in 1994. *Emmerdale* involved a woman who had previously been through all the men in the village (just to make sure?) and went on to 'come to terms with her lesbianism', as *Time Out* put it. In *Brookside* (which had already caused a million lesbians to sigh over the characters of Heather Haversham and Sheila Grant) Margaret got off with Beth, who moved on to an affair with her lecturer. Beth firmly denied to her mother that her previous bad experiences with men had caused her to go out with women. On *Eastenders*, the trendy Della and Binnie became an item, and it was the homophobic Natalie – not them – who got the bad press. *Brookside* then went further by uncovering the lesbian past of Jean Crosby – upright wife of forty years to the insufferable David – as a counterpoint to all these youthful lesbians. On the downside, Roseanne Barr, having battled with the network to ensure screening, gets to kiss Mariel Hemingway in a lesbian bar, and then wipes her mouth. Still, all the characters are popular, attractive women, and we need as many portrayals as possible. Unfortunately, the entrance of lesbian characters has been matched by the departure of gay male characters from the soaps, probably caused by the media's attitude to AIDS.

Lesbians have not all transformed into media-acceptable designer dykes. There is now a range of lesbian identities, in which one might say the only constant was sex with women, if it were not for the lesbians who sleep with men. Some see being a lesbian as an identity, in a similar way to ethnic identity. Others believe it is part of every unconscious. Still others see lesbianism purely as a matter of sexual preference. This represents the acme of assimilationism to lesbians whose sexuality is a political choice and who want to be seen as a threat to straight society. There is no clear aim which is universal to all lesbians. As radical gay and queer sexuality take centre stage, transgression is all, and this must have a further effect on how 'lesbian' is defined.

The scope of *What Is She Like*? involves massive changes to society. There have been many attempts to define each decade by its behaviour, although none of them can be strictly accurate. Edmund White's is a specifically gay perspective : 'To have been oppressed as a gay in the 50s, liberated in the 60s, exalted in the 70s and wiped out in the 80s was a very quick cycle.'[18] Cherry Smyth's *Queer Notions* takes a lesbian perspective : the queer 1950s, lesbian 1960s and feminist 1970s.[19] She sensibly declines to label the 1980s, which might equally be the designer decade or the decade of backbiting, implosion, or sexual rediscovery.

What Is She Like? begins in the repressive 1950s for which Elizabeth Wilson's shorthand in *Hallucinations* was: back in the home, Cold War, and Teds.[20] And what will we call this decade? The Queer 1990s? The lesbian chic 1990s? The *fin de siècle* period has often coincided with a time of sexual libertarianism and experimentation: the signs point towards the end of the twentieth century being the turn of the dyke. It's too early to say where we will go, but this book charts some of the places we have been, and some of the places we are now.

NOTES

1.   Brighton Ourstory Project, *Daring Hearts*, 1992.
2.   Stuart Hall, 'Cultural identity and diaspora', in J. Rutherford (ed.), *Identity: Community Culture Difference*, Lawrence and Wishart, 1990, p. 222.
3.   Hall Carpenter Archives/Lesbian Oral History Group, *Inventing Ourselves*, Routledge, 1989, p. 1.
4.   Pratibha Parmar, 'Black feminism: the politics of articulation', in *Identity: Community Culture Difference*, p. 85.
5.   Hall Carpenter Archives/Lesbian Oral History Group, *Inventing Ourselves*, p. 3.
6.   Stuart Hall, *Identity: Community Culture Difference*, p. 225.
7.   Dorothy Allison, 'A question of class', in Arlene Stein (ed.), *Sexperts, Sisters, Queers: Beyond the Lesbian Nation*, Plume, 1993, p. 136.
8.   Elaine Axton, 'Radical cheek', *Shebang*, no. 2, February 1993, p. 15.
9.   Lillian Faderman, *Odd Girls and Twilight Lovers*, Penguin, 1992, p. 223.
10. Anna Marie Smith, 'Which one's the pretender?', in Tessa Boffin and Jean Fraser (eds), *Stolen Glances: Lesbians Take Photographs*, Pandora, 1991, p. 130.
11. Donna McPhail, in *Shebang*, no. 2, February 1993.

12. Peter Guttridge. 'Lesbian chic is a joke', *Observer*, 8 July 1993.
13. 'Sex survey of 90s women', *Sunday Mirror*, 28 November 1993.
14. Jan Jensen, 'Women who leave men for other women', *Company*, August 1993.
15. 'Tutu', quoted in Isabel Wolff, 'The sauna where London's lesbians take the plunge', *Evening Standard*, 1 June 1993.
16. Elizabeth Wilson, *The Lost Time Café*, Virago, 1993, p. 94.
17. Louise Guinness, 'The love that has learned to laugh', *Evening Standard*, 6 July 1993.
18. Edmund White, quoted in Neroli Lawson, 'Symphony of survival', *Evening Standard*, 1 December 1993.
19. Cherry Smyth, *Lesbians Talk . . . Queer Notions*, Scarlet, 1992, p. 14.
20. Elizabeth Wilson, 'Memoirs of an anti-heroine', *Hallucinations*, Radius, 1989, p. 5.

2
history and sexology
definitions, legislation and popular notions

Current lesbian identity is a temporary mirage.
Suzanne Neild and Rosalind Pearson[1]

I read a friend's copy of Krafft-Ebing and realized that I fitted his description of a lesbian so well that I might just be lucky enough to be one. **Nicole, *What a Lesbian Looks Like*[2]**

Lesbianism is a condition not a career.
***Arena3*, volume 1, number 9, September 1964**

I started looking for psychiatric help – not about being a lesbian, because I didn't know I was, but about not being an actual existing person. But of course now I see the two are incredibly, intimately linked.

Rosanna Hibbert[3]

You got a lot to answer for girl
I never met a man like you before
they say
Get a razor or find a cure   **Sister George**[4]

In this brief look at the ideas of some of the main sexologists whose work on sexuality and the causes of lesbianism has, in popularized form, formed the basis of public opinion, I want to look at legislation and popular notions and how they are still informed by work that appeared almost a century ago. Science has generally defined lesbian desire in terms of pathological deviation. It is also worth pointing out that newer research often goes no further in terms of radicalism.

Radclyffe Hall's *The Well of Loneliness*[5] is dedicated 'To our Three Selves'. Stephen was characterized as a member of the third sex, an invert, born not made, aristocratic, highly strung. An invert's physical characteristics are predetermined: tall, broad-shouldered, handsome, muscular, large hands and feet, with a unique dual vision that combines the male and female perceptions. Inversion being congenital it follows that inverts are natural, that is, following their own, predetermined, nature. Therefore it is wrong and unchristian to condemn 'them' as 'unnatural'. Today all too many Christians suffer from the belief that lesbians can be saved, presumably thinking perversion is a chosen rather than a given vice. This kind of essentialism has prevailed in many circles, and perhaps still does in the pressure to name yourself through your sexual identity. Those who decline to do so are seen as strange and suspect even in the Queer 1990s.

In her introduction to *The Well of Loneliness*,[6] Alison Hennegan writes, 'It's almost impossible now to determine whether the "men of science" created theories which inverts then tried to fit or whether inverts revealed to the scientists theories which they themselves had formulated. Certainly it was a two-way traffic.' Some sixty years after the book was written, is there still a two-way traffic? Hennegan notes that the debates about real lesbians and real women which take place in the book are still running. They are also, in a sense, the underlying idea for this book.

For most lesbians, Havelock Ellis is probably best known as the author of these much-quoted lines: 'masculine straightforwardness ... a decided taste and toleration for cigars ... nothing of that sexual shyness and engaging air of weakness and dependence which are an invitation to men'.[7] *The Well of Loneliness*, which was for many women their first book about lesbians, expounded Ellis's ideas about lesbianism in its characterization, and he contributed a foreword to it. He is also, along with Freud, Krafft-Ebing and Edmund Carpenter, one of the main architects of attitudes to homosexuality and lesbianism of this century, and popular influences have long lives.

Although Ellis went to some lengths in his work to point out that male homosexuals were not effeminate, he went to similar lengths to stress that lesbians were masculine, emphasizing the stereotype rather than undermining it. In this he was led by his belief in masculine sexuality as essentially active and feminine sexuality as asserted through the male. Without a radical reworking of his ideas, he was bound to see lesbianism as a masculinity in women.

Ellis suggested that while female orgasm did exist, it had the function of facilitating procreation, rather than giving sexual pleasure. He believed (without evidence) that most lesbians used dildos and gave little attention to clitoral sexuality. His *Studies in the Psychology of Sex*[8] used only six lesbian case histories: friends and his wife. It is difficult to avoid the conclusion that the paucity of information about lesbian sexuality in his work may not be due only to the difficulties of research, but also to embarrassment at his own wife's lesbianism. Ellis only devoted one chapter entirely to lesbianism, contrary to his claims to give much attention to the subject. Ellis's own sexual tastes ran to watching women piss, which he called 'urolognia' or 'undinism'. This perhaps contributed to his awareness of the diversity of sexual drives and the importance of securing acceptance by society.

This insistence on diversity, and Ellis's belief that the homosexual had always existed, led to a common liberal defence. It is a defence which was repeated in 1994 in support of lowering the age of consent for men. He drew a distinction between 'homosexuality' (any physical relationship between people of the same sex) and 'inversion' which he saw as congenital. This was of course open to the interpretation that inverts couldn't help it while the others, perverts, could. His concern to emphasize the ordinariness of homosexuality paved the way for the imposition of new and restrictive standards of behaviour (for instance behaving in a suitably masculine way). This ideology, though tolerant and liberal, still posits that homosexual behaviour is deviant. It has had supporters ever since, in those who recommend that certain sorts of behaviour will lead to acceptance and assimilation. Ellis's biological determinism was mixed with a freedom from blame, and even a degree of sensitivity. With all its limitations, such discourse began to normalize difference and homosexuality became possible in its modern form.

This approach of 'no problem – no cure necessary' differs substantially from Freud who did not concentrate on inversion in his work, but, coming from a psychological perspective, did see the possibility of a cure. More biological than Freud, Ellis also disagreed with his theory of the bisexual primary state. Freud's theories took more account of the influences of environmental difference that could lead to changes in sexual roles and behaviour. Until the 1930s discussion about lesbianism in Britain was based in the physiological terms endorsed by Ellis, rather than the psychological ones of Freud.

Krafft-Ebing was another contributor, along with Havelock Ellis, to the establishment of the medical model of homosexuality. An Austrian psychiatrist, he compiled a massive collection of 'case histories' in *Psycho-pathia Sexualis*,[9] proposing a genetic explanation. His pejorative views of lesbians focused on differences in physical form, although he failed to find any physiological differences. He explained lesbians who had been pre-viously heterosexual by suggesting an underlying congenital base, precipitated into action through catalysts such as excessive masturbation, or attendance at all-girls boarding schools. He saw characteristic dress, mannerisms and roles as suspicious signs.

There have been too many attempts to categorize and measure, in a pseudo-scientific/medical way, the characteristics of sections of the pop-ulation which society deems unacceptable, for me to go into detail about them all – the criminal's brow, the black person's brain size and shape – and lesbian and gay people have not been immune from this. The perceived signs of the homosexual sickness included skull shape, cerebral characteristics, features of the face and body. Photography has long been used by doctors and police to evidence criminal or pathological tenden-cies. And, as noted in *Stolen Glances*,[10] this unfortunate use of documentary photography has risen again in relation to media use of photographs of people with AIDS: 'homosexuality = disease = death', an equation which then validates all sorts of irresponsible reporting, and further, continues to infect attitudes and behaviour.

J.A. Symonds and Edward Carpenter also wanted their work to help make homosexuality more accepted in general society, along with Have-lock Ellis, and in general their work sought to normalize homosexuality by playing down attributes that society found unacceptable. The approach, which attracts the same opprobrium as organizations such as Stonewall today, seeks to emphasize how similar homosexuals are to everyone else, apart from their unfortunate birthright. All of them contributed to the development of the theory that homosexuality was 'a congenital anomaly, a more or less harmless sexual variation'. This, they believed, was the way towards law reform and public tolerance, the 'sorry but not sick' (i.e. born that way and not curable) model. Inevitably this approach lacked any general challenge to gender and social roles, and so ultimately it failed to satisfy as a radical critique of sexual oppression.

Symonds's *A Problem in Greek Ethics*,[11] which became the basis of a section in Ellis's *Sexual Inversion*,[12] was probably the first serious work on homosexuality published in Britain. Not displaying much interest in lesbian love, Symonds, who believed in homosexuality being discoverable through various congenital signs such as he had himself experienced, aimed to establish that homosexuals could be accepted as a part of everyday life. His work, A *Problem in Modern Ethics*,[13] was the first to link such radical views with the possibility of legal changes. It was Symonds who pioneered the terms 'urning' and 'inversion'. A married man, he never questioned his own adherence to respectability and acceptable social roles. His own ambivalence about his work gave his family room to suppress it after his death, and it was mainly as a result of this that *Studies in the Psychology of Sex* appeared in Britain with only Ellis's name on it, despite their collaboration. Its first printing in English in 1897 led to a court case against the Legitimacy League (a society for sex reform) who stocked the book, and it was labelled scandalous and obscene. As often happens, the court case brought forth the benefit of dramatizing the issue.

Central to Edward Carpenter's argument about homosexuality is that sex is a pleasurable activity whose physical aspects are equally important as spiritual ones. He was also socialist, pro-feminist, an advocate of the outdoor life, rational dress and vegetarianism, all in all a key figure for pioneering socialists, although he lost friends when he set up house with his lover George Merrill. He coined the term 'homogenic passion' to describe the friendships he saw between feminists, which we might call sisterhood, and he believed there was a natural affinity between gay men and (straight) women.

Sheila Jeffreys suggests that sexologists' explanations of homosexuality in terms of innateness and psychology were welcomed by gay men because they undermined the argument about gay male behaviour being seen as criminal.[14] She attributes Ellis's insistence that dildos were widely used to his own fantasy: 'The use of dildos is likely to have been as rare between women in the nineteenth century as it is in lesbian practice today' – which may or may not be her own fantasy. Pre-nineteenth century, it was commonly thought that lesbians had enlarged clitorises that could be used to penetrate other women. A more innovative approach can be found in the *Virago Book of Fairy Tales*,[15] where there are two Icelandic stories about women who use a sealbone as a strap-on.

Charlotte Wolff [16] stressed that most lesbians are seen as wanting to be boys, in a book published as late as the 1970s. She quotes one of her interviewees: 'I am proud to be gay . . . I would not want to be heterosexual unless I were a man. The life of heterosexual women is hardly an existence.'

Karl Heinrich Ulrichs, a German lawyer and writer, proposed a theory of homosexual development of the brain which took place at embryo stage. More recently the gay gene theory has renamed this old concept. The idea of gays being born rather than made has not by any means disappeared. In 1993 scientists in the USA reported that they had discovered a gay gene that could be isolated, and, so the implication went, screened out. There is no concensus about this amongst lesbians and gays in the nature v. nurture argument, although social conditioning is generally seen as a factor in 'becoming' gay. The political and social implications of these findings are of great interest and importance to lesbians and gay men on any number of levels.

Simon Le Vay, the biologist whose research formed the basis of this renewed interest in the debate, was of the opinion that proof that homosexuality could be attributed to a structural pattern in the brain was a positive discovery for gay men. (Lesbians did not figure in this research.) It would, he believed, lead to an end to discrimination since homosexuality is then not a choice which can be penalized. During the few weeks when this was in the news there were many reports that other scientists thought the findings were inconclusive and problematic – certainly the numbers involved in the research were very low. Coming at a time when the reduction in the age of consent for gay men was about to be debated in the House of Commons, it meant greater publicity for the issues. While on some levels this was a good thing, it also resulted in a counter-attack along the lines that, since it had been scientifically proven that gayness amounted to a brain defect, gay men were freaks of nature.

There were some who argued as part of the debate that the age of consent should be lowered because homosexuality was a condition rather than a choice. But this was not considered to be the most radical approach, more a tactical attempt to appeal to the 'tolerant of unfortunates' mentality, as distinct from a civil rights/equalities issue. It did not escape notice that similar theories, widely held early this century, had certainly not stopped discrimination. The strategy did not work; the age of consent was lowered, but only to eighteen, still two years higher than that for heterosexuals. Fears were understandably fuelled about the possibility of aborting 'gay' foetuses which, in a homophobic society, could become the logical conclusion of this theory.

Those who were lesbians in the 1950s were far more likely than lesbians today to have been influenced by and to some extent have internalized the commonly held views promulgated by sexologists. There were, as I have outlined above, several sexologists who saw lesbianism as a congenital condition rather than a sexual or social identity. Freud saw lesbians as a lower stage of development, women who reject femininity, taking on instead masculine identification. Lacan's reading described lesbians as women who refuse to recognize castration: phallic lack being seen as the characteristic of femininity, a negative position. Charlotte Wolff considered lesbianism 'natural' but a tragic condition because it denied the possibility of procreation. Lesbianism as physical deformity; as psychological disease; as unnatural; as abnormal, neurotic, adolescent, inadequate, sad. Less likely these days to suffer from the institutions of psychological treatments to cure us of our sexuality, lesbians still suffer this kind of psychological and theoretical oppression.

The only freely available literature in the 1950s and 1960s did nothing to contradict or undermine this view, indeed it tended to confirm it luridly. Lillian Faderman notes how devastating the literary depiction of lesbianism must have been, both to lesbians and women who were considering lesbianism.[17] This is not to suggest that all who read the literature were taken in by those portrayals of parasitism, sickness and all-round evil which made up a substantial portion of the canon. But such books did have a pervasive message, even if one were confident enough to see through it, and there was nothing more positive to balance out such terrors. Even those authors who were more forward-thinking often had to temper their characterizations with sad endings. Otherwise they risked not getting into print, in a world where expressing anything more positive was seen as encouraging perversion, unless accompanied by a suitably moralistic message to the contrary.

Common in the first half of the century were vampire novels in which twilight lesbians sapped their victims' youth, beauty and energy as well as drinking their blood. Such grossly anti-lesbian tales provided an easily grasped metaphor for lesbians who prey viciously and mercilessly on other women, wreaking havoc in their ordered lives and leaving them spent and empty. Vampire novels are still popular among lesbians, and the vampires themselves are now seen as daringly sexually active (although safe sex is often also an issue), and bravely outside mainstream society.

In terms of legislation, lesbians are still outside the mainstream. As a Lesbian Line press release of the 1980s put it: 'Society prefers to close its eyes to the existence of lesbians. But this apparent indifference is not to be confused with acceptance.' Shere Hite comments 'Neither male nor female sexuality is limited by "genital geography", and it has been one of the greatest public relations victories of all time to convince us it was.'[18] If lesbians were seen as having an aggressive sexuality, in the way gay men are seen, we would be perceived as much more of a threat than we are and probably be legislated against in the same way as gay men have been. 'A lesbian has a more gradual approach, leaving the physical aspect to follow in time.'[19] This is not legislation envy, but it is visibility envy. The reason often put forward by those who refused to vote for sixteen was that boys matured later than girls and so were more at risk of corruption by older predatory men. It should follow that young lesbians should be accepted as mature enough to make decisions about their sexuality, instead of being written off as going through a phase of immaturity.

In *Coming Out*, Jeffrey Weeks mentions that references to lesbianism can be found in medieval church writings, and it may surprise some to hear that lesbianism generally came quite low on the list of sins.[20] There has been a long tradition of seeing 'excessive' (read 'any') sexuality as being against nature, especially for women. For the most part in this century, lesbianism has been seen not so much as sinful but in opposition to the spurious notions of family to which society continues to cling, and as a contradiction to the gendered roles which men and women are supposed to adopt. Legislation is not created by public opinion but it does shape and reinforce it, and there is a certain amount of cross-fertilization, at least in instances where Parliament has a free vote on an issue. This is usually an issue of 'conscience', traditionally capital punishment and, more relevantly and recently, the age of consent.

Weeks identifies several common determining factors in attitudes to lesbianism which can be unravelled into separate strands: the role society allots to women; contemporary notions about female sexuality; and the expression by women of their own sexual nature. Interestingly, these are the same factors on which Faderman bases her ideas on lesbian sexuality and sexual practice (see Chapter 9). Monique Wittig is on hand to take these ideas into another dimension saying, 'lesbians are not women' because 'woman has meaning only in heterosexual systems of thought and heterosexual economies'.[21] This perhaps clarifies the legislative blank which lesbians occupy, and confirms why it is, on a more prosaic basis, that most of the population fear lesbianism.

Lesbianism as a distinct issue in Parliament was last discussed in 1921. The Criminal Law Amendment Act of that year attempted to bring lesbianism under the law. The debates around the issue at the time were, in several ways, echoed by those around the age of consent. Common themes of both Parliamentary discussions, despite the gap of over sixty years, were: corruption (of minors and non-lesbians); the oxygen of publicity (that it was dangerously attractive and should be suppressed rather than promoted); disease (if not a sickness itself that could spread like a plague, lesbians and gay men were seen as carriers of disease); and the extinction of the human race if everyone stopped having sex for procreative purposes.

Minority Rights Group was founded in 1963 and soon stopped its meetings in favour of producing the magazine *Arena3*. Both MRG and Kenric (which started as a breakaway group from MRG, named after Kensington and Richmond where most of the group lived) saw their main function as alleviating loneliness among lesbians. Kenric stressed discretion, a conservative organization, which existed as a kind of buffer for the effects of the guilt and secrecy of most lesbians' lives. Change came in the 1970s and it seems impossible that it could have happened before then. (On the other side of the Atlantic, Stonewall happened in 1969.) There was generally less respect for authority, there was some loosening of sex role limitations, and through various political and support groups there grew up a whole culture through which some women, lesbians and gay men could operate differently in the world and support each other.

> I didn't even consider the possibility that this revolution might make it okay for people like me to sleep with other people like me without being thought of as abnormal or sick; even if things like that had been able to be discussed I wouldn't have known who to discuss them with because people like us had not yet begun to talk about ourselves as a group; there weren't even any names for ourselves except the old, imperial, insulting ones. When I thought about my condition it was always as a condition, a sickness, an affliction that was not my fault, but for which I was forever going to be blamed.[22]

So-called 'homophile' movements of the 1960s were overtaken in the 1970s by a new type of movement which stressed defiance, pride, openness and autonomous activity. Gay Liberation Front (GLF) was itself a short-lived phenomenon beginning in 1970 and all but forgotten by 1975, but the effects of what it started were far greater. Even the title of GLF was important in expressing its departure from previous groupings: each word of it significant, as Jeffrey Weeks notes: gay – positive term; liberation – links with other political movements and civil rights struggles; front – again a word in modern usage to describe political structures.

This was a big change from Campaign for Homosexual Equality (CHE), who were much sneered at by GLF for, among other things, using assumed names when booking meetings and generally being considered closety. GLF's outlook was very much 'we're glad to be gay and fuck you'. The loosening of social mores of the 1960s and the permissive society which it engendered had effects on lesbians' lives just as it did on everyone's, but there were also the well-documented double standards in attitudes to women of the time. The increased pressure on women to be sexually available and compliant cannot have improved lesbian lives. As Janet Green said: 'My sister confided to me that she was going to swinging parties, which were basically orgies. She was telling me about them and I asked if women ever went with women. And she said, "Oh yes, anything goes." So I started going to parties and sure enough women did. On the down side, there was also the expectation that the women there would sleep with the men too, so, you know, there's no such thing as a free lunch basically.' (See Chapter 7.)

It was not until the 1960s that the myth of the primacy of vaginal orgasm fell from favour, although full-scale surveys in the 1940s showed the extent of sexual diversity. Antony Grey wrote how the Kinsey Reports 'opened up the first cracks in the wall of medicinal and legal monopoly of sexual issues. They demonstrated beyond doubt that homosexuality was far more common than had been imagined. . . . It made possible the development of new ways of understanding sexual deviance, and in the 1960s and 1970s a range of therapies blossomed.[23] This development led thankfully away from the prevalence of drastic physical treatments for so-called sexual problems, such as lobotomy, electric shock treatment and behaviourist conditioning therapy. Speaking of gay men, Grey says that AIDS has made sex therapists and counsellors 'discourage sexual spontaneity . . . just the attitudes of mind most likely to dampen the ardour and enjoyment of those who were often hesitant and nervous anyway'. He also sees the more open discussion about sex and sexual practices that were previously unmentionable as a benefit of AIDS.

Despite the use of similar terminology to other alternative political groups, the USA and UK alternative cultures of the time did not 'indicate any rejection of stereotypes of women and gay men'. The ratio of men to women in GLF was high, about 5:1, which is probably little different from the gender ratio in OutRage! Coming out, gay pride and opposition to the concept of sexism which contributed to anti-gay hostility, were the principles of GLF, along with challenging the commercial gay scene. In 1971 they organized an action outside the Gateways Club and the following year saw the first full-scale Gay Pride march.

Tensions around challenging sexism and the tyranny of structurelessness in the organization took their toll, as they were later to do in the women's movement. Weeks also notes that voluntarism (the idea that wanting and willing something to happen was enough) could not itself bring about change and that other forms of anti-intellectualism were rife within the organization.

The 1967 Sexual Offences Act was the first major policy alteration since 1885 when all male homosexual acts were made illegal. The Act partially implemented recommendations of the 1957 Wolfenden Report (which did not address lesbianism). It was based on a slight extension of tolerance for gay men, decriminalizing a small number of offences, on the basis that if there were no victims, there was no offence. It was supported by the liberal establishment, although many supporters of reform were concerned to distance themselves from actual gay men, and to express their denunciation of their lives. Law reform in 1967 affected lesbians too, although less directly, because it opened the door for change, in the same way that the 1994 age of consent outcome affects lesbians as well as gay men.

Work by bodies like the GLC – and the London Strategic Policy Unit which followed it – was based on the belief that any legislative change needed to be supplemented by challenging stereotypes with information about how gay men and lesbians live. Believing that an important way of challenging stereotypes would be through education, they stressed teaching about lesbian and gay issues in schools. Section 28 of the Local Government Act has now made this even more difficult to achieve; the abolition of the GLC, LSPU and ILEA has substantially changed the climate around education, as has the introduction of the National Curriculum. There have been recent uproars about sex education which are likely to make it difficult to teach school-age children anything about sex and sexuality.

Section 28 of the 1987 Local Government Act outlawed 'a local authority from giving financial or other assistance to any person for the purpose of publishing or promoting homosexuality as an acceptable family relationship, or for the purpose of teaching acceptability in any maintained school'. As people first heard about Section 28 there were those political pessimists who saw it as an inevitable, almost deserved backlash: 'What can we expect? We're just a bunch of queers and they want us back in the closet, what can we do about that?'

This was thankfully not the attitude which prevailed: instead the Section had the effect of galvanizing lesbians and gay men into a massive campaign which was, in several ways, ground-breaking. The spectacle of lesbians working with gay men again; the high visibility of the campaign; and the involvement and influence of the Arts Lobby, were all unprecedented for the time. Section 28 has been seen to work through the fear of the possibility of contravention. Student counselling services, exhibitions of lesbian and gay art, and gay groups have had funding withheld on this basis.

It is significant, effects of the Section notwithstanding, that the word 'lesbian' was used in speeches about the Section, although often merely in the form of words 'lesbian and gay'. 'Lesbian' was also posited in some cases against the portrayal of gay male sexuality as predatory and aggressive.

While there was major disappointment and incredulity that Section 28 became law, despite the massed efforts of lesbians and gay men, those same efforts produced feelings of exhilaration. Paradoxically, media visibility of lesbians and gays had increased massively, and there was a renewed feeling of community, the like of which had not been seen for some time. Lillian Faderman, writing about McCarthyite persecution around sexuality in the 1950s, similarly says that it 'also inadvertently helped to foster self-awareness and identity'.[24]

Only a few years after the joint politics around Section 28, Queer arrived, purporting to be the realization of this new-found inclusive political agenda. This brings up questions around lesbian identity. Is it what we are or what we do? Shere Hite takes a definite view: ' "lesbian", "homosexual" and "heterosexual" should be used as adjectives, not nouns,'[25] i.e. not people but activities. There has been something of a hierarchy between women who have always considered themselves to be lesbians and those who became lesbians later on in their lives, and a tension about this ethos of purity has periodically raised its head. Vera Whisman makes the important point that if we engage in the essentialism of 'real' lesbians and lesser ones, we may still be talking about something inherent, or even biological.[26] She believes that lesbians still see and to some extent envy gay male sexuality as unrepressed and somehow more authentic than their own.

Queer is a term with myriad shades of meaning and none: that means a non-assimilationist celebration of delight in being a lesbian or a gay man – or a radical straight or a TV or a TS. It is for all those for whom lesbian, gay, dyke, faggot, zami, poof, were not enough, or who had felt excluded by those terms. Transsexuals or transgendered people have finally been welcomed into the Queer fold, but there is still a prevalent strand of opinion that for many people gender confusion is the result of being unwilling and/or unable to undertake the allotted role. For those who subscribe to this view, willingness to undergo the physical and medical mutilation involved in gender reassignment only confirms the extent of the rejection of gender roles.

Cherry Smyth says, 'Queer is welcomed as breaking up lesbian and gay orthodoxies and making possible new alliances across gender and other disparate identities' but she goes on to say, 'But is the umbrella as all-embracing as queer claims? Are we in danger of denying our heterogeneity in favour of a false "queer nationalism"?'[27]

A couple of quotations from some 1960s correspondence (held at the Hall Carpenter Archive) relating to the Albany Trust suggest the circularity of history, especially if one substitutes 'queer' for 'unisex'. 'Its gimmick seems to be to say, somewhat disingenuously, that homosexuality really doesn't matter, especially amongst the young, because "we are all unisex now".' 'It became smart for non-gay kids to go dancing in the Soho teenage gay clubs.'[28]

It has been noted that Queer is in danger of setting up a new hierarchy of oppression, which (again) subsumes racism, sexism, classism. Already there has been the disbanding of special interest groups within OutRage!, such as LABIA (Lesbians Answer Back In Anger), in order that, in this case, women not be marginalized from the real action. Setting up such groups is seen as tantamount to admitting that the agenda in the main group is strictly male, but its disbanding then allows criticism that women's issues are not and will not be recognized and addressed fully. Which leaves OutRage! in the same no-win situation which left-wing groups used to have around separate organizations for women or black people or gays and lesbians. Already there has been the spectacle of OutRage!'s Rosh Hashannah action, which featured interrupting a (reform) synagogue's business on one of the holiest days in the Jewish calendar, displaying materials that juxtaposed pictures of the undeniably homophobic and reactionary ex-Chief Rabbi Lord Jakobovits (see Sheila Shulman, inter-view, Chapter 2) with pictures of Himmler. Coupled with a fierce refusal to accept that there might have been less offensive and antisemitic ways of doing things, OutRage! privileges the primacy of queer oppression above all else. Their methods are undeniably successful in generating publicity, but concentrating so hard on the end – exposing homophobia – at the expense of the means does not bode well.

Since Section 28, there have been a couple more legislative assaults on expressions of sexuality: Operation Spanner in 1989 when eight men were sentenced to up to four and a half years for consensual SM sex sessions; and, in 1991, Clause 25 of the Criminal Justice Bill which sought to stiffen the penalties for various crimes with which gay men are frequently charged, and was seen as precursor to recriminalization of male homo-sexuality. Paragraph 16 of the Department of Health's guidelines on the placing of children with foster parents included the assertion that ' "equal rights" and "gay rights" policies have no place in fostering services'. In practice, lesbians and gays have always adopted and fostered children, whether or not social services chose to ignore their sexuality. A common criticism of procedures has been that lesbians and gays are frequently only offered children with disabilities, who are thought to be difficult to place. The evident, and offensive, assumption being made by adoption and fostering units is that since queers are damaged themselves they are only fit to be offered such children, whom the organizations also consider to be 'damaged'.

Gay society is growing, incorporating not just pubs, clubs and other social venues, but businesses from complementary medicine to financial advice, papers and magazines, housing and other social service organiza-tions, language, arts production, dress and other cultural codes. This growth can be seen in several ways: the coming of age of a political movement, self-protection in a homophobic world, flexing of the pink pound, a co-option into a Thatcherite individualistic, non-society of consumerism – these are all widely held interpretations. It will be inter-esting to see whether this demonstration of financial power will be what it takes to gain acceptance and civil liberties in the future.

Some people see lesbian and gay male sexuality as the equivalent of an ethnic minority, others see discrimination against it as a class oppression. Both of these approaches are ultimately problematic as the construction and history of race and class oppression are different from that of sexuality. Feminism, as radical in its day as Queer is seen to be now, suffered through seeing 'woman' as a shared identity. What price then inclusiveness?

Feminism aimed to expose how heterosexuality, as well as gender roles, was socially constructed, and so it makes sense to see lesbianism also as a social construct, as an identity which exists in a complex interrelation within the axes of race, class, age, disability. Some who do not subscribe to this view prefer to aim for acceptance of the idea that lesbianism is as *natural* as heterosexuality. The use of the term natural is difficult to accept for anyone who has any kind of progressive political understanding. To reject this aspiration to be accepted as natural is not necessarily a bid for the status of eternal sexual outlaw. There are other options. There are still divisions along the lines of good and bad lesbians: assimilationist, designer lesbians versus SM and lesbian feminists (for very different reasons, these are for once on the same side), whereas it used to be lesbian feminists versus non-feminist lesbians (apolitical lesbians as they were patronizingly called).

There are several issues of importance here: if we all gain entry into the arena of what is called 'natural' in terms of sexuality and sex, who remains in the space marked 'unnatural'? Do we want to be part of this kind of oppositional approach to sexuality? Given our history, do we feel able to decide who behaves naturally and who is unnatural? Is being accepted like this another way of talking about civil rights? Is lack of civil rights all that differentiates us from the rest of the population? Is normalization the acme of our aspirations? Is this a hierarchy we can afford to take our (probably very shaky) place on? Naming is not neutral.

NOTES

1. Suzanne Neild and Rosalind Pearson (eds), *Women Like Us*, The Women's Press, 1992.
2. Nicole, p.45. in National Lesbian & Gay Survey, *What a Lesbian Looks Like*, Routledge, 1992.
3. Rosanna Hibbert, in *Women Like Us*.
4. Sister George, 'Sister George'. Copyright Catcall Records.
5. Radclyffe Hall, *The Well of Loneliness*, Virago, 1991 (first published 1928).
6. Alison Hennegan, Introduction to *The Well of Loneliness*, Virago, 1991.
7. Havelock Ellis, Original Introduction to *The Well of Loneliness*, Virago, 1991.
8. Havelock Ellis, *Studies in the Psychology of Sex*, F.A. Davis, 1924, p. 250.
9. Richard von Krafft-Ebing, *Psychopathia Sexualis*, G.P. Putnam, 1965 (first published 1886).
10. Sonja Ruehl, 'Developing identities', in *Stolen Glances*, Pandora, 1991.
11. J.A. Symonds, A *Problem in Greek Ethics*, privately printed, 1883.
12. See Havelock Ellis, *Sexual Inversion*.
13. J.A. Symonds, A *Problem in Modern Ethics*, privately printed, 1896.
14. Sheila Jeffreys, *The Spinster and Her Enemies: Feminism and Sexuality 1880–1930*, Pandora, 1985, p. 105.
15. Angela Carter, (ed.), *The Virago Book of Fairy Tales*, Virago, 1990.
16. Charlotte Wolff, *Love Between Women*, Duckworth, 1971, p. 200.
17. Lillian Faderman, *Surpassing the Love of Men*, The Women's Press, 1985, p. 345.
18. Shere Hite, *Women as Revolutionary Agents of Change*, Bloomsbury, 1993, p. 67.
19. Dr W.B. Pomeroy of the Kinsey Institute, in *The Ladder*.

20. Jeffrey Weeks, *Coming Out*, Quartet, 1977. I am indebted to *Coming Out* for information contained in this chapter.
21. Monique Wittig, *The Straight Mind and Other Essays*, Harvester Wheatsheaf, 1992, p. 32.
22. Jane De Lynn, *Don Juan in the Village*, Serpent's Tail, 1990.
23. Antony Grey, *Speaking of Sex*, Cassell, 1993, p. 48.
24. Lillian Faderman, *Odd Girls and Twilight Lovers*, Penguin, 1992, p. 158.
25. Shere Hite, *Women as Revolutionary Agents of Change*, p. 85.
26. Vera Whisman, 'Who is a lesbian anyway?', in Arlene Stein, (ed.), *Sexperts, Sisters, Queers: Beyond the Lesbian Nation*, Plume, 1993, p. 54.
27. Cherry Smyth, *Lesbians Talk . . . Queer Notions*, Scarlet Press, 1993, p. 28.
28. Dr L. Compton, correspondence, Nebraska, 4 November 1969. Hall-Carpenter Archive.

SHEILA SHULMAN, FIFTY-SEVEN, IS A RABBI.

I've just got outed in the *Independent*. I should bother to use a pseudonym!

I don't know if you heard anything about the Jakobovits business. Quite a number of reform and liberal rabbis wrote to the [*Jewish*] *Chronicle* saying, 'This is absurd, this is morally reprehensible, this is terrible.' The gay press didn't notice this Jewish response and OutRage! decided to take umbrage at it. OutRage! did a kind of action with posters saying 'Jakobovits equals Himmler', etc. etc. Jack Gilberts and me from the Jewish Lesbian and Gay Helpline protested in the gay press that this was basically deeply inappropriate but also that it played into a kind of British Left antisemitism which always equates Jews and Nazism.

My first relationship with a woman was in the 1960s but by the same token the images in my head dated from when I was growing up, which was Freud and Radclyffe Hall and very little else. So I kept telling myself in this serious relationship that it was bad, wrong and we shouldn't be doing it. It was awful, although I was happy for the first time in my life perhaps. We didn't use the word 'lesbian', although the whole campus where I was teaching was coming out all around me. I didn't notice, I was so paranoid. The first essay I'd ever done when I was at college in 1953, I was a psych major, was on homosexuality. I had all this freight, all this horrendous freight, and between 1950s psychology and D.H. Lawrence and Henry Miller and Freud, this was not a very salutary, salubrious rather, atmosphere in which to think about such things.

When I really came out was in 1972, *à propos* the Acton Women's Liberation conference. It was one of the earlier of the women's liberation movement conferences and by that point I'd read Shulamith Firestone and I'd read *Sisterhood Is Powerful* and in a feminist context it made perfect sense. Veils were falling from eyes at a great rate, you know, and so to be lesbian and a radical feminist made a perfectly coherent and honest sense. Previously I'd been having this aberrant relationship – I wasn't being a lesbian and coming out. But then I came out hollering and that was wonderful.

Since I came out as it were into the women's liberation movement the connection between being a lesbian and being a feminist is very organic for me. Up until then, if you thought about being a lesbian you thought about being a monster, some kind of ghastly aberration, you know. The involvement in Onlywomen [Press] started from about 1973 on. I was involved in a women writers' group of which I think half of us were lesbians. Then we printed some of our own poems. Some of us decided we were going to be printers, control our own production and all that, while technology was outstripping us right, left and centre. So we went to Camberwell Printing College, three of us. We were collectively 'the girls' for two or three years or however long it was. Onlywomen came out of a desire to be able to print and publish and produce radical feminist and lesbian stuff. We realized fairly early on that we wouldn't be able to print books, because the size of the presses and all that was beyond our capacity. So for a while Onlywomen was a jobbing printer and we printed pamphlets and so on, and it became clear after a while that printing wasn't paying – wasn't keeping us ticking over – so we'd better just be a publisher. I was on the editorial collective for years – finally withdrew because I was being shoved in slightly other directions. I'd been keeping going during those years partly on being a machine minder in a print shop, and partly the dole and partly jobs that were just jobs, not work. I more and more wanted real work and the whole business of deciding to be a rabbi was part of that. At no point did it seem to me that I was rejecting any of my past – that was all coming with me for sure. More than not being mutually exclusive, they're mutually reinforcing, I feel.

On a kind of sociological level, as a Jew you certainly learn a hell of a lot about being Other and [as] a lesbian you learn yet more about being Other, as a feminist you learn other things about being Other, so I had a kind of quite complex understanding of otherness. But the other side of that was that all of those specific identities reinforced in my senses the value of starting with your own particularities and that they didn't preclude other people having different particularities.

The religious dimension of it – you have to understand that being a rabbi isn't anything like being a priest, it doesn't mean I have a hot-line nor do I function as any kind of mediator, that is, any literate Jew can do what I do – but I suppose it came out of being in a small Jewish lesbian feminist group for a while and we were spending quite a bit of time trying to figure out what it meant for all of us to be Jewish. It began to feel like the source of more life as opposed to less life, and I was just following my nose at that point. I was terminally bored. It seemed to be where the livingness was, as far as I was concerned, and it was quite a late decision. I was forty-eight before I started training. I applied to the college as a lesbian feminist, I put it down very clearly on my application. I suppose it was some kind of gamble with God, saying if they'll take me it must mean something.

I needed a bigger interpretive grid; while a radical feminist critique is absolutely true and absolutely crucial it is not totally adequate. It was rationalist in that it presumed the possibility of progress which, you know, one begins to wonder about after a while, and it didn't seem to me to conjure with either radical evil or personal despair adequately enough. So while I wouldn't repudiate any of this, it's not the whole thing. I'd become very good friends with a Benedictine nun who kept informing me that I was a religious person, whether I knew it or not. I explained about being a lesbian and a feminist and all that and she said 'Well, my dear, you're in a prophetic position.' I first thought I heard 'pathetic', but no, no, she said prophetic, and somehow the possibility of that linkage really grabbed me and electrified me.

My congregation is identified as both secular and religious: it's usually posited as a polarity but it's a spectrum. Judaism is as intransigently patriarchal as any other religion. My thinking about female sexuality: my tradition can tell me nothing. It's mentally rich in every other area and I love it and I love playing in it but about me as a woman or as a lesbian – zilch, and I suppose the kind of engagement I have is posited on the potential for transformation in that area. I always said I would go on until I hit a brick wall and I haven't quite yet. There is a lot of movement and there is a lot of change but it is exasperatingly patriarchal, of course it is, like all the others. But because in a sense I came to it late with a quite clear lesbian and feminist identity I wasn't going to take any crap. I'm as it were claiming my place within Judaism *qua* woman *qua* lesbian *qua* feminist and it's not going to be me who budges.

One thing it means is that I never wanted to make distinctions between friends and lovers, that is, I didn't want an erotic relationship that is not a friendship and my most intense friendships have always been with women. I care probably at bottom a lot more about friendships than I do about romantic love, which is not to say that being a lesbian precludes romantic love but that is what I care about mostly. I'm trying to explain the political dimension of it, that is, as a woman I feel my primary loyalty is to women. It has a political dimension but I'm doing it out of following my affections.

I know Adrienne Rich does this lovely lesbian existence number and on one level yes, but I never want to be a straight woman's token dyke again as long as I live. That is, I think there is a kind of wanting to have your cake and eat it too amongst heterosexual women. I mean, if you are out as a lesbian you are bound to encounter a certain amount of opprobrium and difficulty and it's not an easy identity to live in, in the world, socially now. It certainly wasn't and it's still not. For heterosexual women protected by their men and their houses and their children to explore their 'lesbian possibilities' is probably all very well. I just don't wish to be on the other end of those explorations and also I think often they don't realize what the cost of being a lesbian in the world can be, or rather they do realize but they're not going to pay it. So of course it's a continuum and of course all the things Rich talks about, the Chinese marriage resisters and all of that, groups of women who choose to be together, are, in a sense, living a kind of lesbian existence, but as a socio-political identity; there's a big difference.

It's a kind of being that gives me definitely a kind of intellectual leverage on what I see, that is what I perceive from outside. I can see things that other people don't see if they've lived within the mainstream all their lives and I treasure that perspective. I have it also as a Jew and they resonate with each other. The things they hear in my sermons, that they find moving and interesting, I learned in a sense in being a lesbian, but it's very difficult in a conventional congregation to be explicit about that. It sometimes pisses me off.

When I was accepted in the rabbinical college, the principal enjoined discretion, so I asked, 'What are the parameters of this discretion please?' And he said, 'You don't say rabbinical student and lesbian in the same breath in Jewish circles.' But after five years I had such a cork in my mouth, I didn't know what was going to come out, but since 1989, I've been clearer and clearer and less hedged about to a very large degree. Now that I've been outed all over the place there's no point in anything. I will change my behaviour to the extent of if I'm doing a wedding or a funeral I will wear a skirt but that's about it.

I think if I'm in the world of identity politics then of course I'm a Jewish lesbian; if we're talking theology it's a little different. It's crucial, and equally crucial to connect with people who are not me, I've spent a lot of time doing interfaith work. The presumption often is, if you're a lesbian you therefore hate men. I was for a very long time a quite extreme separatist, not out of hatred but out of needing to create our own kind of space in which to learn what we had to learn and to unlearn what we had to unlearn. I still very clearly feel it's not women who've created all the trouble in the world, but I'm not ill-disposed, inherently or anything. Because, while politically I may work with gay men in terms of how our sexuality is articulated, gay men are still part of the male power structure and I would always feel more comfortable as a lesbian working with other women, although there are issues on which, clearly, gay men and lesbians have to work together. Separatism notwithstanding, if there was a Gay Pride march we'd be on it. There are a lot of ways in which my gay brothers and I don't have a lot in common, and certainly in terms of how we have each construed relationships it's been very different.

I suppose I am firmly in the camp labelled vanilla. I'm one of those dreadful woolly-jumpered puritans that young queers talk about today as if we had no sexual life, which is absolute rubbish, I have to say. There's this terrible generation gap going on and young lesbians seem to feel they have to invent the wheel all over, or that they have invented the wheel, in terms of sex. So I very much regret that discontinuity. It's all this post-feminist hoo-haa as if there were such a thing as 'post'. As if anything had been accomplished yet, although things have changed quite drastically in some ways.

MARION WILLIAMS, FIFTY-ONE, TEACHES IN A COMPREHENSIVE SCHOOL. MAGGS MCINTYRE, FORTY-SEVEN, WORKS IN THE NHS.

MARION: The issue about whether to use a pseudonym or not is about losing control of the information. I'm a senior teacher in a comprehensive school. I'm out among the staff. I came out to children and since then have decided to never do it again because it was so awful. I'm sort of consultant lesbian on the staff: it's my job to be consulted about lesbian and gay issues.

MAGGS: When I began to work in the National Health I felt I had to keep my sexuality a secret and for three long years I've done that. Being a lesbian amongst others I have an amazing strength. I don't actually have that when I'm not with other lesbians. I feel intimidated, and I feel vulnerable and I think it's because I'm not out, I'm not active and I'm not strong. I really think you need to be active to a certain extent to retain that identity, that sense of community.

MARION: Being a lesbian is about embracing the identity, about joining something. In my thirties I was clinging to heterosexual privilege, by making the assumption that I was only a lesbian if I was in a relationship and since I also had some affairs with men in that period, I called myself a bisexual. When I was living in the absolute closet I didn't know any other lesbians apart from my lover, my ex-lovers and their lovers. It was a very small circle, really unhealthy.

I didn't know anything about lesbian community and therefore I didn't know there was lesbian culture, I didn't know anything about lesbian culture, I didn't know there was fiction, poetry, music, dancing.

MAGGS: Joining the local women's centre was amazing for me, it was a space where I could be myself and just be with other lesbians for the first time. If you're going to come out as a lesbian, you have to have a space somewhere, you have to have contact, you can't sit at home and look at ads and do it from inside the home. For me, the women's centre was a celebration, having all these women around me, that's when I really started to get into my identity – going to workshops and going on demonstrations and meeting other women. It was my life, it was what being a lesbian meant to me at that point in time.

MARION: For me being a lesbian is based on desire not politics. I was a lesbian for years. At twenty-two I first fell in love with a woman and that made sense of all sorts of things from adolescence. She had a very high-profile job which she would have lost if it had been known she was a lesbian, so I got a very rigorous training in the closet. I was taught you didn't write love letters: it wasn't fair because those were the letters that were hardest to destroy, and destroy them was what she had to do the minute she got them. I did write one and we sat together while she lit it with her cigarette lighter and burnt it in the ashtray.

In those days we didn't use the word 'lesbian', the word 'queer' and the word 'bent' as jokes, being deviant and slightly celebratory that we were alternative to society, although we didn't use the word 'alternative' either. I'm talking about 1965 or so. We saw it in terms of being in love and it was also the time of gender-bending and unisex. I didn't think in terms of aligning in any way, I thought of it in terms of loving who I wanted. That was long before, twelve or thirteen years before I met the ideas of the women's movement.

MAGGS: I fell in love with a woman and that was my identity, and from that I grew into the politics, the rest of it came later. That was the beginning of my proper life. I've been through different scenarios really depending on who I was relating to. For me being a lesbian is desire, and also being with other lesbians. The relationship is uppermost in most lesbians' lives. Most lesbians want to have a relationship so they can have a reflection of themselves and celebrate their sexuality. For me that's really important. Over the last three years things have been more different, because I've had to put my identity and my sexuality aside for my job. It does change according to circumstance.

MARION: ... And the politics is about fighting for space for people to be allowed to be that, to be like that. To some people it means, perhaps this has been overtaken by queer, being outside of society and maybe enjoying that. I think political schemata can send you down a total cul-de-sac when you're trying to describe human feelings and human relationships. Those schemes, blueprints about how we're supposed to behave, being right on, being butch. Lesbians change, don't they, depending on who they're in a relationship with, for instance people go from relatively butch to relatively femme, relatively political to relatively not. I think that's how it should be. Those lesbians who're holding down high-powered jobs and shoulder pads and all that, they're wearing lipstick, but those lesbians who live in the country in bungalows and breed dogs, they're not.

MAGGS: You have a code that you can either adapt to or otherwise but it is there for you. Lesbians are much more free in their dress code.

MARION: Coming out at work changed the nature of my relationships, everything changed and I went into a new adolescence in my relationships that was a lot of fun personally. I think it's more that the environment has an influence on my lesbianism than the other way round, because of course my lesbianism is myself. It's a silly way round to put the question: my life is a lesbian life.

At work, I felt that I had expanded to fill up a space that had been allotted to me all the time but I'd been too shrunk and crouched to take it all up. I suppose my lesbianism affected my life in that I'd been twenty years a closet lesbian teacher, never imagining that it was possible to get my life together, never imagining that there was lesbian culture, and that there was the dignity of a whole microcosm of human life in this minority community: I didn't think of it. I was going around with a large part of myself amputated really. But that isn't my lesbianism affecting my life, that's society affecting my lesbianism. Silly question.

MAGGS: I like to identify as a lesbian a lot of the time. I'm quite happy to wear clothes that make me look dykey, in fact I quite get off on that.

MARION: I spent twenty years as a closet lesbian thinking, 'If I say that, will they think I'm a lesbian? If I wear that, will they think I'm a lesbian?' Dissembling was absolutely essential to survival. So when I came out I had this huge liberation and it was only then I began to devise a style of clothes for work that I felt expressed me and I've done that now. I find the whole gender-bending thing – for me that's a left-over from the 1960s rather than the new notion of queer – very exciting and increasingly I'm learning to enjoy clothes as a mode of fancy dress. I love looking at Maggs. Yes I do love looking at you [Maggs] looking dykey. I'm not a femme dresser myself. My last partner before Maggs was quite femme in her appearance. I find it all very fascinating, cross-dressing is an interesting phenomenon. I'm not sure what it is about men's clothes that's such a turn-on. Must be the power involved. Just like men in drag; part of the drama is that he's treated like he's not worth very much. And gay men calling each other 'she'. There's a lot of politics in all that. I don't like it all but I do think it's fascinating.

MAGGS: We don't want to be femme and mainstream. We're stuck outside of that and if we wear waistcoats it immediately makes everybody think, is this a butch dyke or a lesbian? And there's a lot of that with me darling. I wear clothes a lot of the time so I can be identified outside. I want people to know I'm a lesbian.

MARION: So how does it feel then in a lesbian event to be dressed with lipstick and …

MAGGS: I think it's OK because I think we know what we're doing and if you're seen to be a lesbian it doesn't matter what you're wearing in a lesbian environment. But outside I want people to think, 'She might be a lesbian,' without me telling them.

MARION: I wear a labyris a lot of the time because I want any dyke within eyeshot to know and I do that quite consciously at school at parents' evenings, in case there's a lesbian mother.

MAGGS: I say 'dyke', it's so strong. It seems to annoy straight women and men, they don't like the word, they find it obscene and ugly. It's got impact and it makes people stand back and think. I like using lesbian but that's a watered down label for me. But dyke I think, yeah, I'm a dyke.

MARION: It came along with feminist alignment for me, and when I started using it, my therapist of the time (a straight woman) said, 'Do you mean you're becoming more masculine?' and a couple of heterosexuals quivered a bit. It's a word of aggression really, an in-your-face sort of word.

MAGGS: You can hide behind 'gay', can't you? We're accommodating them really, aren't we, with words like that, but with 'dyke' you're not accommodating anybody, you're actually throwing it at them.

MARION: I knew both 'bent' and 'queer'. Bent means something quite different now from the 1960s when it was more self-deprecating. I can't do this on tape but there was a kind of crooking of the finger – I'm bent. It was ironic but it went along with quite a lot of internalized homophobia.
   We'd been to ballroom dancing classes and I said that the idea of leading a butch dyke across the floor was exciting to me and you said that's Queer. I have met lesbians who really enjoy being outside society, being subversive, being alternative, but most of my life I have hated being outside society. It's still my dearest ambition to live as a lesbian in the mainstream of society, to have society adapt to accept me and you as the people we are, loving as we do. There's a lot of things about it that I want to change but I don't particularly want to live outside it.

MAGGS: You can live outside it with a group of people and feel really strong in that network and you can survive quite well but as soon as that breaks up …

MARION: I see that as a coping mechanism, not an ideal, and to be really Queer you've got to see that as an ideal.

CAROL USZKURAT, FORTY-FOUR, IS A WRITER, RESEARCHER AND TEACHER, AND LIVES IN LONDON.

It's very interesting where historically you begin to desire other women and how that is interpreted when it happens. So there was me in the 1970s and it was my husband who first noticed my desire for other women, or made me acknowledge that that was the case. I think he noticed because of my interest and excitement at the soft porn film, *Emmanuelle*. I had always had attractions towards women and I knew they were not allowed. I had a dream when I was seventeen, a very erotic dream about somebody else in the upper sixth, and I woke up in a cold sweat thinking, oh I've had this dream but I mustn't tell anybody. This was 1966.

At one time I would've said that it dawned on me that I was lesbian. But, looking back now, those historical circumstances led me towards a confirmation of a desire into an identity because of the time I was in. If you'd interviewed me ten years ago I would've talked about it differently, I would've said, 'This is when I came out, this is when I found that I was a lesbian'. It's standing in a different position to your desire for women.

I had trouble in the 1950s as a girl because I was a tomboy. I had two brothers and I found being a girl very boring, but that might have been something to do with the fact that my mum went to a mental hospital for the first time when I was eight. I've been thinking about it recently and I might've taken a dislike to the feminine because of my mum being unstable, that might have influenced me, I don't know. There have been times when I've looked back at being a tomboy and said 'oh yes I was kicking against the patriarchy' but I don't think necessarily ...

I went to the London Women's Workshop for the first time in about 1974 and there were all these women, dressed in clothes that were too big for them, nonchalantly draped over piles of rubbish and piles of books. It had squat ambience. I found it really weird because by that time I'd been teaching drama for about several years, having worked really hard to go to college, get off the housing estate and all that. To walk in to something that was wilfully messy, I just couldn't understand it at all.

I can remember going to see this friend and telling her about how I'd come out to a man I worked with and taking it all really seriously, and it was really serious! It was to do with the way lesbianism was constructed through that whole discourse of 'you come out, you acknowledge this is what you really are, you read everything in your past life as something that either got in the way of your lesbianism or something that gave you a glimpse of it'. And I just find that unsatisfactory. But it makes it quite difficult because the lesbian community as constituted in grass-roots terms tends to deal in that.

I look at it very differently. I don't know if I am one sometimes in the accepted sense of the word. There's all these different varieties around now, so you then have to decide where you go socially in relation to what you think. For instance if you go to the Lesbian History Group. That is extraordinary, it's like going back in time, they all look exactly the same, they all dress exactly the same, they all think exactly the same. Desperately seeking out incontrovertible proof that she was a lesbian, that's what the Lesbian History Group is about. I quite liked it for a while. I'd just come back from Bristol having done my degree and also at the end of a disastrous relationship where the woman I was with had gone off with a man, which I think coloured the political position I then took up, which was into separatism and radical lesbianism. I think the distress and anger I felt informed that position. It took me a couple of years to rethink.

They were talking about Emily Dickinson one time and I said, 'Well she might not have had any sexual inclinations whatsoever,' and this went down like a cup of cold sick. So that's one sort of lesbian I don't want to be. Just thinking about it in terms of finding someone to have a relationship with, which is quite an interesting way of doing it, I wouldn't want to have a relationship with someone from the Lesbian History Group because you'd be rowing all the time. In fact there was somebody I did have a relationship with through going to that group who kept in intermittent touch with me and got very fed up with the way I was changing my ideas, couldn't even maintain a friendship.

The other thing is the word 'being' – it's not so much what I am as what I do. Lesbianism is what I do. I read a lot of Kinsey at the beginning of the year, and it was fascinating. It's very flawed research-wise. For the time it's very humane and open and one of the things he says is, 'Lesbianism and homosexuality are not a problem, they're only a problem if you disapprove of them, then they become guilty for the people who do them.' The way he was talking about it as something that people do, that made me start to think about it. It's a perceptual thing, and it happens to be where I'm doing my own research. In it being something that I do, as opposed to something that I am, in my own thinking, that then makes it a far more fascinating area to look at.

Whether it's me doing an academic distancing thing because I'm being infiltrated by the structure of the academy, I don't know ... but I don't see it as something I am, which is why I can't hold identity. The coming out stuff makes me uncomfortable. And also the stuff that went on in the 1980s about 'extra identities' – I have a working-class background and I have a whole range of interests that are not necessarily lesbian. Things like the Enlightenment and how that changed people's way of looking at human nature is an interest of mine, and the Poor Law, and so many things I'm interested in, literature in general. If you are something, I would suggest, you are not anything outside of what you are. So then that's not a matter of being; it's an aspect of being as opposed to your being.

Also from all the stuff I've read about, the classical stuff, it's something that's been produced not out of joy, It's been produced out of suffering. It's made in response to that negativity and the problem with that is that you then acknowledge the nastiness. No, you don't so much acknowledge it, you uphold it and strengthen negative responses because you diametrically oppose yourself to them. And then the whole Pride model; that then makes for lack of debate because you consolidate yourself against the outside forces and it can be very stultifying. Which is where a lot of it seems to be at the moment.

I'd bought a couple of skirts, which was really heavy stuff at the time, and groovy hair and everything, blonde highlights, and I went out to International Women's Day in 1982 or 1983. I had this red shirt on and this nice top, and this really sharp pair of black corduroy trousers that came in at the bottom and had zips up the side. I walked in the door and this woman lumbered up to me, she must have been about fourteen stone and she still managed to wear clothes that were too big for her, lumberjack shirt on, baggy jeans and a surly face; her hair was – well let's just say it hadn't been allowed to grow – and she walked up to me and she said, 'You look too feminine'. And this might be my arrogance but underneath her disgust there was a trace of attraction. In telling me off she was telling herself off. I remember going to this straight lesbian club where all the women were into butch and femme and I heard this woman say to another, 'Leave that cunt alone, that cunt belongs to me'. What were you to do? There was either this very restricting lesbian feminism or this hobnail boot business, there didn't seem to be anything else. There is a proliferation of lesbian contexts now, but I suspect each one has its own set of rules – you couldn't wear dungarees to an SM bar, which in a way is just as bad.

I find the scene really difficult now because with hearing aids I can go into a lesbian bar and it's impossible, you can't hear anything. Well you do but you have to really work hard at it. I'm getting old aren't I, but then in a sense having the hearing aids is partly a sign of that. But the Older Lesbians Group, oh my god. They're all about in their seventies; one of the leading lights wants a return to the women's liberation movement, no transsexuals. So I tend to socialize with a small group of friends.

Don't talk to me about disability politics! Disability politics I found very similar to radical lesbian politics. The women who are involved in both lesbian and disability tend to be radical lesbian separatist feminists. Whereas that sort of thinking separates the world into straights and lesbians, now you separate the world into able-bodied and disabled. I'm so furious about it all, I'm thinking about writing a play or a satire about equal opportunities for the dead, I'm so fed up with it.

What I like about Queer is that it provides a critical umbrella for all human relationships that are not essentially procreative, so it can take in transvestites and transsexuals, and the theory of it, that there are a variety of sexualities, and the idea that genders are performances. About a year ago in Waltham Forest there was a pre-operative transsexual who wanted to swim in the women-only sessions and this was taken umbrage to. But under the Queer umbrella that would have been all right. Ideally it's got that open-mindedness which I prefer to the closed orthodoxies of having allegiances with a particular lesbian group. When identity politics started to arise in the early 1980s, when it was to do with extra identities for lesbians about race, class, Julia Penelope said that lesbians were going for each other because they were attacked by the world, and they couldn't fight the world so they were attacking each other. I actually think it's more complicated than that.

I do like the idea of Queer, I'm very interested in the history of that with the stuff about AIDS. The revolutionary lesbian feminist line says all the campaigning that lesbians have done with and on behalf of gay men has infected them, not with AIDS but with heterosexual values. According to revolutionary lesbians, gay men are heterosexual! Sheila Jeffreys has got this thing, along with other women, that gay men have infected lesbians – bit of an unfortunate metaphor, but I don't know if that's what she used or my interpretation of it.

I first heard about SM through the anti-SM lobby. I read that book about sado-masochism, since then I read widely around it. Sheila Jeffreys seems to treat it as bad behaviour lesbians have picked up from gay men, that's why they've all got into SM. It doesn't hold water anyway, because if you read Pat Califia's *Coming to Power* it says that they've been involved in it since the 1970s and it gives this fascinating account of how the group got together. It's very much like a lesbian coming out thing but it's coming out about sado-masochism now.

I don't see it as a problem, lesbians sleeping with men. There was a time when I would have done. The idea of a lesbian who sleeps with a man not being in the bisexual category I find really interesting. I wonder what it would be like if it wasn't taboo. The fear that happens, the waves of distress when the whole thing about 'she's gone back to men' happens. It's just the same as the waves of horror that are said to occur, that do occur in many instances when 'my daughter's a lesbian', oh shock horror. It's the same response. I remember in the late 1970s hearing about women who'd gone back to men and feeling really frightened, because I had moved from marriage and come out as a lesbian and I was supposed to have this identity now. Seeing yourself as immutable is about security.

I remember talking to this woman who'd written a piece about coming out stories, and I asked her what happens to a coming out story if a woman then goes back to heterosexuality, what then does a coming out story become? One set of behaviour sets itself up in opposition to another which then says you can't do this, and you then reproduce the same structure, the same delimits. It's very interesting with lesbians in relation to anything sexual, because how far does the fact that it's become a public identity place restrictions on you as a woman, never mind you as a lesbian? You then become restricted in a completely different way when it comes to desire, you are restricted about what you can talk about, what fantasies you can share, what dreams you can talk about, very difficult. I wonder what's going to happen, in a hundred years time, how we'll look back. The other thing is, lesbians who've had babies without knowing who the father was, what will happen when the children want to know who their father is and the mother says, 'I decided you wouldn't know', and the child says, 'Why did you have the right to deny me?' It's an interesting one because in terms of lesbian feminist politics, those women did that as a political act. And we don't know what's going to happen in ten years' time, when we get adolescents and the shit hits the fan in terms of 'I want to establish my own space, and I want to be a person in my own right, and where did I come from?'

3 **s**isterhood?
lesbians, **p**olitics and **f**eminism

I feel that my eventual ability not to be afraid to say I was a feminist was important later to accepting my lesbianism. For me, being lesbian (or, at first, accepting the possibility that I might be lesbian) developed from my raised feminist consciousness.   Susan, What a Lesbian Looks Like[1]

Then I read the infamous Leeds Radicalesbians pamphlet ... if lesbianism was like that, with all that vitriol and guilt and shit throwing, I wasn't having anything to do with it.
Margaret, What a Lesbian Looks Like[2]

Fascist feminists say you can't be a lesbian unless you eat houmous; there's only one thing you have to eat to be a lesbian and it's not houmous.
Lea De Laria, interviewed by Frances Williams, *Gay Times*, issue 179, August 1993

Veils were falling from eyes at a great rate, you know, and so to be lesbian and a radical feminist made a perfectly coherent and honest sense. Previously I'd been having this aberrant relationship – I wasn't being a lesbian and coming out. But then I came out hollering and that was wonderful.   Sheila Shulman

I think Kenric's lasted so long because it's not political.
Kenric member

There is a photograph by Val Wilmer of the National Women's Liberation Conference in Birmingham in 1978.[3] A large crowd of women, some standing, some sitting, are voting on the sixth demand of the women's movement: 'An end to discrimination against lesbians and a woman's right to define her own sexuality.' As we know, the vote was passed. Neither of its tenets has become a reality, indeed, none of the demands of the movement has been met. Those demands were:

- Equal pay for equal work
- Equal education and job opportunities
- Free contraception and abortion on demand
- Free twenty-four-hour community-controlled childcare
- Legal and financial independence for women
- An end to discrimination against lesbians
- An end to discrimination from intimidation by the threat or use of male violence

The photograph has its own importance as a document of that particular event, an important piece of history. It serves to remind us that there was an organized feminist movement, which could be exciting and energetic – the women too engrossed in the vote to notice the camera. Some women will scan this photo to see if they recognize anyone, others will comment on the clothes, the haircuts, the look of the scene, in the same way they would with old family pictures.

Nearly twenty years later, the gains which were made towards those demands have been diminished. They have also been seized upon as the cause of many of today's social ills. In mainstream Britain, feminism is seen as having already achieved a better position for women, and is also scapegoated for the parlous state of society: crime levels, unemployment, impotency, depression levels and more.[4]

Almost all the women I interviewed at least mentioned feminism. One of my questions was whether their lesbianism had any political meaning for them. Even if the interviewee was strongly critical of feminism, and defined herself and her lesbianism in opposition to it, it was as if no one could talk about lesbianism without referring to feminism.

During the heyday of lesbian feminism, this would have been expected. There was a pattern of detailing and defining one's politics (which meant one's relationship to, and involvement in, feminism) at the outset of any discussion. But the backlash against feminism has been at least as strong from within as from outside feminist circles. Given this, I was surprised that almost all the interviewees talked about feminism. If the mainstream backlash against feminism is positive evidence of its importance and effectiveness, perhaps there is a parallel strand among lesbians.

There were clear-cut differences along age lines in interviewees' attitudes to feminism. Lesbians who were young adults in the 1950s came out into a very different environment from young lesbians coming out now. Some younger women loudly resent the limitations of attitude, politics and lifestyle which they feel older lesbians would like to impose on them.

Many older lesbians, who were involved in feminist politics which informed their sexuality, regret younger women's apparent rejection of their gains. As they might say: 'I didn't woman the barricades and spend some of the best years of my life going to meetings so that you could drink expensive European lager in London cafés.'

There are only two black women in Val Wilmer'spPhotograph. Feminism failed for a long time to take on the issue of racism, underestimated and ignored its importance, and did not know how to adequately approach issues about racial and cultural difference. 'I felt that there was little support in helping me integrate my identity as a Black lesbian and ended up feeling totally alienated and with a complete loss of my self-confidence.'[5] Individual white feminists often did not know how to welcome black women, or create an atmosphere which encouraged black women to show up.

While racial identity was often ignored for fear of saying the wrong thing, or of being seen as racist, a common approach to avoiding the perceived perils of class difference was downward mobility. Some middle-class women tried to pass as working-class by adopting lifestyles and habits which sought to belie their middle-class backgrounds and unacceptable privilege. For a long time there was little questioning of feminism's norm, the white middle-class woman; inevitably, that meant a particular perspective and a set of priorities which excluded many women.

For some lesbians who had been involved in the bar scene, the women's movement was seen as a saving grace, and as an exciting opportunity to be who they really were, make a new politics and change women's lives. Feminism politicized gender and sexuality. To lesbians who had grown up in a society which would have them believe they were aberrant, inverts, third sex, unnatural, or sadly born that way, this was a huge advance. Many women found that coming out as lesbian enabled them to come out in other areas of their lives, to examine and redefine other identities, as

Linda King notes in the *Lesbian Archive Newsletter*.[6] If a woman feels settled about one aspect of her life, she may feel more able to explore another. Indeed, any major change will involve some kind of reassessment and realignment in relation to others. While it is easy and fashionable to trash feminism, its aims were very ambitious, the stakes high and the opposition enormous.

In the late 1970s to mid-1980s, political affiliation was seen in some circles as a definitive expression of identity. The slogan 'The personal is political' was distorted into a means of turning personal animosity and envy into political argument. Many women were damaged by what followed, which has also been seen in other political movements in other times and places: the use of political power to settle personal scores; personal inadequacy and hostility; the imposition of confession-style 'self criticism' as the path to political wholesomeness; the wholesale reification of all people from certain backgrounds, and the denigration of all those from others. If, as some people maintain, these are necessary stages in a process, perhaps the only way to move onwards is to see them as stages and not irretrievably bad endings. The scars still run deep, and strongly influence some women's attitudes to feminism. For a substantial number of lesbians this history has led them to join the backlash against feminism. Other women are still strongly involved in what some would describe as feminist activity, while rejecting the label 'lesbian feminism' because of its connotations, largely around race and sex.

In feminism's attempts to correct the racial and class omissions, the explosion of grouping around sameness probably engendered the very fear and rejection of difference that it sought to end. Lesbian feminism concentrated so hard on taking on and responding to issues of difference that it produced a politics of identity, with safe places for some, ghettos for others. Particular and multiple oppressions came to be worn by some as unassailable badges of superiority. Perhaps this was necessary, to shock lesbians into awareness of issues of race and class identity which it had previously been too easy to gloss over. But, while this may have been a useful strategy in the short term, many women retired hurt without the will or the inclination left to work for change. The introduction to *Radical Records* puts it, perhaps over-diplomatically, 'In the lesbian feminist communities issues of multi-oppression have been most vigorously debated, to the extent that they have become, in the mid-80s, central to most of the discussions about what it is to be a lesbian.'[7]

Experience was all, and there was a feeling that no one outside that experience could be allowed to have anything cogent to say. The disclaimer in Sue Allen and Lynne Harne's piece in *Radical Records* is a case in point here – they felt it necessary to say that they did not presume to speak for anyone else.[8] The anti-intellectual nature of the movement intensified that approach and the feelings which surrounded it. The one essentialism of lesbian identity was then broken down into many others. Suspicion and its attendant segregation all but stopped the possibility of mutual discussion and understanding. Political cliques and social groupings became enshrined into fortresses of identity, which many feminists saw as less than progressive: 'To concentrate on the differences and divisions between us in a way that breaks rather than strengthens the link is no strategy for progress.'[9] Judging by the responses of several interviewees, there are still barriers and walls to be climbed. It seems clear that the rules surrounding lesbian identity have changed, but the judgemental attitudes of other lesbians continue.

Janet Dixon says in *Radical Records*, 'Lesbianism and feminism were synonymous, either one without the other was untenable. A non-feminist lesbian was just a failed heterosexual. A non-lesbian feminist was just a male apologist.'[10] Separatism was, for some, the logical conclusion of their lesbian feminism, the only pure way of living their politics. This caused problems and resentment for lesbians who had other political allegiances: black lesbians who were involved in mixed black groups, women with male children, socialists, and so on, who were effectively being told they were not sufficiently committed, and were under false consciousness.

After the split from the Gay Liberation Front (GLF) in the early 1970s, it was not until the mid 1980s that women again started working with gay men in substantial numbers. The right sort of lesbian just did not do that, because the ethos of separatism had a wide impact, even on those who did not subscribe to it. Separatism was seen as a benchmark by which everyone else's commitment was measured. Also, gay men were still men, and thought to be too busy having fun and having sex to have politics. 'We feel we have little in common with gay men or with the sexual politics which is centred around the freedom of sexual practice.'[11] But wasn't sex as a political issue what lesbian feminism was all about? On some level, yes, but there are immense difficulties in women focusing on their sexuality, lesbian or straight. Other issues took precedence, and, for a long time, lesbianism as political identity received far more attention than lesbianism as a sexual identity.

Many lesbians who had been involved in the GLF moved over to the women's movement, responding to the Front's lack of commitment to working against sexism. Political involvement with men was looked on askance by many for a long time. 'Some women who are lesbians and feminists work closely with men on the male left ... they are not woman-identified and gain privileges through associating with men and putting forward ideas which are only mildly unacceptable to male left ideology.'[12]

Many lesbians started doing work around AIDS and HIV issues during the 1980s. Others responded to AIDS with attitudes which resembled those held by the far right. 'When I went to work for the Terrence Higgins Trust in 1985, there was only one woman said it but I think more thought it; and she said, "Why are you going to work with men? And actually what does it matter if they all die?" or something deeply unpleasant like that.' (Janet)

Other lesbians were not only working with gay men but supporting trade unionists during the strikes in the mid-1980s. As one Lesbians & Gays Support the Miners leaflet put it, 'Bonds of solidarity have been made that no one would have dreamed possible a year ago.'[13] Indeed. Of course there always were lesbians who were socialists, but this group, and the Lesbians and Gays Support the Printworkers group which followed during the Wapping dispute, did feel like big departures. 'We have a long way to go before prejudice and discrimination is a thing of the past. In order to achieve equality we need allies and the way to win allies is to fight alongside others struggling for their rights. If we want support for our rights, we must support the right for jobs and basic rights. We're offering positive support to the sacked print workers, and presenting a much more positive image of lesbians and gays than most pickets would otherwise see.'[14]

Neither miners nor printworkers were known to be especially concerned about rectifying gender inequalities and discrimination, and the printers were still more likely to be found busily excluding women from 'the print', but the relentless onslaught of Thatcherism had changed attitudes. These new lesbian and gay alliances were further cemented during the campaigns around the passage of Clause 28.

In the face of disillusionment and withdrawal from the women's movement, together with the galvanizing effects of Section 28, the high profile of AIDS and HIV work and direct action groups such as ACT UP and OutRage!, mixed politics are now again firmly centre stage. The advent of Lesbian Avengers may change this. In 1994, the Avengers, a direct-action group already very active across the USA, began organizing high-profile actions in London, aimed at raising lesbian visibility and attacking homophobia.

Separate, autonomous political organizing has often been used by groups and movements working against various oppressions. Queer, by contrast, takes as its platform an inclusiveness of gender and sexualities, in opposition to the separation of the 1970s and 1980s. Queer has also reappeared on a cyclical basis, albeit in different guises. In the atmosphere of the 1920s, it was fashionable to be a bit queer, it was another daring, flighty, outré thing to do. In the 1950s and 1960s, queer, used in a self-denigrating rather than reclaimed way, signified an outsider status which did not offer the possibility of assimilation. Whereas Queer now, as a politics, would spit on any offer of assimilation, and flaunts and revels in its difference.

For some feminists during the late 1970s and 1980s, a positive choice for lesbianism was a reaction against misogyny and heterosexism. 'Feminism is the theory, Lesbianism is the practice' read badges at the time. The *Political Lesbianism* pamphlet from Leeds, which demanded that feminists become lesbians as a demonstration of their political commitment, was merely symptomatic of the general climate of the time: 'Our definition of a political lesbian is a woman-identified woman who does not fuck men. It does not mean compulsory sexual activity with women . . . Lesbianism is a necessary political choice, part of the tactics of our struggle, not a passport to paradise.'[15] In the letters section of the pamphlet, one woman responded, 'Are they telling us that an orgasm with a woman doesn't mean she is controlling me?' This and other papers took the line that, if you were not a lesbian by inclination, becoming one by political rectitude meant you were taking your politics seriously. And if you didn't follow the line then you weren't a good feminist. Some made a choice to be political lesbians. This could mean that politics led the way and bodies and heart followed, but for some it signified political rather than sexual action.

Later, to choose was no longer enough, and the term 'never-hets' was heard. In this hierarchy, women who had always been absolutely clear about their sexuality were suddenly 'real lesbians', as distinct from those who had taken longer to discover their sexuality. And, according to this same rubric, lesbians who were mothers, or who wanted to become mothers (those who had had, or who wanted to have, sperm inside their bodies), were not lesbians at all.[16] From the same camp came the term 'hasbians', for those who had chosen in haste, and returned to heterosexuality at leisure. More recently, the term 'post-lesbians'[17] has been coined, an ironical, self-referential style sign of the times. *Phase* has also weighed in lightly with 'pre-queer' – a response to 'post-queer' as coined by Paul Burston – in their third issue (which featured Madonna): 'Don't ask us what we mean – we just wanted to make sure we joined in the fracas before it went away.'[18] Is 'pre-queer' simply a reworking of the old, and very unqueer, 'any woman can be a lesbian'?

During the late 1970s and 1980s, if every aspect of life was seen as patriarchally infected and formulated, then rejecting that meant starting over, with no history and only a certain lesbian future. 'We have to stop reflecting the decadent values of the patriarchy around us', said an editorial in Artemis (no. 3, 1983) who saw even wearing trousers as evidence of co-option into masculinity. Heterosexual pasts, family background and ties, and other political solidarities were all left behind.

Lesbianism was seen as the acme of sisterhood, but sisterhood has no sexual connotations and lesbianism is also about female sexual desire. For some women, sisterhood was powerful but lesbianism was bad publicity. Others found that, although feminism gave a context to their lesbianism and enabled them to be more positive and less isolated, sisterhood had sharp teeth.[19] The issues of feminist sexuality, discrimination against lesbians, support from straight women, respectability, caused massive upheavals within the women's movement in the 1970s.

In the 1980s, class, race and sexual practice came into the spotlight. Lesbianism was seen as giving feminism a bad name: 'And I could see it in my own women's group, I remember hearing someone in the bar saying 'Well, we're not all lesbians, only one of us is.' (Jayne, Chapter 4)

The London Lesbian Sex and Sexual Practice Conference in 1985 brought bubbling resentments to the surface. The three major topics of the conference were SM, class and disability, but the SM debate completely overshadowed the weekend. Lesbians with disabilities, angry about the way issues of disability continued to be sidelined, and how they themselves were therefore marginalized, were trying to use the conference as a way of opening up debate. Anti-SM dykes (who were the conference organizers) were denying SM women – or even those expressing interest in SM – the right to speak. As a kind of counter-plot in this scenario, some middle-class women were giving their cheque books and credit cards to working-class women in a bizarre effort at redistributing wealth and overcoming their class privilege. Instead of bringing differences of political opinion and/or sexual practice into open debate, this conference drew up battle lines. Pro- and anti-SM groups proliferated, organized, demonstrated and put out leaflets.

The London Lesbian and Gay Centre was the site of a long-running battle about whether lesbians and gays who were into SM should be allowed to use the centre (and also whether bisexuals and transsexuals should be allowed entry and, if so, should be able to use the women-only space). The Fallen Angel pub in Islington (now the Angel) also saw demonstrations and suffered boycotts because an SM group used the upstairs meeting rooms. Lesbians Against Sado Masochism (whose acronym, LASM, was often mispronounced 'lash'em') produced a leaflet in about 1985, *What is this big fuss about sado-masochism?*, which set up this definition of SM: 'Sado-masochistic sex is the eroticisation of power, pain and humiliation in a relationship based on domination and submission.' It then answered a set of questions it had set:

But if it's consensual why is it anyone else's business?
But you're just being prudish – isn't vanilla (non-s/m) sex rather bland?
But isn't lesbian and gay liberation about freedom, not more limitations?
But can't it act as a kind of release of these oppressive feelings?[20]

At around the same time another leaflet appeared from SM Dykes, although as both were undated it isn't clear whether it acted as catalyst to the previous one or was a response to it.

SM is power and trust
  self-control
  erotic
  role playing
  fantasies and fetishes
  fun
  fucking brilliant and brilliant fucking
It's important to realise that the singling out and scapegoating of SM is part of a much bigger move to censor and control groups and people who don't conform to the aforementioned 'mainstream' sexuality.[21]

Ten years on, outlooks have shifted considerably, but these are still issues. A letter from Lesbians Against Pornography appeared in the *Pink Paper*[22] suggesting that SM dykes have 'a hold over the gay press'. It continued, 'This has really gone too far now ... the constant barrage of self-hatred and homophobia being acted out in porn and sm is evidence of this ...

You aren't going to have it all your own way any longer.' New developments will be awaited with trepidation.

Mainstream party politics, and those who were active in that sphere during the late 1970s and early 1980s, were looked on in a derisory way, as irrelevant and diversionary. Those who called themselves socialist feminists were largely seen, in the ascendancy of radical feminist politics, as misguided, wasting their energy in a struggle where women's issues would never be given the primacy they deserved. The stereotype of socialist feminists was that they were not concerned with sexuality. In return, radical feminists were held to be uninterested in class issues. Socialist feminists might be lesbians, but radical feminists were unlikely to be straight, or not for long.

Labour councils were attempting to activate their new-found commitment to equal opportunities through funding centres for women, black and ethnic minorities, and lesbians and gays, as well as sections and committees in their own bureaucracies. The aim was to provide services that fulfilled needs for all their constituents, and took account of minority needs instead of just the mainstream.

For a long time after the possibility presented itself of local and regional council funding for some of the work that had previously been done at grass-roots level, debates raged about co-option. If we got used to having a photocopier, wouldn't we become softened up and then be lost once the council took it away? If we started to pay wages for people to do things they had previously done for free, then would anyone do them when there was no more money? We wouldn't be able to run things in our way any more, we'd have to abide by their rules.

Femi Otitoju puts it so: 'Mainstream party politics were nothing to do with the aims of my struggle as a feminist and a woman identified woman. Local government was a smaller version of government, and both were to be fought, demonstrated against and challenged at every available opportunity. It [local government grants] undermined the very idea of autonomy and could well turn into a monster that could devour us.'[23]

This is not the place to discuss whether or not we were had. Most equal opportunity policies are well-intentioned but inoperative, though they have led to raised standards in some quarters. Whether or not local government devoured us becomes a moot point because it was the Tory party which chewed up local government as fast as it could, alarmed at all that money being spent. Quite a lot of this spending improved people's lives. Looking at some of the reports published by councils and committees, and in particular, the GLC, the *sine qua non* of municipal socialism, it is clear how much wider a brief local authorities then held. A vast amount of this work has now, after nearly fifteen years of Tory government, become the province of the (underfunded) voluntary sector.

In *Changing the World, Tackling Heterosexism* and the GLC *Women's Committee Bulletin Special Issue on Lesbians*,[24] the subjects range through housing, parenting, services, advice, transport, employment, social and cultural issues. At the time, the authorities saw their remit as not only to provide services for all sections of the population, but also to acquaint residents with the reasons why they were pursuing such policies.

According to Ann Tobin, 'When the GLC was abolished, the response of much of the Labour movement was to blame the GLC's support for gay rights. When Clause 28 was introduced, many gays blamed the loony left for going too far.'[25]

Feminism's ambitions for change were massive; and not all of them, by any means, have been achieved. The methods employed in feminist politics were faulty, and were a stumbling block for some of the women involved. But the intentions, the transformations which were envisaged, have to be considered before any judgement is made on feminism. The dream of a sisterhood with a common purpose and a shared identity is now unimaginable to most people, including, or perhaps especially, those who believed some twenty years ago that they would be part of that dream. A shared identity in that sense now looks unattractive. Perhaps this is an effect of the individualistic 1980s, rather than anything specific to feminism. Many women now feel that if they do not want to conform (at least not entirely) to the straight world, then why should they want to conform to their lesbian peers? This was recognized some time ago in *Sequel* magazine: 'Let's face it, as lesbians, we often have very little in common – except the obvious sexual/emotional and social aspects of our lives.'[26] But at the time that *Sequel* was publishing, mainstream lesbian feminism did not put forward such views.

Since my own first tentative steps into the world of feminism as a student in the late 1970s, I have heard two completely different sets of women use the line, 'I'm not a feminist but ... '. The first time, it was used by women who thought feminism was too strident, went too far, and was too off-putting. More recently it is used by women who think feminism has served its purpose and is now redundant, and that invoking it is hardline and uncool. It may seem a major indictment of feminism that, within this fifteen-year cycle, it should have been unattractive to both sets of women. However, the line is most often used to introduce an idea which is actually feminist – perhaps it is the personification of the feminist which is being rejected, rather than associated ideas. And as a fifteen-year period is only a few years short of a generation, it is not so surprising that feminism is rejected by women at both ends of it.

Seeing lesbianism as a lifestyle rather than a politics, as many women do now, need not be negative or regressive. Living the life can be seen as something more than who you sleep with. Those who regret the passing of lesbian feminism *à la* 1970s and 1980s should take heart from the fact that the loss of a label does not necessarily translate into wasted decades.

NOTES

1. Susan, in National Lesbian & Gay Survey, *What a Lesbian Looks Like*, Routledge, 1992, p. 47.
2. Margaret, *ibid.*, p. 60.
3. See Rosa Ainley and Belinda Budge (eds), *Postcards from the Edge: Lesbians Looks*, Scarlet, 1993.
4. See Susan Faludi, *Backlash*, Vintage, 1992.
5. Gerry Ahrens, Ahmed Farooqui and Amitha Patel, 'Irrespective of race, sex sexuality . . . ', in Susan Hemmings and Bob Cant (eds), *Radical Records: Thirty Years of Lesbian and Gay History*, Routledge, 1988, p. 29.
6. Linda King, 'We have always been here', *Lesbian Archive Newsletter* (n.d.).
7. Susan Hemmings and Bob Cant, Introduction, *Radical Records*, p. 9.
8. Sue Allen and Lynne Harne, 'Lesbian Mothers: the fight for child custody', *Radical Records*, 1988, p. 181.
9. Jan Parker, 'No going back', *Radical Records*, p. 264.
10. Janet Dixon, 'Separatism', *Radical Records*, p. 77.
11. Sue Allen and Lynne Harne, *Radical Records*, p. 181.
12. Leeds Radicalesbians, *Love your enemy? The debate between heterosexual feminism and political lesbianism*, Onlywomen, 1983.
13. Lesbians & Gays Support the Miners leaflet, Hall Carpenter Archive (n.d.).
14. Lesbians & Gays Support the Printworkers leaflet, Hall Carpenter Archive (n.d).
15. *Love your enemy?*
16. Julia Penelope, *Gossip*, no. 1, Onlywomen Press, 1986.
17. Thank you to Gloria Heswall for this.
18. Peter Cummings and Helen Sandler, editorial, *Phase*, issue 3, May 1994.
19. Wendy Clark, 'The dyke, the feminist and the devil', *Feminist Review*, no. 11, 1982, p. 31.
20. Lesbians Against Sado Masochism leaflet, Hall Carpenter Archive.

21. SM Dykes leaflet, Hall Carpenter Archive.
22. *Pink Paper*, 30 July 1993.
23. Femi Otitoju, 'The should we, shouldn't we? debate', *Radical Records*, p. 223.
24. GLC Gay Working Party, *Changing the World*, (n.d.); GLC Women's Committee, *Tackling Heterosexism: A Handbook of Lesbian Rights*, (n.d.); GLC Women's Committee *Bulletin*, Special Lesbian Issue, issue 17, June 1984.
25. Ann Tobin, 'Lesbianism and the Labour Party', *Perverse Politics: Lesbian Issues*, *Feminist Review*, no. 34, 1990, p. 66.
26. *Sequel*, no. 18.

VAL WILMER IS A WRITER AND PHOTOGRAPHER. SHE WAS BORN IN 1941.

At the moment I'm writing about the involvement of local black musicians in British jazz and popular music. Some of these people were gay, but one of the problems that I have in talking about this is when straight people question it. They say, 'But they were married.' Yes, well, people were married. You had to be – otherwise you'd be more or less dead, you know. It's only in recent history that people have been able to be safe, to be unmarried.

I like being with women and I enjoy the company of women: the things we talk about, our ways of seeing, the strengths women have, but I don't like excluding men from my life. I like excluding them from particular situations, of course, but men do, to a great extent, dictate the way that society is, and I want to be part of society, I want a fair share of the action. I'm certainly not a separatist, I've never thought about being one for a second. But although I'm a very political person and I've taken a decision to talk about my lesbianism at any opportunity I have, I don't think that I feel as strongly political about being a lesbian as a lot of people do. Because I have access to the media, I feel it's my social responsibility to talk about my sexuality – when it's appropriate, obviously. At the same time, I know I don't feel as devoutly part of 'the' lesbian culture as maybe I should. And at fifty-one years old, I wonder what that says about me.

And there's another aspect of my attitude to men. I know there's a fashion now for straight women to hang out with gay men, but I've always found some men attractive. For my sins, I occasionally had sex with men until about ten years ago. At one point I felt perhaps I shouldn't do this, but I think I was responding more to a culture that told me not to, rather than feeling it deeply. I have always mixed with a lot of black people and that thing about 'consorting with the enemy', the way some black people described sex with whites, was something I'd heard so often. I could see that having sex with men was the same thing.

I sometimes feel that the lesbians I know are obsessed with middle-class ideas – except they're not all middle-class. There's this kind of coy lesbian world – god knows what some of them are like in bed! For some people you're only supposed to behave a certain way and not step over the mark with enthusiasm. Well, we might as well be little old ladies sitting around in bonnets, having tea! I don't really drink any more, but even now, when I go to some women's things, though I don't get 'out of it', I sometimes feel I have to tone myself down. This may sound like paranoia, but I know how some people think about me because they've said, with surprise, 'oh, you like flowers', 'you can cook', that sort of thing. I just look at them and think, what on earth do you think I am?

If people think I'm aggressive it's only because I've been used to hanging out with all these heavy guys. I didn't want to be the woman in the corner so I developed a style. Plus, I came out of the old bar culture, where you did not behave like a shrinking little violet unless you were an out-and-out femme. I came out of those two different worlds, plus there was the struggle to be an independent woman at a time when no other women did the kind of work I was doing, writing about jazz, taking photographs – or very few. You develop a certain way of being.

Nearly everywhere lesbians socialize is around drinking. It's a problem for people who drink and it's a problem for people who don't drink, but, on the other hand, I wish there were still bars to go to like the Gateways. I used to hate it, but now I wish it was there, even though I hardly drink at all now, and didn't have a drink for five years. I think whenever you came out, as you get older, you feel the need to be near the culture of that time. Not that you want to live in the past, if you're sensible and especially if you've got a progressive mind. Nostalgia is pointless. But why should we have this nostalgia for that kind of closety existence? I suppose it's like why men have sex with strangers in public toilets, it's because it's secret. It's a perverse side of human nature. I think really the idea of sex being jolly fun is a drag. It's got to have an undertone, a current. Sex without a bit of sleaze (for want of a better word) is the antithesis of what I want on any level. The truth of it is that I don't feel that I speak the same language as many of the lesbians I meet. I feel uncomfortable because of it. And as I've got older I have often felt more at ease with straight people – except when they're talking about things which underwhelm me. Often I find myself having more in common with them, which is very strange. We have not built an alternative culture – well we may have, but I'm not very happy with it.

Today's world is so materialistic and consumer oriented, it's inevitable that the lesbian scene should take that on. These are very cold times we're living in; the idea of sisterhood or anything like that is out the window – which is a shame. There was a time when sisterhood really was a reality. It was about having a place to go in your mind, where none seemed to exist before because of feeling so marginalized through being a woman. The idea that we were building a new world, ho ho, was very attractive. I thought it was the most wonderful ideal. A feeling of solidarity and being part of something, which is always attractive, especially if, for whatever reason, you've always felt marginalized.

I'd always had lots of sex in my life both with men and women. Sex was very much part of my daily life. God, that sounds so grandiose! You develop ways of being sexually. My ways of being were to do with the lesbian scene of those days, the area in which I had grown up and the people I had moved with. Well, here comes sisterhood, this wonderful feeling.

But with it came all these prohibitions about the way I was. I don't want to give you the idea I was some rampant sex fiend, doing it twenty-four hours a day, but suddenly it was, 'don't do that, don't say this, don't touch me'. Now you know, at the moment of sexual desire, and especially at the moment of your heart's desire, that is the most dreadful thing someone can say to you. You know, slap in the face, kick your teeth in, punch in the stomach, all at the same time, and it doesn't go away when the bruises go away. That happened to me several times and I wasn't being particularly over the top. This sexual culture grew out of the women's movement about 'we will not be like men, we're going to be lesbians, we are fighting against the ways men want us to be'. Fair enough. Of course the movement was very young at that stage, but these reactions were terribly hurtful to me, and I know that they damaged a lot of other people as well. And some of those people didn't necessarily have the same resources as I had.

To be on the receiving end of that kind of thing was really awful. For a while it made me feel there was something wrong with me. I wanted to belong to the gang but obviously I didn't have the credentials. I feel quite tearful just telling you about it. It made me try harder but it made me retreat too. I've been treated badly by men and abused in various ways. I didn't want it from women and here I was getting it. I suppose they felt the same way about me. I was arrogant too, and it seemed to me that my life had been a lot more interesting, and wilder, and filled with passion of all kinds, than theirs had. Now I look back and I feel that I shouldn't be too judgemental. But that's too simplistic. They were fucked up, even more than I was. It was quite a long time before I thought of myself politically as a lesbian – the women's movement came first. For a long time I couldn't really come to terms with the idea that lesbianism, homosexuality, gayness, whatever, was a political statement.

A lot of people have a need to belong to a culture, and I've had this need very desperately all my life. Also, having been a freelance for so many years, you need a centre. People started being less friendly, less helpful, less loyal. People's lives changed, some went off and had children, some were lesbians, some weren't. Political events, social events, the whole world changed – meaning Britain. People ran out of energy too.

Politically, I think we have to support each other on everything, even on things we don't necessarily like or approve of. I think it's absolutely vital, in the sense that all oppressed groups should support each other. I think lesbians who turn their back on gay men must not be surprised when gay men turn their backs on them. Do we want a fair share of the pie? Yes please, we want exactly the same. Or do we want to be separatist? I don't. Gandhi said, 'I do not want the windows and doors of my house to be closed. I want the cultures of all lands to blow freely about my house, but I refuse to be blown off my feet by any of them.' I want to go to my grave being part of the action, right? I don't want to be in a ghetto.

They may write about designer dykes, but what about the majority of lesbians out there, whose reality is down the dole, up the tower blocks, married, all sorts of things? My last lover lives in the countryside and she's a teacher. She had a child, her mother lived nearby and she wasn't out. That was a turn-up, going to her house and having to pretend we weren't lovers! So, designer dykes, so what? Same as designer anything, it's for people who've got money. Once again I'd support them on the barricades, but would they support me, I wonder?

Coming from my generation, I still dislike the word 'queer'. There's a parallel to be drawn with the word 'nigger'. Richard Pryor, who made quite a career out of that word, went to Kenya and, when he came back, gave an interview to *Ebony* magazine. He said, 'I went to Kenya and I didn't see any niggers', and said he wasn't going to use that word any more. We have always used the words 'dyke' and 'queer' as a kind of in-joke. Now when I see 'Queer Nation', I understand why they do it, but I don't like it.

And then the word 'dyke' for people of my generation, especially people who've been to America, is also a word of insult. I use it with other women, but I don't want any straight person saying it to me, although they do. I heard the odious Richard Littlejohn on LBC – he hates women, *hates* women – saying, 'What is it about a bunch of sadassed dykes?' and I thought, yeah, that is the way it's generally used. A lot of people, even a lot of lesbians, don't realize that it's a word of insult that we took and turned into a word of pride, like African Americans use the word 'Black'.

I don't really like the word 'lesbian' all that much, but I feel it's necessary for us to use it simply because it is such a taboo word. For most people of my generation it was almost impossible to say. We referred to ourselves as gay women and that was the end of it. 'Dyke' actually sounds much nicer. I don't like the word 'homosexual' because that implies that all we ever do is bonk. Really it should be 'homoemotional'. After all, that is what identifies us: our emotional attachments, not that we have sex with people of our own gender. Lots of people have sex with people of their own gender and frankly, that doesn't make them gay. That is one of the great myths of all time. Only gay and lesbian people know just how many straight people do it, the rest of the straights out there don't believe it if you tell them. They just think you're exaggerating, or that it's special pleading, whatever.

When I was younger, and a bit more zappy, straight women were always throwing themselves at my feet. Gay men of a certain kind can't walk the streets without men jumping on them, and yet it's the one of us who is out who is always seen as the predator. I find this fascinating, but the more knowledge of it you amass, the more you realize the diversity of sexual behaviour, and the more you do wonder about the validity of identifying as one thing or the other. I think this radical gay sex and lesbians having sex with men stuff is just another thing to do. Women are terrified of being identified as feminists or as lesbians – it still is so – and so will do anything they can that gets away from dungarees and no make-up. It's safe for them to say, 'Hey, I'm not really like *those* people.' And I think a lot of people were repressed by the politics of the period.

I was staying with a friend in New York and she had all these pornographic books beside her bed. While she was away I read some of the books and got turned on. It started me thinking and I realized that the whole atmosphere there was much more sexually charged than in circles in England. Some of her friends were SM kind of people, and I asked her, 'Why do you like these people, why are they your friends, do you really like all that stuff?' And she said, 'It's not really that, but most lesbians have such dreadful sex lives, and the whole press about lesbian sex is so awful, that we must give freedom to these means of expression, anything we can do to make it on the agenda more.'

I was a bit taken aback but I've thought a lot about it since. All the lovers I've had, there's only been a couple I can say that I really *really* clicked with. It's always exciting of course, and if you want to be with someone, it doesn't matter what you do. But I think English people in general are not very good in bed. I mean, I've had lots of good times, but with some of my lovers there hasn't been that much imagination. So I think if the Pat Califias of this world are out there writing their dreadful books, at least it makes people talk about it. It's an awful thing to say that your own people are bad lovers – maybe what I've said is a little unfair – but it all comes down to what you actually like. I guess it's OK if someone wants to stand on opposite sides of the room and when they look at each other, they come on the spot. But that's not for me.

The Gateways was, for me, a mixture of excitement and resentment at it being a ghetto. And the Englishness of it all. My own lover was black, but there were very few other black women around that scene, so there was little contact. I can think of a few other black women in those early days, just four or five. I got to know a couple briefly, but the others – I can see their faces but that was it. Going down there I always had mixed feelings. I was always excited, but at the same time I hated the fact I was going, which, I suppose, comes from a lack of self-worth about being a lesbian. The truth was that it was kind of sordid because of the way you had to be, but still there was a terrific ritual involved. Even where you parked the car was important; there were several places where it wasn't safe to park the car. Now I look back on it, it was nothing. A few jeers, but nothing like what could happen today. After all, it *was* in Chelsea.

The thing that upset me most about it was that you couldn't really talk to the people around you. Conversation ranked low, it was more about posing and drinking. And if you did try, they thought you were after them. I palled up in the end with some women who were very ordinary. They worked in garages, betting shops, and so on, but they were the ones who would talk to me. I'm talking about the 1960s. There were quite a lot of people there who were older than me, born in the 1930s, and they were ordinary women of a certain kind who worked in shops and factories. It was very very straight. For those women to put trousers on and leave their make-up at home was quite something. For us it was too. I can remember Terri saying, 'I think we can start wearing jeans.' Honestly! And I wasn't a kid, I was about twenty-five.

I can remember exactly what I wore, too. I had this gold watch, which I thought was just wonderful, and camel-coloured trousers, flared, and a crew-necked pullover in grey. I had my hair just so, and I really thought I was the bee's knees! That was when I thought I could pull anyone – I found out I couldn't. Cross-dressing then was a totally different thing, you know. Buying a man's shirt must have been a terrifying procedure before the days of chain stores. Sort of Armani versus Littlewoods *haute couture*. Those women who put on their Burton suits and went into a man's shop and bought their shirts put their lives on the line. It was dangerous.

Going down there and meeting all those people was a very formative experience for me. Later on, a lot of puritanical attitudes came out of the women's movement. Some of the ideas about sexual desire revealed a total lack of understanding of how most people lived – working-class women, married women, black women. Women didn't earn much money and they'd save up sometimes for weeks to go down to the Gateways. It would be packed on Saturdays sometimes, and people would go, 'Oh look, the army's in', and that was a signal for some of the middle-class women to split, because they couldn't stand the heavy butch brigade coming down the stairs.

The other thing I didn't like about that whole lesbian scene was the role-playing. I didn't feel that way, didn't really understand it I suppose. I didn't want to be identified with these real butch types, and I certainly didn't fancy or want to be one of the femmes. There was this woman called Cheryl, a bit of a 'Sloane', very tall, long hair and stylish. I hit on her one day, and she tossed her head and said, 'Don't let the hair fool you, darling.' She was butcher than me, oh god.

The truth is that here I am between these worlds but it was, and is, seen as really strange to think like that: you really had to be one or the other. And, despite the women's movement, you still do. I still find myself attracted to women who're butch, and I'm attracted to women who aren't as well. I found the femmes mostly so dimbo-ish. I remember going down the Gates one night and saying hello to this woman I hadn't seen for a while. She said, 'Well you know what it's like, when you've got a butch. They've got to have their meat and two veg on the table when they get home.' And this person lumbered up, thumbs stuck in her braces. She looked at me with this 'don't come near my woman' kind of look. I won't forget that till the day I die. I'm sure that, away from the public gaze, people like that were quite equal in many ways, but in that place it was the ritual thing they felt they had to go through. But the idea of having his dinner on the table is ... pretty heterosexual.

The other thing I'll never forget was when I got together with this woman who used to call herself Frank. She was going out with a friend of mine and we always used to go, 'Nudge nudge, wink wink, we'll have a date one night when the girls are away', type of thing. So one day we went out, had a few drinks and went back to her place. I said, 'How about it then?', and we got into bed. It's hard telling you this story, but I think I have to tell it to show just how awful and how different things were. She was a very slim attractive woman, very butch, and she automatically went into her thing. Well, I couldn't deal with it like that. I kind of reversed proceedings, made love to her and she had an orgasm. This was a long time ago, I was very young. I asked her, 'Do you usually come?' and she said, 'Well, I always let the woman come first.' It's not funny. At the time I couldn't believe she'd said it, and telling you now, nearly thirty years later, it still hurts me when I think of her saying that. When I started to consciously think of myself being part of the women's movement, I thought about her a lot. I felt I would never again have to be with somebody who thought that way, because really my heart broke for her. She ended up getting married and having a child.

HAVVA IS A TWENTY-FIVE-YEAR-OLD BLACK WORKING-CLASS LESBIAN.

I had a relationship with a woman when I was thirteen, a school-friend of mine. I knew the word lesbian, but I didn't think that was what I was, because, at the end of the day, I always thought I was going to grow up, get married and have children. The reason I – I use the term – split up with this woman at fifteen was because it was getting to the stage where people were starting to talk about us, calling us things before we were labelling ourselves like that. So I said, 'Look, I think I want to tell people how I feel about you', and she couldn't handle it, so that was it. It was on the bus going home from school, and I gave her back her ring and she gave me back my ring. It had got to that stage. We were physical together in lots of other ways, but we didn't have sex in the traditional sense.

I was devastated, cried for three months. And then it was Zitta. Between the ages of fifteen and eighteen we had a relationship, which was turbulent to say the least, and for lots of reasons, which now I look back on: our age, different backgrounds, the fact that I wasn't allowed to go out, because I was from a very strict Turkish Cypriot family. She was the woman I had my first proper sexual relationship with. It was in that relationship that I became a bit more aware of what was happening, and the fact that I really did find women attractive and it wasn't just a fluke with one woman.

I started to develop ideas, and, politically, I started to define myself in lots of ways. I started thinking about whether I was black or white. I'd never felt completely comfortable – or comfortable at all, in fact – with thinking I was white. But black meant something different to me. Politicization in that way, that happened around the age of eighteen: talking to people about historically defining yourself as black and all the other stuff that comes with it. Also, looking at things in terms of class and all that. So I do define myself as a black working-class lesbian.

All sorts of things started happening then, in terms of politicization, becoming aware of everything. I suppose a lot of people would describe me as quite hardline about a lot of things. I think I'm loosening up a bit as I get older. A few years ago, I made this decision that I wasn't going to have relationships with white women any more. I made that decision for obvious reasons. I still feel like that, because I find that there are lots of problems, particularly in dealing with racism, and I don't want to have that in my relationship at home. I don't know if I'm going to keep feeling like that. I tend to have quite clear ideas about my politics. I mean, I'd be more upset if you called me liberal, probably, than if you called me right-wing.

For a long time, I said that there's no such thing as bisexuality – as far as I'm concerned you're heterosexual but you like the occasional fling, and it's not got any particular … I'm not sure if politics is the right word. I don't think being a lesbian has to be particularly political. I think you could be a lesbian if you just want to sleep with women.

I want to be with a woman because I want to create something – oh God, this is going to sound so wanky – a kind of move away from the whole heterosexual stereotype of what relationships are supposed to be like. I want to try and move towards … I don't know what the word is. Equality, perhaps. I've never been heterosexual. I never slept with men – if that means I've never been heterosexual, whatever.

That's why I feel very strongly about SM, because they're not doing anything new – they're doing what straight people do all the time, which is abuse power constantly. I don't see it as moving forward or liberating ourselves. Like lots of things, because something's happening across the world, it doesn't mean it will never touch my life. So, people's argument that it goes on behind closed doors – that doesn't sit with me, because everything's got a knock-on effect.

Some lesbian sex is boring, but I've had lesbian sex that's not boring as well. I think the point is that SM is not something that some people do only in terms of certain scenarios they carry out. The whole power play goes on every day in everybody's life. I acknowledge that we are all holding up what is sexy, what is attractive, what is a turn-on, and how it's OK in certain situations to have power over someone else. I just don't think that's an OK way to continue. I don't think we're going anywhere. I'd like to know what freedom of choice is. If someone can tell me, I'd be really interested.

I'm involved in a group of women called Lesbian Response. I don't know if you've seen our postcards. We just got together to try and do something about violence in lesbian relationships, the whole power-tripping thing, because it's another thing that's just not talked about. I think if SM has done anything it does mean we're able to talk about sex much more … complete opposite to the lesbian feminist line.

There were quite a few of us who were sick of going out and seeing SM dykes all over the show, covered in their regalia. Even if they weren't, just the whole intimidating way that they can be in groups. A lot of us were getting really pissed off with violence in lesbian relationships never being talked about. Another thing was to talk about race, and talk about the sort of images we have of black women: the way we're portrayed on the scene, and in books, and so on. It's generally a lot of negativity. The group is mainly black women, mainly working-class women. We're not coming from the whole 'you've got to be really straight and not have fun and not talk about sex' attitude. That's really not what we're like.

We've had a few dances where we've had very clear dress codes, but we've also had leaflets at the door about the group, talking about what else we're going to be doing. We've had quite a lot of interest, quite a lot of women coming and arguing with us, sometimes actually at the dances. They've been there three hours, and then they've decided to come and start an argument with somebody. And we say, 'OK we'll give you your money back', and they don't want to go. What we don't want to do is turn away women who may be thinking about why they're into SM. It's not the women, it's the act, the stuff in the mind that goes on, that we want to challenge.

When I first came out, I looked so completely different to how I look now. I had really long hair, and I always used to wear full make-up, and I used to shave my legs and have skirts and court shoes. Right through my teens I looked like that — even when I was sleeping with women and thinking about who I was, I never changed the way I looked. I never thought I should do. Up to nineteen, I'd always thought, I can look how I want to look. At seventeen I left home, so at that point I could do what I wanted. It meant I could go to clubs and meet loads of other lesbians. I didn't go mad, I went out a couple of times a week, on a Friday and Saturday. I hit the scene and I saw all these women, and loads of attitudes and different opinions.

It was the whole attitude, thinking that because I was with a woman who had short hair, and I had long hair, it was assumed immediately that it was butch and femme. And that pissed me off, and I also found that a lot of butch dykes would slap my bum and things like that. It used to really wind me up, you know. Now I laugh at it, but then I used to get so het up about it. So I cut my hair, and I stopped shaving my legs and wearing make-up. I just looked very different. And I felt comfortable about it — it was only a few years later that I thought, 'Why the fuck did I have to do that?' I don't think I'd ever feel comfortable wearing full make-up again, but I don't feel judgemental if you want to look a certain way, in that sense. I also think, culturally, and in terms of class, there's lots of different opinions on what you should look like, and I don't think that the whole white lesbian feminist look is for everyone.

There's also a whole thing about how my parents brought me up never to look rough. If I was going out, my clothes should be ironed, they should be clean, my hair should be clean. And I think at first I used to question that all these women who — mainly white middle-class women — really looked like they hadn't washed all week. You know, the Greenham look. I used to wonder what was going on. The whole downward mobility thing used to really wind me up. I didn't know what it was then. I used to wonder, why did they look at me because I wanted to look a certain way. Black people in this country have to try harder at everything, and try and look good, because you have to constantly be making an impression. So I think, for all those reasons, we're expected, we're told we have to look better. A few years ago, when everyone was wearing ripped jeans, my mum and dad would go into one if I ever turned up with ripped jeans.

Around Clause 28, I went on loads of TV programmes. There was *Kilroy*, *A Time and A Place*, but there was one where you could actually see just me – that Channel 4 programme, the women's programme. The whole thing started off when the presenter turned to me with, 'Havva, you're a lesbian.' And I remember just grinning, and I thought, this is it.

Someone at my mum's factory said to her, 'I think I saw your daughter on the telly last night – I think she was saying she's a lesbian.' My mum rang me up saying, 'Havva, were you on the telly saying you were a lesbian last night? Why are you going on the telly saying things like that?' And I said because it was true. And she just went into one, screaming round the house. And she said, 'So does that mean' – and I'll say it literally as it translates – 'Does that mean you're the sort of woman who lick women's cunts out?' And I thought to myself, how do you know?

Queer: I just think, where are these people coming from? We try and make ourselves accessible to all sorts of people, be trendy and be different. If you talk about the whole argument about whether we are genetically lesbian or gay, or whether we make a choice: if we go down the line that we are genetically lesbian or gay, then, yes, some people might say, 'they can't help it'. So maybe that's a way to get our rights, but I don't think that's the way to go about it. I think we should be talking about having some choice about who you want to sleep with, but I wouldn't want to go down the libertarian road, and I think that's what it is. Even around HIV and AIDS, I don't particularly like working with gay men. We're fighting a very similar battle in one sense, but you know, gay men are men, they just get involved with other men.

I don't know if I'm on the scene. I suppose I think of being single, I don't think of being in a relationship. I tend now to go out where there are mainly black women, so I might go to Shug's on a Sunday, or I might go to the Vox, or to WKD. I won't go to places like Venus. I don't go out as much as I used to. I've got a lot of Turkish Cypriot lesbian friends, so that's important to me – that I can keep some semblance of family and community – because, obviously, I'm excluded from a lot of stuff that goes on. We do a lot of that, we have barbeques, which is what I did at home. I'm going to end up being just like my mum, I know. We like eating together, going round each other's houses, and going for walks, going to the theatre, whatever, but I'm not a clubby clubby type of person.

When I first came out and I was going out on the scene, I always felt uncomfortable for various reasons, and that is to do with feeling a lot of racism, and not being sure about what was going on. It was only when I met other Turkish Cypriot lesbians – it didn't matter if it was other black women. They 'understand where you're coming from', and all the clichés – but they're true. Not that everyone I meet I feel really warm and loving to, because, obviously, there's differences there as well. In a lot of senses it's a family that we've created for each other, because all of us have got very similar experiences of not having that, or being excluded from lots of things that we would normally be part of. All sorts of stuff involving the whole family network, and it just stops as soon as you leave home or you come out of the family by disgracing them, by doing something that means you bring shame on the family. I've done all those things, really.

My work is in supported housing/counselling. I get a lot out of it, it's not me thinking I'm doing some great deed. I do a lot of helpline stuff because I speak Turkish. Sexual abuse counselling, and HIV and AIDS information, and pre- and post-test counselling, and all that. I think that's got a lot to do with my lesbianism as well. I feel like all these issues are so linked, so intricately linked. I see it all to do with who I am.

I say 'dyke', I say 'lesbian', I use the word 'zami', though it's not the first word I'd use about myself. When I'm with Turkish women, I use a Turkish word, which is *sevici*, the technical word for a lesbian or gay. It translates as 'same sex'. That's the word that most people know, common terminology for me. I think 'gay' is very male, and not political. I see it as a very 'let's just have a fuck' type of word.

sexuality and other identities

race, class, religion, weekend lesbians, going straight

Lesbian is something I do, not something I am.   Carol

He was just someone who reminded me that I wasn't a total lesbian.
     Jayne

Lots of black lesbians I know won't use the word lesbian, because they see it as a white word.   Helen

I can't separate off Buddhism and lesbianism, they're both a part of my life, they're both very important to me.   Natalie

What if I was to sleep with a man one night, does that make me not a lesbian any more?   Tiz

I remember how, in the early 1980s, as a freshly minted twenty-two-year-old dyke, being a lesbian was everything. All I wanted was to be with my girlfriend and to do dykey things, which meant going out a lot and going to meetings. Anything else – my work, my background (which was politically unsound for the times), my past (a less than wholesomely lesbian-in-the-making one) – was quite unimportant.

I then worked with a lesbian who clearly felt very differently. She never said she was a lesbian, although this eventually became clear to me, and she looked different from most of the lesbians I knew and saw. I was puzzled as to why she would not say. It was clearly not because she had problems with her sexuality, nor because of an intolerable level of homophobia in the workplace. One day she talked to me about how she and her girlfriend had decided to define themselves as artists. At the time

I thought this was mighty strange behaviour, felt a little threatened by it, and put it down to pretentiousness. It was a while before I knew what she meant.

In retrospect, my younger self's way of seeing seems part of the time – using 'lesbian' always as a single noun, rather than an adjective or part of a list of nouns. Defining myself solely through my sexuality was a necessary and mainly fun phase, but it delayed my looking at the wider context of who I was, who I wanted to be, and what I wanted to do. Quite a few interviewees said that when they first came out they were only interested in being dykes, in being not straight. After a while, other aspects of their lives asserted themselves. Problems arose where these were at odds with mainstream lesbian life. A lesbian identity, once formed, was supposed to grow purer and stronger, it did not involve change. A lesbian who defined herself through other systems, perhaps related to work or some other system of beliefs, or, heretically, refused to define herself as anything, was considered to be 'not up to scratch', or even self-hating.

Lesbians now see their identity – sexual, social, political – in as many ways as there are lesbians. While 'lesbian' to some means an all-encompassing identity, to others it is but one element in a multi-faceted self-definition. In the writings of 1970s and early 1980s feminism, 'lesbian' itself was supposed to say it all. But the exclusions of feminism meant that this was problematic for a huge number of women.

Lesbians who pre-dated second wave feminism had been used to a very different set of cultural norms, partly informed by a web of issues around visibility and personal safety. They may well have been interested in feminism, but their behaviour was different. These lesbians were told they were wrong to live as they did. Butch and femme identities were unacceptable. The twilight world of the bar dyke was often depicted and discussed with disdain – women who were not, by the standards of the time, out, who behaved like men and who had no politics. They were seen by many as the dinosaurs which feminism should make extinct, and if they were unwilling to make changes, they were shunned.

In the late 1980s, with the massive disillusionment on all sides with lesbian feminism, there was a partial reclamation of butch and femme, and a tardy fêting of those who had been there and done it. 1987 saw the publication of Joan Nestle's A *Restricted Country*[1], and strong and positive publicity was elicited by her speaking tour in this country. There was also an academic reclamation of the novels of the bar dyke zone (known as lesbian survival literature in the Lesbian Herstory Archives in New York), which many women had continued to need, read and enjoy regardless.

In the early 1990s lesbianism, in its popular image at least, is no longer transgressive. The media has made PC the new monster (missing both the joke and the importance), and predictably has thrown out the equality of opportunity baby with the politically correct bathwater. Predictably, now that we're just people and individual achievement is all, it is that much harder to vocalize or try to improve awareness of inequities and discrimination without being immediately labelled as a 'PC fascist'. So the reasons why aspects of identities were ignored, for the greater good of political progress and changed lives, have not been overcome but are positioned firmly on the backburner.

Lesbians who had come out in earlier decades were not the only ones who had difficulties with 1970s lesbian feminism. Lesbian identity was expected to subsume all others. Other aspects of identity, which were of at least equal importance to many women, were seen as diversionary and divisive, and as attributes of the patriarchal systems which divided us against ourselves and would be swept away. Examples are being black, working-class, disabled, socialist, femmy, distressed, rich, upper-class, sexually adventurous or sexually outspoken. Looking back, it seems less clear what exactly lesbians were supposed to be, but very plain what we weren't. The limitations on women's lives of the 1950s had been partially overcome, but 1970s feminism unintentionally became a new straitjacket.

By the mid 1980s, little was published from the lesbian feminist perspective which did not give details of the authors in terms of age, race, class and disability. This was a reaction to being belittled through male writings, and to the voices of women – in particular working-class, black and ethnic minority, young, older, disabled, mothers – being denigrated and considered invalid. But, as a strategy, it was dangerously double-edged: can the reader find all she needs to know about someone with these details? How can she avoid making unhelpful assumptions? For instance, assumptions about the differences between black and white working-class women; women of working-class origin with and without further education; black women born in this country and elsewhere.

As there had been a straight/lesbian explosion in the 1970s, so, in the 1980s, there were explosions about racism and classism to which the mainly white and middle-class women's movement could not adequately respond.

Certainly I won't obey that lesbian mafia nonsense that one must dress in a certain way or cut off one's hair to be real. Those are all the superficial rules, silly. I no longer believe that feminism is a tool which can eliminate racism – or even promote better understanding between different races and kinds of women. I have felt less understanding between different races from many lesbian women than I do from some straight people. At least their heterosexual indifference allows me more freedom to be myself.[2]

As a reaction to lesbianism's denial of other aspects of identity, a tendency developed for women to regroup around different identities, retiring to arenas where there would be no such ignorance around. The titles of many of these groups were specific to the nth degree.

There was a pervasive expectation that black women should choose whether to concentrate politically on race or gender, as if the two were easily separated and mutually exclusive. Here are two responses: 'I can't call myself a "lesbian feminist" because to me it is a whole concept that says you subsume everything to patriarchy.'[3] And, 'The pressure to be either Black or lesbian make it very difficult and confusing to develop being Black and lesbian.'[4] If a woman was seen to choose race, she was thought not to be serious about her feminism:

> ... while my sexuality is a part of me, it's not the only thing. My race and class are equally important ... If you don't have the same politics as some white lesbians and are seen to be politically involved with Black men, then they somehow patronize you and think you haven't quite made it yet. And they believe themselves to be at a much higher stage of consciousness because according to them they are women-identified and you are still male-identified.[5]

Black lesbians calling themselves 'black lesbians' or 'black lesbian feminists' makes explicit the solipsism that the use of 'lesbian' or 'lesbian feminist' generally excludes black women. This linguistic exclusion, as an index of more general denial, has led to some black women rejecting the use of the word lesbian (and feminist) entirely. Despite the proliferation of women's publishing enterprises during the last twenty years and the supposed commitment to equal opportunities and challenging racism, it took until 1993 for the first book about black lesbians living in Britain to appear.[6]

Caught between the body beautiful ethos and ableism of the commercial scene, and the heterosexism of disability politics, lesbians with disabilities are another example of 'other-identified' lesbians who may organize separately. These women often find themselves excluded from mainstream lesbian activities. The venue may be physically inaccessible, or the event may not have been structured so as to be attractive and welcoming to women with disabilities.

> I don't like to meet people because so often they're unsympathetic and ignorant, and they say, 'Oh you look perfectly fine', or 'It's incurable, isn't it?' or 'It's mass hysteria, isn't it?' I get all this kind of crap all the time and it does put me off meeting people. I don't want to get back in touch with some of my peers because they say things like, 'How can you not be better yet?' 'So you're not better yet, why don't you do this or that?', and when I need to ask them for help they get stroppy or they're not nice. (Annie)

Alisa Solomon talks about a three-year plan for improving access that was published in Boston in 1989.[7] This included advertising events as scent-free and posting sniffers at venue entrances to ensure compliance, and making sugar-free drinks available at all times along with signs 'indicating that the presence of sugar-free drinks is not an endorsement of the diet industry'. She noted that women took great exception to the authoritarian tone of the manifesto, although this was coupled with an awareness of the desirability of improving access. 'Though their responses have ranged from dismissal to ridicule to disappointment to anger, all have tempered their scoffing with sympathy.'

Sisters Against Disablement (SAD) helped put access issues firmly on the map in this country. For a time, during the 1980s, all venues – community-based and commercial – had to give access codes, in SAD-defined format, for their ads to be accepted in newsletters and magazines. SAD no longer exists. Gemma is another long-running group: 'If you're a lesbian or bisexual woman, with or without a disability/illness and over 16 years old.'

Although the dyke scene is largely too commercial to be interested in access issues, the disability movement has of late taken on some issues around sexuality. The Tokens, a cabaret act performed by lesbians with disabilities have become well known on the disability cabaret circuit.

Awareness of the needs of people with disabilities and long-term illness has possibly increased as more lesbians and gay men experience friends living with HIV and AIDS. This has not yet translated into changes in how the scene operates.

It used to be that a lesbian's politics said everything about her that anyone needed to know. Now a lesbian's style is often taken as a window on her beliefs, lifestyle, politics and background. In these postmodern times, when there is so much talk about playing with style and image, it is a little surprising that style is taken at face value. Perhaps this is an indication that no one watches *The Late Show*.

Feminist Review produced an issue in 1990 entitled *Perverse Politics* in which the contributing authors were falling over themselves to assert their belief in a polymorphous identity, that is, one that takes or passes through different forms or stages. It was as if, now that identity politics had been discredited, it became acceptable to acknowledge that identity is not fixed. Inge Blackman and Kathryn Perry noted that 'there are more ways of looking like a lesbian than ever before.'[8] And went on to question, 'But do they have anything new to say about our identities and politics?' They talked about how wearing items of different ethnic styles from countries of origin, within a western cultural context, could assert racial and cultural identities. Mixing up fashion in this way allowed the display of varied allegiances as well as origins: DMs and saris, head wraps and leather.

Whether to take images and representations of women at face value has also been a major issue with regard to attitudes towards sexual practice. SM women have been criticized for appropriating lesbian sexual imagery. They have advocated as a liberating force the making real through playing out of fantasy. Anti-SM women have often fallen into the trap of blurring the actual and fantasy, reacting to the latter as though it were the former. Both pro- and anti-SM lesbians have voiced their feelings of exclusion from the lesbian scene as, at different times, certain sorts of sexual practice are held up as OK, right, hip or exciting, depending on who is speaking.

In the current climate of sexual exploration outside of the duality of straight and lesbian sex, there has similarly been upset in both quarters. 'How much longer, in an age when only sexual honesty and self-respect will save our lives, are we going to keep on pretending . . . that we all stick to the gay and narrow?'[9] Some lesbians have spoken about their fears of no longer belonging if they are not inclined or not prepared to sleep with men. Others who have 'experimented' or moved into heterosexual relationships, have been ignored, excluded and written out of address books.

Some older lesbians talked to me about feeling ignored by younger women, and excluded by current lesbian images of sex. In straight society, older women are thought to have no sexuality, and now the same messages were coming from lesbians, who might have been expected to have a more radical, forward-looking attitude.

In *Women like Us*[10] older women described feeling that they were not seen as lesbians unless they were overtly sexual in their behaviour and dressed in a fetishized fashion.

There are now many older lesbian groups, lesbian history groups and projects around the country, although certainly fewer young lesbian groups than in the heady days of local government funding in the early 1980s.

While club culture is the dominant mode of the lesbian scene, younger women will have primacy. Even so, they object to the ghost of feminism's past which, as they see it, dictates what is acceptable in terms of behaviour, sexual practice, and leisure pursuits. They also feel limited by lesbian culture which, they claim, labels some activities as wrong and unlesbian.

There are many organizations for lesbians and gays who have religious beliefs. These beliefs often serve to position them as piggy in the middle, between an increasingly hedonistic lesbian and gay scene, generally disinclined towards the religious and spiritual, and a largely disapproving religious scene. *Gay Christian* sets out its platform:

> It is the conviction of the member[s] of the Gay Christian Movement that human sexuality in all its richness is [a] gift of God gladly to be accepted, enjoyed and honoured as a way of both expressing and growing in love in accordance with the life and teaching of Jesus Christ; therefore it is their conviction that it is entirely compatible with the Christian faith not only to love another person of the same sex but also to express that love fully in a personal sexual relationship.

Many lesbians' experience of religion, particularly in relation to their sexuality, is less than positive. There has been a proliferation recently of lesbian- and gay-friendly meditation and Buddhist groups. There is still disagreement about just how friendly such groups are, and a pervasive feeling that this kind of activity is not part of the Life.

Arguments about religious belief and between co-religionists some-times surface in the gay press. The *Pink Paper* has a column, 'In Belief', which covers a range of related topics, such as the increasing numbers of out priests and vicars, and lesbian ex-nuns. The issue of women priests featured in a *Pink Paper* article about Quest, the lesbian and gay Catholic group, and caused controversy at the group's twentieth anniversary. Quest is billed as a traditionally conservative group, unlike the Catholic caucus of the Lesbian and Gay Christian Movement, which challenges the hierarchy. There is a Jewish lesbian (and gay) community of congregations, organizations, helplines and discussion groups. There are now lesbian rabbis, lesbian deacons and lesbian vicars (although, as noted in 'In Belief', it may be difficult for deacons to come out without fear of spoiling their prospects, given the scarcity of posts they will be chasing when they become vicars). The Metropolitan Church in south-east London had a tent at Pride 94 in which they were officiating over wedding or commitment ceremonies. In the USA there are far more lesbian and gay religious groups. One called Dignity exists nationally and has about ten groups in New York alone. It will be interesting to see whether this trend will cross the Atlantic.

Since the 1960s there has been a huge growth in alternative religous practices: lesbians interested in goddess worship, matriarchal religions, female spirituality. This probably reached its height during the activism at Greenham Common. During the early 1990s, perhaps as part of the eco-aware culture and the move away from the cut and thrust individualism of the 1980s, I have again come across many articles and references to goddesses, witches (a group of whom apparently sort out the weather each year for Pride) and female shamanism.

Lesbians have psychics, healers, therapists, counsellors and gurus. Since sisterhood is no longer expected to be able to solve everydyke's problems, therapy and personal growth have become acceptable if not requisite pursuits among lesbians. There used to be, and still is, a section of lesbian opinion that remains totally opposed to the idea of lesbians seeking therapeutic help. The main arguments for this opposition can be separated into three strands. The history of psychiatry in relation to lesbians – and women in general – is hardly a glorious one, and the brief history of sexology in Chapter 2 shows clearly the sources of this. Secondly, it was anathema to pay an 'expert' to help you sort out problems which, in the thinking of the 1970s and early 1980s, were caused by a patriarchal and homophobic society. Thirdly, the dominant strand of lesbian feminism was anti-intellectual and could not, therefore, see any usefulness in psychoanalytically-based work.

Unless a lesbian has always known her sexual identity, and never felt forced to try to change it, she will have gone through a period of change from heterosexuality to lesbianism. Some women have had sudden flashes of realization, or fallen in love to such an extent that no further exploration or explanation was needed. Many others remain unsure for years of where to position themselves on this axis.

Now there is the option of Queer, which could be seen as a hipper version of bisexuality, in spirit if not in deed. Bisexuality has long had bad press and a bad reputation in lesbian lore. But what about those for whom sexual identity is not a defining feature, or who are unable to make it one: 'I just like women', 'I'm not a lesbian, I just love this woman' (cf. Margaret in *Brookside*). It is impossible to know the chances of these women going on to adopt a lesbian identity. Anecodotal evidence suggests it is very common for those first 'not-a-lesbian' relationships to break down when one partner has to go off and see if it is really just about that one woman.

Lesbians going straight is an issue which can arouse big emotions and strong talk about betrayal and respectability. There is, however, a growing number of lesbians who do not throw up their hands in horror, but react instead with, 'So what?' or 'How exciting'. Conversations about lesbians having relationships with men inevitably bring up a lot of questions about what we mean by lesbian and how we view the construction of lesbian sexuality. Some women still call themselves lesbians while involved with men. Others immediately swap labels.

Sally Munt asks if, although we might believe that lesbianism and lesbian identity are influenced by social and cultural change, we feel and behave as though there is some immutable essence of lesbianism.[11] And the answer is an unequivocal yes. Comments like 'I never thought *she* would do it', or 'I'm not surprised about *her*', or 'I'm just having a heterosexual relationship at the moment', imply there is an essence of lesbianness, a true lesbianism, which is forever (and which is suggestive of the congenital theories for lesbian existence outlined in Chapter 2).

The new plurality of definition around lesbian sexuality and behaviour has been met with relief from those who think it is a more honest and possibly liberating attitude. There is a certain amount of sadness and derision from others, who feel that it will lead to their lives being diminished and marginalized. The newly formed twenty-two-year-old version of myself would surely have been appalled; her older version is caught between a rejection of lesbian essentialism and a touch of that old dinosaur feeling.

Anecodotally, it seems some of the most outspoken and visible lesbian feminists of the past are the ones who are having sexual relationships with men. This should not be too shocking. Firstly, we are more likely to hear about the lives of the most famous women. Secondly, given the level of dissatisfaction with the prescriptive nature of feminism, is it surprising that those who inhabited the sharp end found it more limiting than most?

Apocryphal tales abound of white weddings, hidden lesbian histories and getting his dinner of nights.

The reactions to a woman being unfaithful with a man are vastly magnified in popular lesbian wisdom over an affair with another woman. On an immediate emotional level this makes sense. The two are not choices of equal worth in the eyes of society, and this has heavy implications for how lesbians will react to them. But what exactly are we saying here? That sleeping with men is such a desirable thing, so tempting, that someone has 'fallen' when they succumb? Are we saying lesbian sexuality is better, or that we ourselves like it better? Do we believe it is morally and politically preferable? Are we still saying that the real lesbian is the woman who has always been one and will forever stay one? What happened to the right of women to define their own sexuality? Was that a Utopian ideal? Do lesbians still not allow change in people's lives? If Queer can subvert the hetero/homo dichotomy, could this dilute some of the tension and anger around this subject, without also diluting the notion of lesbianism? The range of behaviours and practices that can now be included under the heading 'lesbian' could lead to a more open, broadly based attitude to sexuality.

NOTES

1. Joan Nestle, A Restricted Country, Sheba, 1987.
2. Cherie Moraga and Gloria Anzaldua (eds), This Bridge Called My Back, Kitchen Table Press, 1984, p. 69.
3. Gail Lewis, in 'Becoming visible – black lesbian discussions', in 'Many voices – one chant: black feminist perspectives', Feminist Review, no. 17, 1984, p. 66.
4. Gerry Ahrens, Ahmed Farooqui and Amitha Patel, 'Irrespective of race, sex, sexuality', in Bob Cant and Susan Hemmings (eds), Radical Records – Thirty Years of Lesbian and Gay History, Routledge, 1988, p. 128.
5. Pratibha Parmar, in Becoming visible – black lesbian discussions, p. 59.
6. Valerie Mason-John and Ann Khambatta, Lesbians Talk: Making Black Waves, Scarlet, 1993.
7. Alisa Solomon, 'Dykotomies: scents and sensibility', in Arlene Stein (ed.), Sexperts, Sisters, Queers: Beyond the Lesbian Nation, Plume, 1993, p. 210.
8. Inge Blackman and Kathryn Perry, 'Skirting the issue: lesbian fashion for the 1990s', in 'Perverse politics,' Feminist Review, no. 34, 1990, p. 67.
9. Lisa Power, Pink Paper, 2 July 1993.

10. Suzanne Neild and Rosalind Pearson (eds), *Women Like Us*, The Women's Press, 1992.

11. Sally Munt (ed.) *New Lesbian Criticism*, Harvester Wheatsheaf, 1992.

**HELEN: I'M THIRTY-FOUR, I'M BLACK, I LIVE IN BRIGHTON.
TINA: I'M TWENTY-SEVEN, AND I LIVE IN BRIGHTON NOW. I'M
GREEK.
TIZ: I'M TWENTY AND I WAS BROUGHT UP IN YEOVIL, WHICH IS IN
THE SOUTH-WEST.**

TINA: I'm out here, but not out in Greece. I'm out to my parents, and to my close friends. I'm not always out to groups of people I meet here, for a variety of reasons. I find it hard to negotiate what it means to be a lesbian in a Greek way of thinking, so I'm very aware of the image I put out. In Greece the image of lesbians is more or less the equivalent of Radclyffe Hall, that's the nearest. Highly undesirable, mannish, lusting after everything that's got a skirt on, very praetorian and distasteful. The image is changing in Greece, very slowly.

The other thing that is important for me is that there is no sense of lesbian history, lesbian community, lesbian continuity in the way that there is here or in the States. The use of the word lesbian in Greece is a term of abuse, the same as queer used to be here, amongst the general population, and amongst lesbians has been so until very recently. Now it's changing in more or less the same way that queer is changing here.

HELEN: Coming out for me was a very long process. I came out, then I went back to being straight, then I came out and then I went back to being straight. It took several years. I think partly I didn't meet the right person who would spearhead me into the lesbian community. Once I'd initiated myself into a drunken lesbian fling I could say to myself that I could do it, but that wasn't a lesbian to me. A lesbian was somebody who desired women because she found them sexually attractive and could envisage having long-term relationships with them, not because you've been abused, because you've been fucked over by men, because you've got a thing about the patriarchy – but because there's something that made you think women were better than men in terms of having relationships.

TIZ: I decided I was a dyke at fifteen and that was that. Just did it, shagged lots of women and that was that. Shagged a bloke and thought, fuck this, I prefer the birds. I didn't know any other dykes, then my schoolteacher clocked on to me, and so I thought, fuck that, I'm not a dyke if she is. There was this club in Yeovil where all the girls got together and either fought each other or slept with each other. I don't have a problem with dykes who've been het, but I have a problem if they're still quite straight, if they act very girly.

Designer dykes in London must have a lot of money, they must hold down very good jobs. I mean they're wearing Destroy gear, not Caterpillar boots –

oh no, we don't go for Caterpillar boots, you mere mortals use them. Designer dykes are also the ones that integrate the club scene, they're the ones that, in a way, almost try and play the fag hag. They go to all the gay boys' clubs because it's really stylish. You can get your traditional dyke, she goes out and she may wear your trainers and the style stuff that's in, she may wander around with a little bomber jacket and the cap, and she may listen to the good stuff and go to the clubs. But she's not a styler, not a real, 'Hey, you can't look at me unless you earn twenty grand a year'. It's shit. It's like a fag hag looks at a dyke.

I'm a bit of a label girl and I like my labels, even though I can't afford them. I like the stuff I wear, I take pride in it. And you get other dykes that don't care what they wear, don't give a shit, aren't colour coordinated, '501s, what are they?' I think you just get sets and sets and sets, and this lot seems really upper-class dykes. Unfortunately, that's what the London scene is at the moment, it's like, let's take on a straight persona because we can do that too. I suppose it has to happen, just like white people had to have afros in the 1970s, but I think it's just really sad. But it's all very discreet, isn't it, that glance over you, to see what's she wearing. I wouldn't like to have the attitude, but I think the clothes they wear are really nice.

TIZ: The thing with dykes, I've realized, is that if it's something dyke-run, they feel they can complain about it to you and expect you to change it straight away. If it's something that's straight-run or gay male-run, they won't complain. It's such a pain in the arse. I've been running this club for a year and a half and we just can't get our heads round the way they complain. 'It's too SM; it's too vanilla.' They don't get off their arses and do enough about it. Either we play too up-to-date music or it's too hard. 'It's not chart stuff; the other club's bigger; that banner's abusive to women.' I feel like crying after I finish at Shameless Hussies [club in Brighton] sometimes. I buy all this really nice music, top-notch stuff that I spend my dole on. I end up playing all the old shit and it's upsetting. Which is why you get all the good DJs in London or Manchester.

HELEN: Do you think that because, in general, women haven't been used to choice in terms of social events and socialization ... when they get a choice, they don't know what to do with it?

TIZ: Yeah, and also a lot of dykes don't seem to go to London, and that's what we're trying to provide is London in Brighton. So they don't know what's on, and if they were to go to Venus at the Fridge, and there'd be all this new music being played, they'd probably dance to it because it's a London club and they spent a lot of dosh getting there. Tina can't talk about her clubs because they're illegal.

TINA: Tiz has said it all, I'm not really a club girl. You can't expect people who moved here from smaller places to suddenly shift into the urban designer feel. The sense of community in a place like London is much more transient, although gossip is rife.

It was my first relationship in Canterbury with Helen. I went through being a radical feminist, goddesses, the whole range, but after a while it just didn't work.

It's only the last year and a half I've started moving towards a distinct SM crowd in London, and going to clubs through that, and at the moment it seems to be more the kind of attitude I was looking for. Sexual attitude and sexual urges as well, but of all the scenes it seems to be the most transient. That is not really what's happening in Brighton. Moving here, I have to constantly justify a position, even before identifying myself as SM.

HELEN: It also means your community in London isn't down here, so you have to travel to be accepted as an SM dyke.

TINA: It seems to me that in small places, people who've been here for years, maybe negotiated a previous heterosexual life, have come out and have struggled to maintain a position that for a lot of people coming from the cities is passé. For me, cities work better, because I have no history in this country, and no sense of community other than the one that I wish to identify with, so it's much easier to live with a sense of anonymity.

HELEN: I think I have a regional understanding of community, a regional community of understanding, which is to do with race, politics and acceptance and colour. Having lived most of my life in London, a supposedly cosmopolitan place, one would have thought I'd be well placed in London as a black dyke. But there are other reasons why I don't want to live in London: partly it's too big, blah, blah. I sometimes find the community of lesbians is much more segregated, particularly for black lesbians. I'm not a separatist, but I find that I'm in a sense mingling with white people as opposed to any other people of colour, and at times this creates an identity slippage.

In Canterbury, where I lived for four years, it seemed very homely. Everybody had relationships for fifteen years, that kind of atmosphere, and to a certain extent I was mothered by older dykes, which was OK, but sex was not on the agenda at all. As a new dyke I wanted to explore sex and sexuality and it needed to be at the top of the agenda, together with race. If it hadn't been for my very good friend Akua I don't think I would have been able to last the four years really. She protected me against black homophobia, particularly in the black student society circles. I ended up gravitating towards the black side, and Akua and I created our own society that allowed anybody who had a genuine interest in anti-racism in. We found the women's societies as separatist as the black societies were.

Coming to Brighton was a complete explosion because sex is on the agenda, right at the top. You go into a pub or a club and there's this incredible sexual energy in the atmosphere; and it seems to ride on the back of gossip, short-term relationships, a constantly renewing influx of new students and new people. Community here, for me, means spending a hell of a long time thinking I should live in London again, because Brighton's so white and so ignorant.

I think the political battles within feminism in the 1980s instilled a sense of guilt in white people, which is not really the idea, is it? What I think it's done – all the race awareness, all the arguing and conferences and clubs and pubs and books – is instilled some sense of guilt, which of course stops white people trying to integrate. And they integrate to the best of their ability but don't go any further, just in case they make a boo-boo, just in case they say something that's racist, just in case.

So what comes out of it is that the colour is ignored, even though they're not ignoring it inside. For that reason, it's very difficult for white dykes to actually talk to me as a human being in Brighton, and the ones that do become my friends are very few and far between. I should imagine it's very similar with dykes who've got SM 'tendencies'. Most people want to belong to a community, you need to find people who are going to say whatever tendency you have is OK with them. Otherwise you become isolated and ... it's very similar to being black really.

TINA: I think there's a big difference, because the whole SM thing has got a series of labels to do with a kind of denial of the feminist movement.

HELEN: So has the black movement, in a different way, but the outcome is the same: the denial of the white feminist movement of the 1970s. When there were all those big bust-ups in the late 1970s, early 1980s, the ones who were left were the lesbians, the SM dykes and the black women.

TINA: I'm fed up with having to explain that I don't want to be a man, having to explain myself ...

HELEN: ... Like they do if you're black, they ask you to explain your relationship to feminism – 'why are you fucking white women?' And if you have SM tendencies, 'Don't you realize this has great connotations with slavery of our past, and you're bringing the side down.' From the little experience I've had of being a lesbian – because it isn't very long really – I get the feeling that women are very scared of change, of exploring their sexuality. They seem to think that sexuality is a label they can attach to themselves to be accepted into a particular group of friends or whatever, just like a password that says 'yes, you can come in'.

But that's as far as it goes, and when it comes to talking about sex and what we do in bed and all that ... I mean there's so many jokes about it aren't there? The younger women I've met recently, through Tiz, don't seem to have the same fears about expanding on their sexuality and just having a good time, because their parents were 1970s and that's a completely different set of attitudes. It seems to me that younger women are much happier to be upfront about lesbianism at a young age than women of our age. I'm sure we have some forms of feminism to thank for that.

Tiz: Mandy and myself had a helluva problem being accepted as dykes in Brighton. We couldn't get into the scene. It's not just about politics, it's like if you're not ... boring actually. We had to join Pink Parasol, which is like Lesbian Strength, so we met lots of dykes and we started doing political things that we didn't believe in that much. You get a lot of baby dykes in Brighton and a lot of them are baby butches, very fresh turnover, and they're very impressionable, so the older dykes go, this is where it's at kid, you do this, don't step out of line and you'll be sorted. It's got this real rising up through the ranks mentality. For instance, I say, 'go out and check some chicks', and this woman just nearly fainted, and I said, 'yeah, babes'.

Another thing you find with a lot of girls is once they find a girl they kick themselves off the scene. It's like a predatory thing, isn't it? You hunt round for the woman, hit her over the head, drag her back to the cave and you're sorted, and she stays there. Then you have problems and you come out and start to have friends again, and it's such a crock of shite.

It's like everything: you get out of a drugs phase, you go into a celibate phase, you go into everything, don't you? But the thing with dykes is they don't seem to understand that. It's like if you're bisexual you don't wear the lesbian badge, it's so defining. If I fuck a man one day a year ... am I a dyke still? And you get all these straight girls coming on to the scene, that like to dabble and go, 'Ooh, I'm not sure.'

[Do you see yourself as part of a particular group of lesbians?]

Tiz: Yeah, I do, we're all club and music girls, that's my thing.

HELEN: Yeah, I think I'm a club girl. I don't get on with the academic dykes, because they just talk about it and don't do it. They hide behind academia really, which I find frustrating. I want something more down to earth, so I tend to hang around with people I used to work with as a care assistant.

TINA: Surely there's a problem there as well, because they don't appreciate the academic part of you. ... It's the same: I don't feel like I identify with a social community, although I would say I'm in the SM community, but then I have the excuse that I'm not British. I'm interested, seduced by the academic circle (not necessarily a lesbian circle at all in my experience), and then seduced by the SM gang, but then there's a price. It is political but at the same time it is viewed, from all the communities I'm part of, as a profoundly unpolitical statement, because I refuse grounding. I refuse to make an overt political statement. My political statement, if you like, is a hybrid. I think you can't be a hybrid, an exile, without paying the price. It's the price of 'What brought you here? Why do you speak this language? Why do you look the way you do? Why do you have these preferences which mean you can't identify with a straight Greek scene, a lesbian Greek scene, a lesbian English scene, a straight English scene?' That's also why, in a way, I like London as a non-Londoner, because I feel I can have the space to survive there, whereas if I made my home here, I'd suffocate.

HELEN: I've found it pretty difficult myself.

TINA: Yes, but you're coming from another London, not my London. The other side of that is that being a hybrid is a particularly commercialized and saleable thing, it's what makes the covers of *Vanity Fair* and so on, and that's totally apolitical and all the rest, so ... mainstream, so het.

TINA: I have changed the way I dress and that was more London influenced than SM influenced – about having money and having a job, being able to buy stuff. I changed from putting everything I could find on top of my body and trying to hide it, to trying to be sexual, physical, sexually visible, and trying to show as much flesh as I possibly could.

HELEN: Your flat was a playground, wasn't it, because you weren't associated with anybody here, you could come here and fuck around.

TINA: That's right, I was free, I could fuck around, and then I was back in London, and that was a kind of ideal situation for a while.

HELEN: I've changed my image in terms of wearing less clothes as well, I used to be the hippy dyke in Canterbury. But it's completely not on to wear that kind of thing here. I found it very difficult to be accepted into the community anyway, like Tiz, but for different reasons, mainly because of my age and my race and my ... whatever. So I found myself completely unconsciously getting into leggings and t-shirts, and what have I done, I've cut all my hair off.

TIZ: Slightly your lover's influence I feel ...

HELEN: Well, I've had influence from other lovers, but it hasn't made any difference. I think it's partly to do with really wanting to be accepted into the community, but also I like playing with the idea of seeing people view each other, I find it fascinating, watching how lesbians interact with each other here, how people look.

TIZ: You're turning into a style baby as well though – look at that corset you bought, it's beautiful.

HELEN: That's something to do with enhancing my sexuality and coming out more, because I don't think coming out is a stationary process. I find that I'm coming out all the time, and going from one thing to another, and looking at a circle of femme dykes and seeing what I can get out of them, looking at a circle of black butch dykes and seeing what attracts me.

TIZ: But it makes you feel good, doesn't it, to wear different things ... for instance, why are you blading all your hair off? Is it to prove something? It's not just because we want to shave it off for you – you want to shock.

HELEN: People are shocked anyway. If I sit in a pub, people are very tentative about coming up and talking to me. So getting laid as a black dyke in Brighton is pretty slim on the scene really, unless you act white like some black women do here – never talk to other black people, try to look as white as possible, and never talk about race.

TIZ: It's not just that people see your colour as unapproachable, and worrying they might slip up, it's also because you're so fucked off with the scene, you make yourself unapproachable.

[Which names do you use to describe your lesbiansim?]

TIZ: I use 'dyke' or 'dirty lesbo'. 'Queer' just means straight now, actually, which I think I'm feeling a bit upset about. 'Lessie' or 'lesbian' I find very boring and 1970s, and 'gay' is crap ...

HELEN: It's a dilution, isn't it, of 'gay and lesbian' ... But it's interesting the word dyke is completely rejected by, particularly, black separatist dykes, black separatist lesbians or black separatist zamis. It's considered to be associated with fascism. Because the dyke, in the 1970s realization of the dyke, was supposed to be big, butch with maybe fascist tendencies; and lesbian is a white term so ... I call myself a dyke, because I live in Brighton and that's what the term seems to be here, and it doesn't bother me. If I was in Manchester and part of the black lesbian scene there, I'd probably call myself a zami. If you get a group of women who belong to a particular subculture then they want their own name, it's important.

TINA: A lot of white lesbians would never call themselves lesbians ... gay women, gay ladies. ...

TIZ: We used to put that on flyers for Shameless Hussies when it first started up – gay ladies, gay girls – never used to put dykes, and never used to put queers, or lesbian. As soon as we established ourselves, we started putting 'clit licker' on the flyer.

HELEN: I enjoy wearing the clit licker badge, particularly if I'm in a very straight sort of environment.

TINA: I quite like queer actually.

HELEN: Queer is very popular with SM dykes isn't it? Well, it used to be. Is it passé now?

TINA: What does Della Grace call herself now? Sexual outlaw? No, it's pussy-licking sodomite.

TIZ: I think young gay people as a whole need – I really needed – confirmation. And when I discovered *Out on Wednesday* or whatever, and *Portrait of a Marriage* and *Oranges Are Not the Only Fruit*, I just felt like, phew, there are more gay people. And that was when I was seventeen, eighteen, and that was too late, I needed it at fourteen, fifteen.

HELEN: The idea of the lesbian safe sex video was obviously really good, when it started out. I see things as carrying on from one another. You develop things, and at least something's out that can be progressed from.

TIZ: I was embarrassed because the worst clip was the two white women ... the others were quite good actually. I thought the Victorian woman with the strap-on was all right, 'Bend over love ... while you're down there.' Let's talk about herpes, and then let's talk about going down on her with a piece of cling film – it's like, so what? And like in the club scene, I don't know many girls who carry rubber gloves, I know you do [Helen], but then I take them off you at the start of the night so you can't shag anyone.

TINA: I think safe sex is important actually, but it was just not shown in an interesting way, in a sexy way.

TIZ: All those DJs and they couldn't even get some decent music ...

JAYNE EGERTON IS THIRTY-FIVE AND WORKS IN TELEVISION.

The first time I slept with a girl was quite extraordinary really. I went away with my boyfriend when I was sixteen, and he got shingles and had to go to hospital overnight. While he was there I got picked up by a much older woman. She was called Lola, an anarchist in her thirties, she was a completely wild creature. I don't really remember what the sex was like, but I was bowled over by the fact I was doing something so *risqué*. There was a sense in which I thought I was building up an intriguingly diverse sexual c.v. The truth was I didn't tell anyone. I also slept with a couple of girls at boarding college, but was quite unmoved by it. Really, I was very bound up with men. I think there was always an undercurrent in my life that lesbianism was something I could do, an identity I could move towards.

In my late teens I began to get involved in radical politics. This wasn't an affectation or a stage. I've hung on to a core socialist analysis of the world even now, which makes me feel like a dinosaur. My feminism grew out of what I had seen and experienced in my family; it was natural, organic. I remember women's liberation bursting onto TV when I was twelve, when the Miss World contest was disrupted. It stayed with me.

It wasn't easy to join the Women's Movement. Like being a hunter going after an exotic, elusive species – you knew it was out there somewhere but you didn't know how to find it. I would loiter around shyly on demonstrations, Reclaim the Night, abortion demos. I remember going to a National Abortion Campaign meeting when I was twenty-one. I felt like a kid swooning at the prefects. I realized, rather excitedly, that some of these remote, magnificent women were lesbians. I was driven more by the desire to be part of that charmed circle, rather than an urge to clamber into their beds. Lust came later. I had a long relationship with one of these women several years later. Not so remote after all.

I got involved with Women's Aid while I was still heterosexual. Seeing women so badly hurt by men affected me deeply. I used to come back from the refuge and want to punch my gentle, ineffectual boyfriend in the mouth. I decided, in a deliberate, pre-meditated fashion, that I wanted to give up men. Some of the lesbian feminist writing of the time made this sound no more difficult than throwing away that last packet of Marlboros. The kind of anti-male violence feminism I was attracted to was not renowned for its welcoming attitude to straight women, unless they were 'in transition'. Lesbian chauvinism was the order of the day. There was also anti-lesbianism amongst heterosexual feminists. But this was not a problem in the circles I moved in.

In 1981 I went to a Leeds conference on sexual violence, with the full intention of cutting my sapphic teeth, and by the end of it I had got off with someone. I remember I wore this charcoal boilersuit with a purple leather jacket and little hints of make-up. I adjusted my clothes to suit anticipated reaction. I really wanted to be one of the girls, I wanted to be accepted. I was young. I didn't want to go in the clothes I would wear normally and say 'just accept me as I am', because I had a horrible feeling I wouldn't be accepted. I regret that anti-male violence politics came to be identified with political lesbianism. I heard of someone at the conference saying, 'Well, that was pointless, there were women in the room who were still straight.' It had the potential to draw in so many women.

I joined WAVAW [Women Against Violence Against Women] after the conference. My best friends all come from this period of my life. Plenty of sensible, intelligent women were drawn to these politics, contrary to what the most sectarian of the socialist feminists would say. We attracted women who wanted to 'do' something. WAVAW came to represent the outer fringes of feminism. In political terms, I went from A to Z. Probably I could have done with something gentler, but for a time, I had this genuine desire for uncompromising feminism. There were all sorts of other areas of life in which women were disadvantaged, which were thought not to be sufficiently swashbuckling. No one even wanted to talk about equal pay – yawn yawn, let's get back to pornography and violence.

But there was something thrilling about mixing with women who always called men 'fuckers'. I unlearned deep-seated habits of deference to men, for which I'm eternally grateful. But my individual voice fell silent: I was complicit in the abuse of other women who did not 'fit in', who were not lesbians 'yet' or who were the 'wrong sort' of lesbians.

The lesbian feminist scene of the early 1980s had some very negative and scary elements. There was a great deal of harassment and intimidation, often done in the name of a grand political principle. Race, class and sexuality came to be sticks with which to beat other women. There was a rush to identify as more than a lesbian, to clock up an additional oppression – was my grandmother Irish etc.? I remember the daughter of a famous academic calling herself working-class on matrilineal grounds. So-called self-definition was all. I think separatist politics of any description are very prone to internecine warfare. Much of the lunacy and in-fighting seems like a function of living in a goldfish bowl, an unreal world.

I find it difficult, in the end, to work out what I did think and feel politically, or sexually really. I fell into a certain political network, got involved with women. It all happened at lightning speed, I didn't have very much time to reflect. I got involved in a long-term relationship when I was twenty-two, with a woman I was in love with. Sexual questions that remained just got buried. I had prematurely taken on an absolute lesbian identity and adopted a scorched earth policy to my heterosexual past. It was 'Lesbian Year Zero'. I felt stimulated and excited in the lesbian environment I found myself in, about all the new ideas, and then, over time, I felt restricted and I realized I'd closed down all sorts of options for myself.

My first sexual experiences with women, post 'coming out', were not a blazing success. I was absolutely clueless. Although I had had these early sexual experiences with girls, I couldn't really remember them. I think my experiences with men had been real normative heterosexuality, a lot of fucking and not much else. I think there were a lot of women who had wider sexual repertoires than I did then, who could transfer some of their heterosexual experience into a lesbian sexual context, but I couldn't even do that. The woman I got off with was really, 'hey I'm a seasoned lesbian', but it turned out she'd only just given her boyfriend up. She had a very convincing appearance. I suppose when women talk about that definitive first time experience, I never really had that. A sense of sexual homecoming – I just had a sense of confusion.

After four years, I ended up sleeping with a man I had been involved with some years previously. Questions I had thought answered erupted in a spectacular and destructive fashion. Sex with Gill had petered out by this time, so either of us might have been in the market for a bit of sexual excitement, but the fact I chose a man was devastating for us both. I felt that it had the quality of looking back over my shoulder, and that was how I presented it to myself. I thought, I can just find these things out about myself, exorcize it once and for all, and then I can get back to my lesbian existence. We had the most terrible, terrible time after that. We had this weekend when we chain-smoked and drank coffee, it was all played out against the backdrop of Band Aid, I remember. I promised I'd never see him again. I realized he wasn't what I wanted, but he was a catalyst.

By the time I met Allegra, I'd dropped out of heavy-duty politics; I'd seen enough grotesque behaviour to last a lifetime. I was involved in a lesbian oral history project, and she was a new volunteer, surly but gorgeous. I'd often felt like the object of desire in sexual relationships, and here I was, in wild pursuit, being the active desiring subject. It was a very passionate relationship, and at that point everything came together for me, and that was when I thought, 'I'll never sleep with a man again.' I used to say that to Allegra, and she used to say, 'Well, I don't really need to hear you say that.'

I remember us lying in bed one night, and telling her the story about the man, in full uncensored detail, and she said that was the first moment that she felt she loved me. I thought this was wacky in the extreme, because a lot of other women would have just jumped out of bed and said bye-bye. It was the intimacy and the honesty of it, and she's very good about acknowledging doubt and ambivalence. She always thought I was an opinionated old bag because I had such strong opinions about everything. She used to say she hated to think she knew everything about the world already, because that's the end of so many conversations.

Paradoxically, she was the one who made me feel I would always be a lesbian, but she was also the one who gave me permission to think heretical thoughts. It would've been liberating if I'd allowed it to be. It was a very stormy relationship, but we fucked like angels and that was a very revelatory thing for both of us. So to that extent I thought it was the end of the story. She used to joke with me, because she's the sort of person who always wants to throw a spanner in the works, 'I think you probably will end up sleeping with men.' I used to be, 'How can you say that, of course I won't.' She had quite a few friends who were ex-lesbians, who I was very hostile to, so I feel kind of ashamed by all that, because I was hoist by my own petard. By the mid-1980s a number of the 'nouveau' lesbians had returned to the heterosexual fold. My antagonism towards them was rooted in reluctant identification: it could've been me.

When I did get involved with a man again, it seemed to destroy the very foundations of my life. I had these periods when I'd want Allegra back, but fear of my own ambivalence meant I left it until it was too late and she'd moved on. The truth is that I didn't really want him either. He was just someone who reminded me that I wasn't a total lesbian, and that I probably never would be, although I certainly would be able to have very loving intense relationships with women. He just reminded me that there were other possibilities. I was attracted by his attraction to me, and by the sheer novelty value of masculinity. But I threw away my life for a man I did not want.

I was one of those people who worked in the voluntary sector, and I was a bit snobbish about it and thought, really I'm a journalist, I should be doing something more creative. I think a lot of people in the voluntary sector feel like that. I think I did do very socially worthwhile work for a long time, because it seemed inevitable that I would. And I got a lot out of it. I worked predominantly with lesbians, and women who became lesbians. The truth is, as far as sexual choices are concerned, that what happens at any moment is dictated by what's on offer. I never really met any straight men, so it's all very well for me to say I lost any attraction to straight men, but I didn't meet any.

Over time, I've realized that my desire for a fixed sexuality is part of a yearning for the coherent, solid sense of self, which evaded me when I was growing up a chaotic, lonely, injured child. Even if I have relationships with women in the future, I've given up on the fiction of ever possessing a pure lesbian identity. It's not me.

When I look at the behaviour of some 'women who went back to men', I'm grateful that I didn't go to such extremes. You heard of women who had been lesbian separatists, who then had white weddings. And then you think, leaving aside the question of their lesbianism, whatever happened to their feminism? How did we create such a straitjacket for ourselves that the only way some women could liberate themselves was to go completely off the rails, in a way that can't have been healthy or good for them? There were women who just fled lesbianism and grabbed the first man, who might as well have a paper bag over his head and personality, like, any man will do. There was a trend amongst some women, to take the edge off a man's masculinity, to go for a man who was in some way 'disadvantaged' – gay men, black men. Some rash choices have been made. It's very sad when women deny their lesbian pasts.

The other thing I think we didn't really bargain for was women who really wanted to have children, and somehow couldn't set themselves up in a situation to have a child with a woman, or simply thought it's much easier to do it with a man. I've had two abortions since I started sleeping with men again. I'd describe these pregnancies as willed accidents. A few years ago I would have denied any longing for a child. Knowledge of my own needs has been a long time coming, I'm still at the early stages. But I'd say to any woman with ambivalent sexual feelings: face them, because I can promise you that, if the repressed returns, it's with a vengeance.

I had a brief period of going to bisexual women's groups to see if I could find some new identity. But really it left me cold. I always associate it with ridiculous personal ads – 'bubbly curvaceous girl seeks other' kind of thing. I don't find the very angry bisexual movement attactive at all, it means nothing to me. I think the word community is over-used anyway, but when it's used by bisexuals it means fuck all. If I had a relationship with a woman now, I would call myself a lesbian again, because of the political importance. But it wouldn't be a statement about how I feel inside.

The lesbian scene has changed beyond recognition since the 1970s. There's been a violent backlash to the 'party-pooping' feminism in which I was involved. There's now a libertarian fundamentalism, which takes us back to the 1960s before women's and gay liberation even began. But then history has an unpleasant habit of behaving like a revolving door. It's easy for one straitjacket to replace another. A few years ago, the revival of butch and femme seemed like a healthy antidote to the 'let's all look like delivery boys' school of lesbian feminism. But it's romanticized 1950s roleplaying, and in sexual terms it over-simplifies attraction and power differences between women.

I'm amazed by the cross-fertilization between lesbian and gay male culture. It never looks like an equal exchange – unsurprisingly, boys seem to come out on top. It also seems like a capitulation to the idea that men are the ones with the sexuality. The old lesbian scene gets derided as unsexy, a sea of check shirts and identical haircuts; but being expected to shave your head or pierce your labia is just another kind of conformity. I hate the self-conscious naughtiness and decadence of some 'queer' culture.

I still feel a lot of anguish and uncertainty about sexual identity. In many ways I would leap at the chance to have another relationship with a woman, but, looking at my track record, I'm rather an off-putting prospect. Sexually, I've found it difficult being with men again. Camille Paglia can only think heterosexual men are sex gods because she doesn't sleep with them. The truth is that most men are rather ordinary, and the idea that they are tempting forbidden fruit is something that we should discourage amongst ourselves, but they get set up in that way. It invests them with a power that they don't have. A frequent complaint of thirtysomething women like me is that men are much less sexual than they are – a far cry from the revolutionary feminist-type analysis. But then real life is messy and complex, and has a way of undermining cherished political orthodoxies.

5 *l*abelling *o*urselves

*q*ueergirls, *c*ompanion
*l*overs and *d*iesel *d*ykes

So. Lea De Laria's mother says, 'Why did you have to go on that show and say you're a queer or a dyke? Why couldn't you say you're a nice lesbian?'   Drill Hall performance, 1993

As far as much of the rest of the world is concerned we're all just a bunch of queers.   Lisa Power.[1]

DYKE If you're poor / then you're a dyke / if you're rich / you're sapphic // but if you're neither one nor the other / a lesbian, a lesbian is what you'll have to be // if you're weak / you're sapphic // but if you're neither one nor the other / a lesbian, a lesbian is what you'll have to be // if you're earthy / then you're a dyke / and if you're aesthete / you're sapphic // but if you're neither end round the middle / a lesbian, a lesbian is what you'll have to be.   Eleanor Hakim.[2]

dyke queer lesbian gay diesel femme zami lesbian boys baby dyke SM dykes lesbian chic sapphic queergirls daddy dyke khush butch passing woman lesbian feminist drag dyke queens (and kings)

Adopting labels can be a shorthand method of description. Having a language to describe yourself means you exist. Identities that have been secret and stigmatized necessarily take on enormous significance, and an insiders language, (like Polari, although much more widely used by gay men) is often an important part of the secret. Labels may have different meanings in time and culture, and can move in time from subcultural argot to mainstream banner headlines. Some have long-term currency and some stay firmly locked into their original usage. The importance remains even if the label is qualified, or altered depending on circumstance and audience.

There are also labels that are ascribed by others, as a rigid categorization used to contain and dismiss. Labelling can be a method of belittling that which is feared. *Making Black Waves*[3] points out that labelling has always been a feature of colonization. Even some labels used in this way have been reclaimed by black people, as 'dyke' has been.

In an interview with 4 Non Blondes[4] Linda Perry said, 'I consider myself very open minded. I'm not a "lesbian" – I hate that fuckin' word in the first place – I'd rather be called a dyke if anything. But I'm attracted to a lot of people; I do not limit myself.' Not liking the word 'lesbian' is not unusual because the sanctions against it are so high: it can be unsafe, some women think it is an ugly word, or do not want to be pigeonholed, or dislike its 'feminist' connotations.

Perry's use is interesting because it sees women-only sexual encounters as limited, and demands to be able to use 'dyke' and sleep with men. Della Grace appearing in Camille Paglia's *Without Walls*[5], talking about lesbians having sex with men, very succinctly added to these sentiments when she said, 'It doesn't make you bisexual, it makes you adventurous.' There is massive contention among lesbians about this. Some see it as an acceptance of lesbianism as a lesser sexuality, as a dilution or as a denial of hard-won choices.

Now that lesbians feature more often in the media, there exists a new arena for the creation of trends and terms. A certain amount of cross-fertilization takes place – lesbians and the media are not mutually exclusive. The media simplifies the division into lipstick lesbians (news: young, attractive, fashionable, employed) and lesbian feminists (not news: older, ugly, dowdy, angry, poor).

There is another division, aside from that of the labels coined for lesbians and by lesbians. Many of them can be separated into the sexual and non-sexual. Taking the sex out of lesbianism is a criticism often levelled at lesbian feminism. The late 1980s and 1990s have been credited with putting the sex back in. On one level this is nonsense. It suggests that feminist lesbians were too busy going to meetings to fuck, or that they were all 'political lesbians'.

During the 1970s and 1980s some women saw lesbianism as a political rather than a sexual identity. They took on the label 'lesbian', without having had any sexual contact with women and without necessarily having any intention of doing so. For some women, appending 'feminism' to 'lesbian' made it easier to cope with.

Many interviewees referred to political lesbians in terms usually associated with endangered species: 'I haven't met one of those in a long time.' Several women commented that the tide of lesbians 'turning' (going straight, the opposite of 'she's on the turn' referring to women coming out as lesbians) had included a sizeable proportion of 'political lesbians'. Many women discovered that sexuality is not that simple, not something you can just make a decision about, political or otherwise. To follow those feelings back to heterosexuality may be seen as unsound, but to ignore and repress them can also cause all sorts of problems.

There have long been problems around self-definition. In the 1960s *Artemis* offered this advice to readers: 'Think twice before sticking a label and a stereotype on yourself.'[6] The lesbian continuum idea, devised by Adrienne Rich, meant women-loving-women of all descriptions, and not necessarily sexual, could be welcomed into the lesbian sisterhood. Other lesbians, clearer about their sexual identity and practice, objected to this on the grounds that it desexualized lesbianism, making it more palatable for general consumption.

In the nineteenth and early twentieth centuries, being lesbian in the modern sense was not a cultural possibility. The term 'passionate friendships' was used to describe fervently emotional relationships between middle- and upper-class women[7]. Redolent of nineteenth-century fiction, passionate friendships inhabit the tail end of Adrienne Rich's continuum. Many would argue strongly that such women are not lesbians. Given that they had no outlet for sexual feelings and little unsupervised contact with men, their emotional attachments focused on women. Others assert that lesbianism is not just about sex, and that since their primary attachments were to women they should be included under the umbrella of lesbianism. Anne Lister, the Regency heiress from Yorkshire whose letters and diaries detail kisses and orgasms, is one famous example. Perhaps her financial position allowed her the possibility of such extravagances, protected by her position in society, as were the members of the Bloomsbury group. In most cases there is no way of knowing whether women 'were' lesbians, and it may well be wishful thinking.

Another historical example comes from a pamphlet called *Feminist Practice Notes from the Tenth Year*.[8] This includes a piece by Amanda Sebestyen entitled 'Tendencies in the Movement', which was written because:

It seemed to me that our political alignments had got so inextricably mixed up with separate friendship and sexual networks that it was getting harder and harder to see the real points of political difference between us. *In fact, there's often a resistance to facing up to all the implications of adopting a particular label.* (My italics.)

The chart which accompanied the piece looks at thirteen different groupings from 'equal rights' to 'female supremacist', taking in 'Altusserian' and 'Redstockings' along the way, outlining their different positions on causes and responses. There were some handwritten deletions on the chart – apparently Reclaim the Night was off the agenda of actions for the tendencies 'Firestone', 'Cultural Feminist' and 'Female Supremacist'. (Attitudes to lesbianism feature in the columns, but as an aspect of political action, rather than desire or sex.)

Plainly, labels are not always used in such a serious way. The new, upmarket media tags are fairly flippant, but they still provide pointers to the habits of a particular group. A contemporary version of the 'Tendencies' chart might define the finer distinctions between forms of consumerism and sartorial style. This is not to say that defining ourselves is limited to shades of lipstick and who makes the best leather trousers, just that these are some of the most evident characteristics. The effects of mainstream influence and broader cultural options from which choices are made are evident everywhere: one example is the Left's transformation from corduroy jackets to sharp suits and red roses.

The difference between a lipstick lesbian and a designer dyke is hardly of crucial significance. They're coined as lightly self-mocking labels in the main, with little meaning apart from what you wear, where you shop, or the lifestyle you lead. Certainly 'lifestyle' (another, very successful, 1980s media term) has come to signify self-seeking indulgence, a pastel Sunday supplement existence oppositional to any kind of political consciousness or understanding.

A term which has not yet crossed the Atlantic is 'power dyke'. It has the advantage of not resting on something as ephemeral as lipstick. Power dykes have status and the influence to get things done. Again, this is media-led language, often used by lesbians with a knowing smile. The smile could be about how partial and therefore meaningless these terms are, or that lesbians will ultimately be able to use the situation to make more substantial gains. A 'you don't know the half of it, Jack' smile. Perhaps this is an indication of how far we've come. We can use these ironic labels for ourselves, and they are essentially labels of acceptance.

This is a first for lesbians who have been more used to reclaiming labels of abuse.

Coverage in the lesbian media around this has been understandably substantial. The coverlines on the first two issues of *Lip* magazine offered articles on Lycra and lipstick lesbians. The title itself suggests a knowing-ness – a little bit of lippy, lippy lesbians, and so on. The editorial of the first issue begins: 'I haven't got time to be a lipstick lesbian.'[9] This is actually about how time-consuming it is to produce a magazine.

The same spread features a series of responses to the question 'Do you like lipstick?' Responses include: 'I dress in black and wear lipstick as a spot colour to contrast with my leather.' 'I never want to be a painted doll and I never want to kiss one.' 'I'd never wear it myself but I love it if my girlfriend puts it on.' The whole is rounded off with a photograph of a woman, wearing flares, platforms and of course lipstick, at the Wow Bar in London, the natural habitat of the designer dyke.

The second issue's editorial piece provides more background for the topic:

> Yes it's true there's a generation of women who don't feel the need to justify their sexuality in terms of world revolution or saving the whale ... Younger lesbians give the thumbs up with their feet – on the dance floor ... Horrors! You mean we're pandering to the superficialities of consumer culture? Our answer is yes, Yes and YES.

These new developments were not universally well-received. Jane Solanas's column in *Shebang* offers some clues to the backlash:

> With my disposable income and my disposable girlfriend, I dress up in the mirror in my pretend S&M gear and carefully apply my lesbian make up. Such a lesbian act, to wear make up. Makes me more of a woman than a heterosexual woman could ever be, and my girlfriend, who's got a 6" dildo permanently in leather trousers, is more of a man than the men I despise.[10]

Mixed in its messages, this column entertained by saying something different, and cutting through the swathe of media-friendly scene bull-shit.

In a later column,[11] Solanas suggested that the media's introduction of 'designer dyke' as a phrase 'coincided nicely with media neurosis about AIDS [which] rendered heterosexual sex a suddenly difficult topic for the media and homosexual sex almost a taboo subject.' Solanas thinks 'lipstick lesbian' as a term appeared in the 1990s. The chronology may be uncertain but her ideas about the genesis of the terms are credible. The Gran Fury slogan, 'Read my Lipstick: lesbians get AIDS' underlines this. It introduced safe sex discussion among designer dykes. It targeted service providers who might be unaware of lesbians' particular needs. It used Bush's electioneering 'Read my lips' slogan, and also cashed in on lesbian media acceptability.

The *Pink Paper*'s version of the *Guardian*'s 'Notes and Queries' column carried this response to the question 'Where does the term "dyke" come from?':

In the Wild West of the 19th century, young men, usually workers, were said to be 'dyking up' when they dressed up smart on an evening to take out a girl. In those days great numbers of women 'passed as men', for many it was the only way to achieve economic independence and/or give expression to their sexuality. Apparently – and quite naturally – the term 'dyke' came to be used to describe these 'passing women' ... I love it because it implies that 'dyke' means somebody stunning and gorgeous.[12]

There are other less mainstream labels which mean lesbian. Monique Witting and Sande Zeig offer several winsome and cryptic definitions in their lesbian dictionary.[13] 'The companion lovers are those who, violently desiring one another, live/love in peoples, following the verses of Sappho, "in beauty I will sing my companions."' 'Companion' immediately suggests a cosiness, like romantic friends, but this is not a sexless definition. Other entries in the dictionary include:

LESBIAN   Before the night of the vanishing powder, lesbian meant she who was interested by 'only' half of the population and had a violent desire for that half. A lesbian is a companion lover, or a companion lover is a lesbian. The lesbian peoples had been called such after Lesbos, the most beloved center of their culture. The word is still used in the Glorious Age, despite its geographical meaning.
BUTCH   A tough companion lover is called a butch ... At present it is often said of a little companion lover who goes travelling alone. [Baby butch perhaps?]
VANDYKE   During the Concrete Age this name designated all lesbians. It meant that they were of the vanguard. The companion lovers agree that all the lesbians before the Glorious Age were vandykes.

Mentioning 'the verses of Sappho' leads on to 'sapphic' with its artistic, ethereal, and aristocratic connotations. Sapphic appears only very occasionally, most often in situations where it would be too coarse to say lesbian. It has more poetic than sexual connotations. In the film of *The Group* by Mary McCarthy, Lakey (played by Candice Bergen) returns from Europe with her German lesbian lover. Harold asks if she has always been 'a Sapphic'. Sapphic could have been used because Harold was a pretentious aspiring writer, or because 'lesbian' could not be said on screen.

Labels move from the cutting edge to the mundane, from the unacceptable to the embraced. 'Girls', which used to be a word to spit at, now means lesbians. 'Leather girls' was once the acme of lesbian outlawism. It is now applied to leather-trousered designer dykes – almost from the backroom to the boardroom. Elizabeth Wilson, describing her 1960s lesbian life, called herself an outlaw. She meant that she saw lesbianism as necessarily bohemian, an 'awkward mingling of the masculine and feminine; mannish gestures clashing with a smooth dress and seamless french pleat hair do, or a lacy jumper with a short crop.'[14] In contemporary parlance 'outlaw' is usually preceded by 'sexual'. It continues to mean radical but now has overtones of sleaze rather than culture. Wilson's description of getting her identity together from a assortment of genders and options would be called gender-fuck in the queer 1990s.

There are also a few labels which are seldom used in self-description, like 'baby butch', 'diesel', 'tankie' and 'passing woman'. While there can be little contention about the meaning of the last three, baby butch is more elusive. Does it mean a young butch, an aspiring butch, a small butch? Similarly, to say, 'she's butch' in the post-modern era could mean someone who is it, looks it or plays it. Diesel, as yet unreclaimed, the ultra-butch word, is used as an insult by lesbians and straight people alike.

'Pink Pound' has come into use as a term describing the consumer clout of gay men (rather than lesbians who are subject to gender-based employment discrimination). This has only relatively recently been exploited as a fertile market. The success of the Gay Business Association and the development of Old Compton Street in London's Soho, an area more known for sex shops and Italian delicatessens, into Queer Street, or even Queer Town, met with ambivalent responses from the communities it is supposed to serve. Supporters applaud the establishment of gay-owned and -run businesses, while some detractors complain about the business ethos behind them, and the low level of lesbian involvement. Pink it may be, business it remains.

There was a flurry of new magazine launches in 1993–94: *Diva*, *Lip*, *Attitude*, *Phase*, and the relaunch of *Shebang* (see Chapter 8). This led to prolonged debate, and some in-fighting, about whether gay- and lesbian-owned meant better. The launch issue of *Phase* ran a readership profile survey, which included a question about supporting gay-owned businesses. The overwhelming majority of the questions were about how readers spent their money, presumably towards fashioning a marketing-useful profile. More suprisingly, the magazine's anti-PC editorial –'We're not going to tell you what to think. Really, who's got the time?'[15] – was belied by the limited options for readers to describe themselves: gay, lesbian or other.

For some lesbians, the emergence of the gay business phenomenon is further evidence of mainstream assimilation and co-option. This has led to the use of 'pinkpounders' as a new insult. And for some it may be enough to cause them to run screaming from the patisseries of Old Compton Street. Criticism about consumerism, and taking up American trends too easily, has been levelled at everything from the music scene to the ubiquitous rainbow flag to Pride.

There are annual debates about whether Pride – no longer called Lesbian and Gay Pride – has become just another 'colourful' summer festival, thus safe for heterosexuals. The march, known by some as 'the political bit', is now separate from the brewery-sponsored party in the park. This means that a lot of people no longer march. For many it is still a massive buzz to walk through central London: we are the majority and a bewildered public looks on.

The combined might of London Transport and British Rail conspires to make the journey to the park as slow and difficult as possible. As dicussions got underway about 1995's Pride, the organizers recognized this journey, perhaps a touch over-optimistically, as another exciting element of the day. Lesbians and gay men flood through stations, taking over whole trains, deafening and embarrassing other commuters who provide a backdrop of incredulous looks and double takes as they realize with whom they are sharing their carriage.

In 1993, following President Clinton's assertions about equality in the forces, a US Army colonel led the march. This meant that some people who felt more strongly about the US forces' aggression and imperialism than they did about homophobic discrimination in the forces, decided not to come to Pride at all. Their attitude was, to borrow a Queercore expression, 'Just because you're gay doesn't make you OK.'

Queer has become the label of the 1990s, so far. Its progress through stages of acceptance, diversification, backlash and rejection says a lot about the quick mutation and turnover of some labels. It is now so over-laden with meaning that it almost needs to come with a definition attached to each use. Julia Parnaby suggests that this is 'a direct consequence of post-structuralist arguments around language which claim that the meanings of words are constantly redefined each time they are used by the individuals who use them.[16]

In its most common current meaning (discounting homophobic insult) Queer is about inclusiveness of all expressions of sexuality outside the conventional. Queer is for those who decline the acceptance and assimilationist path, and for those who seek the breakdown of the homosexual/heterosexual polarity. There is Queer with a capital Q – 1990s in your face inclusive sexualities – and queer as a reclamation of the 1950s hate word. Queer is a word of the 1990s, 1950s and 1920s. The 1990s use is a celebration of what the 1950s feared, in a rather neat demonstration of the generational slogan, 'We are the people that our parents warned us against.' In the 1920s only the wealthy upper classes could afford to be *risqué* and a little bit queer. In the 1990s it is still very much about having fun, but it is also angry and deadly serious.

Steven Wells described the driving force of Queercore in NME as 'Anger and a desire to confront and shock.'[17] Queercore, played by bands like Sister George and Tribe 8, joins queer and Hardcore rock. 'We're on the dole, we hate discos, we're queer and we exist,' said Sister George. Their lyrics cover virus envy, handlebar moustaches and the author Jane Bowles (a self-ironic label queen who called herself Crippie the kyke dyke).

This is a welcome promotion of lesbian and gay issues in rock. Queer-core has received a certain amount of hype in the gay and music press, deliberately positioned as it is on the margins of both the gay and music scenes. Success could be a problem for Queercore. It would involve the bands in risking, as Jon Savage has said, appropriation by that which they have built their reputation on despising.[18]

Both Queer's supporters and critics have focused on its inclusiveness. Its supporters applaud it while critics complain that to include everyone who is not straight in the broad sense of the word, dilutes the idea to meaninglessness. The other most frequently heard criticism is that it pays little attention to ensuring that women and black and ethnic minority people are involved, and their concerns heard. In *Sisters, Sexperts, Queers,*

Vera Whisman asks whether a lesbian queerness can be real queerness in that it 'does not immunize us from things like rape, harassment or poverty'.[19] This is a transatlantic echo of Suzanne Moore saying (reassuringly often) in her various columns that the need to address childcare isn't very queer.[20]

A letter from Peter Tatchell in *Lesbian London* had this to say about Queer and sexism:

> The homophobic fear of being branded 'queer' encourages many insecure heterosexual men (and some closeted gay men) to adopt an exaggerated machismo as a way of publicly asserting that they're 'not queer'. This machismo, with its aggressive and domineering attitudes, has a particularly damaging effect on women's lives. By opposing homophobia, we challenge the fear of being labelled 'queer' and thereby undermine the basis of much of the destructive anti-women machismo in our society. In this sense, the fight against homophobia is also a fight against the macho culture that sustains the subordination and ill treatment of women.[21]

Critics would argue in response that Queer has its own machismo, that it is not a trait limited to closeted gay men.

The demands of the closet, the historical secrecy of lesbian lives and the concomitant lack of public places to meet, socialize and mate, have probably given lesbians more reason than heterosexual women to use classified ads to meet lovers and friends. Until the 1950s, when living and working outside and away from the family became more of an option, there was less opportunity for an urban bar-culture to exist. For those outside major urban areas, the problem remained. Contact ads have long since lost their taint of social failure.

The language used in the ads shows a clear development from isolation to a position of confidence in looking for other lesbians. Looking at this and contrasting those from different journals and papers is revealing in a study about labels and identity. The personals operate using narrowly defining words and phrases for aspects of identity in both seeker and sought. But language is an elastic and changing thing, and so they retain an ambiguity.

> Sex Queen, sadly abandoned needs new, exciting busty playmates. No vanillas, no waifs please.

> Solvent? Dyke seeks sugarmum. Discretion assured, photo essential. Tell me what you want. It's OK.

Wild musical lesbian seeks others. Swap ideas, make music, love, revolution, rhythm, rock. No drugs or country, only sex.

Alluring young feminist, Sapphic, aesthete, desires vibrant, cerebral, stylish women friends, utterly lacking in stereotypical attributes. Romance perhaps.

Boy (dyke) seeks boys/girls for hanging out, casual safe fun, black 'n' blue, being the queerest girl (?) on the block. You might take some beating!
(All from *Pink Paper*, 1993–94.)

Versatile leather dyke seeks similar for hot toy fun and role reversal games.

Young streetwise dyke, boyish and cute, seeks an older dominant femme (25–35) who knows how to treat naughty boys.

American dyke, into fun and games in a big way. I keep cruising but nobody seems to be into casual times. Where are you?
(*Capital Gay*, 1993.)

Warm and witty lesbian. Varied interests, attractive sexy and fun, seeks honest, affectionate, together woman with sense of humour for happy healthy relationship.

Lesbian feminist. Irish working class roots. Not into therapy. Non-smoking mother (daughter 11 years). Reading, writing, friends, activism, music, the planet, animals, spirituality. Friendship & sharing/possible future relationship.

Lesbian feminist wants companion, colleague, partner, soulmate, to share dreams, vision, ambitions, successes. I care about world change, business career.
(*Lesbian London*, 1993.)

Hardly known any gay women. Never had a lesbian relationship. Have come out to one or two friends. Age and status not important, but should be free for overnight weekend stays in Blackpool.

I am age 35 but as I am extremely young both in looks and ways maybe someone younger would be all right as I have always wanted both an older sister and a younger sister.

I am Butch, good sense of humour, and kind nature. References good – was with one woman 8 years, another 7 years and another 4 years. Would be grateful for just a friend, another Butch even, or a nice lady.

Cultured European woman, middleaged likes women's company, not necessarily physical contact. Free afternoons, no commitments of any kind. Enjoys strolling in the park, taking afternoon tea.
(*Sequel.*[22])

'Rachel', interviewed in *Shebang* about classified ads, said, 'Perhaps for some women who are not used to going to bars, or who are not yet completely sure about their lesbian identity, ads may be an effective way of meeting other lesbians.'[23] The opposite may also be true. Postal introduction leading to a one-to-one meeting may be easier for unconfident or inexperienced women. On the downside, it cuts back on the possibilities of eye contact and other physical pointers of active sexual chemistry. For some, these can provide the incontrovertible evidence they need to be be sure about their sexual feelings, and act on them.

Many ads come from women who, far from being uncertain, have honed their sexual identity to very precise definitions, and who use ads to find someone complementary to fulfil those specific needs. Few advertisers would deny, though, that meeting someone on the basis that they satisfy a list of specified attributes is no guarantee of any kind of compatibility.

Both advertisements and labels have developed from those of thirty years ago. Then, the majority were simply looking for other 'gay women', whereas now advertisers can be either ultra-specific or luxuriously ambiguous about their requirements. The language of the classified ad has developed in line with lesbian visibility.

Using signs, abbreviations and labels, then, perhaps comes as second nature to lesbians, an integral part of the life, whether those labels are inspired by celebration or insult, and whatever the overlaps and generational differences in their perceived meanings. The media's capricious gaze finally looks kindly – admiringly even – on lesbians. Whether this proves to be a brief interlude or not, it could be a positive force. A higher media profile, while certainly a respite and a boost for lesbian visibility, does not of itself give lesbians any greater legal or social standing.

NOTES

1. Lisa Power, 'Voices in my ear', in Bob Cant and Susan Hemmings (eds), *Radical Records: Thirty Years of Lesbian and Gay History*, Routledge, 1988.
2. Eleanor Hakim, song, 'Lesbian play for Lucy, large country, first continent, concrete age', in Monique Wittig and Sande Zeig, *Lesbian Peoples: Materials for a Dictionary*, Virago, 1980.

3. Valerie Mason-John and Ann Khambatta, *Lesbians Talk: Making Black Waves*, Scarlet Press, 1993.
4. Ray Rogers, '4 Non Blondes' dark roots', *Phase*, issue 1, March 1994, p. 14.
5. *Without Walls*, Channel 4, 3 May 1994.
6. *Artemis*, no. 3, 1983.
7. See Lillian Faderman, *Surpassing the Love of Men*, The Women's Press, 1985.
8. Amanda Sebestyen, 'Tendencies in the movement', in *Feminist Practice Notes from the Tenth Year*, In Theory Press, 1979, p. 16.
9. *Lip*, issue 1, 1993.
10. Jane Solanas, *Shebang*, issue 4, Pride 1993.
11. Jane Solanas, *Shebang*, issue 5, August 1993.
12. *Pink Paper*, 29 October 1993.
13. Monique Witting and Sande Zeig, *Lesbian Peoples: Materials for a Dictionary*, p. 35.
14. Elizabeth Wilson, 'Memoirs of an anti-heroine', in *Radical Records*, p. 45.
15. *Phase*, issue 1, March 1994, p. 3.
16. Julia Parnaby, 'Queer straits', *Trouble & Strife*, no. 26.
17. Steven Wells, NME, 5 Feburary 1994.
18. Jon Savage, quoted by Steven Wells, ibid.
19. Vera Whisman, 'Identity crises: who is a lesbian anyway?', in *Sisters, Sexperts, Queers*, Plume, 1993, p. 57.
20. Suzanne Moore, in Cherry Smyth (ed.). *Lesbians Talk Queer Notions*, Scarlet Press, 1992, p. 34.
21. *Lesbian London*, no. 17, June 1993.
22. *Sequel 2*, no. 3, 1963.
23. Lisa Sabbage, 'Desperately seeking', *Shebang*, issue 8, February 1994.

ALICE STEIN (NOT HER REAL NAME) IS SIXTY-SEVEN.

When you came I started talking about going to college. What I didn't tell you was that when I was at college I had an affair with a woman. The other women in the house where I lived hated having locked doors, they wanted togetherness twenty-six hours a day. When they found we were having a relationship they got very angry and upset about it, because it was with another woman – we're talking about 1946.

I had actually gone to this university with a woman I was incredibly in love with, and I think for ten years of my life my whole internal life was being played out in the conversations I had with her that took place in my head. We spent almost all our time together, we were extremely close and when we went to university, she said she didn't want to continue our relationship which was only friendship. I became more and more desperate, she totally dominated my inner life. Finally she said, if you wanted to see less of me I could see more of you. Classic statement. So she moved and I decided to spite her by having an affair with another woman.

In 1946, when you applied to the University of Michigan, they sent you lists of accommodation which were either non-starred, one-starred or two-starred, I forget which was which but one set of stars were for Jews and one for blacks. The Dean didn't make it clear that there were co-ops which were interracial.

So the result of having this affair and being discovered was that they wanted to throw me out of university. Let me say I was a good student. I had two options. The first was to be thrown out of the university; the second was to see the college psychiatrist. So obviously I chose to see the college psychiatrist and lied and lied and lied, finally told her that it was a passing phase. I can still remember, I have an image of this woman, in the best transference tradition, silhouetted against her window with her arms raised, fixing her hair and I thought, 'My god, she is lovely,' but I never told anyone that.

All through school and high school I'd always had crushes on women and I knew I couldn't tell anybody, and so that was the secrecy. I don't know where that knowledge came from: I didn't know any other lesbians. I was the only lesbian in the world.

After working at Macy's that summer I had to go back to university to see Y and see if we could get going, and she told me she didn't want anything more to do with me and she was marrying the guy who was the bartender where we had worked. I think she was scared shitless by what we had done and by the intensity of the relationship. I felt at that point that being a lesbian was really disgusting – she thought so, the college authorities thought so, there was no one to tell me it was OK.

I was married twenty-five years, and during that period there was a woman I knew through various different people, and I very much fancied her but nothing ever happened. I think she had an idea there was something going on.

He was mad about me and decided we were going to get married so I did. I didn't know how to escape these expectations, I was only twenty or twenty-one. I thought, 'This is real life. I have to grow up now, I have to be responsible.' It was quite interesting we both had a secret life, my husband and I. His secret life had to do with his past, who his parents were and where and how he grew up. He didn't want this known. My secret life had to do with my inner life, my emotional life. To be a lesbian was my secret life.

I think I might have told him about Z, but I never told him I was still thinking about her when we married. It took me ten years to stop thinking about Z. When I say thinking, I mean relating my internal story to her in my head, day by day, hour by hour.

After the marriage was over, I started coming out. It took me a long time. It took me a long time to realize it was now my life. I had to come to terms that I had a life of my own, which was a frightening discovery. That was the naughty bit of me, that was the satisfying part of my life and it was too good to be true.

It's peculiar, because on some levels I was very aware. My friends say I was always politically aware of what was going on in the States in terms of civil rights. I worked for a guy who was doing a book on discrimination and housing and he was the first to take up that issue. Gay politics I hadn't a clue about. There weren't any. They didn't exist, right, when did Stonewall happen? Well, after I left the States in 1956.

I always knew I was different, peculiar. My oldest friend told me that I was continually telling her about having crushes on this woman and that woman, who I worked with, but we never named it, never said lesbian. That period in the bookshop, I got myself pregnant and I had to get myself an abortion. I fancied this Hawaiian woman. She was going out with her boyfriend and she asked me to double-date. And this horrible man insisted he wanted to have a relationship with me. I kept saying no, he kept saying yes, and he raped me. So I had to have an abortion. So all that was going on in my external life. I was keeping it together, I made it work, I made a living, I was able to afford my life.

I was in therapy. I had thought I had a wonderful analyst but six months ago my friend told me that in New York therapeutic circles, as far as he was concerned, he was the toast of the town because he had 'cured' this lesbian woman. He believed he had cured me because I was getting married.

In a sense I felt I lived up to that ideal of 1950s femininity, I met it. I was a great actor. I was living a straight life. I think this kind of splitting was a consistent pattern in my life. As a child even, I remember thinking, it would be wonderful if I could talk about what I was thinking and feeling to anyone. I felt I could never tell anyone. My mother used to fix up dates for me, with her friends' sons, these awful pimply Jewish youths from Brooklyn, and made me put on lipstick. I couldn't tell her, there's this girl in my high-school class I fancy. It still influences me, I think I'm still a very split personality.

It's off-putting when people behave like I'm going to get on with them because they're lesbians, it's embarrassing actually. It's a parody, like drag is a parody. It's disrespectful also.

When X came to live here, my son said, 'Well, Mum, are you having her here because you're in love with her, or because you think it's politically the right thing to do. Are you trying to be trendy?'

What does it mean to be a lesbian? What does it mean to come out?

LOU MARSHALL (NOT HER REAL NAME) HATES WORKING AND LOVES GOING OUT. SHE IS TWENTY-THREE.

I don't know if I'd ever say I came out, it seems like making such a big deal out of something that doesn't have to be any more. I mean, I know it wasn't always like this, and people still get beaten up and all that stuff, but to say 'I've come out', I think it's like setting yourself up really. 'Look at me, I'm a lessie, I'm really discriminated against, give me some attention.' For some people it's a real struggle, I know, teenagers, married people, but I didn't have any trouble, and there wasn't any great realization, you know, one morning I woke up and knew I was gay, or anything like that. Maybe that's why I wouldn't say I came out, I don't feel like there was anything I came out of.

For sure, I wouldn't be able to say this was the day when It Happened. I'm sorry, it just seems so ... silly to me. And I'm not going to make some big commitment (to who anyway?) that this is how it's going to be for ever and ever. I hear people talking and read about it, 'We had to do this, and now these young people, they don't care,' and all that. I don't see why I have to care about the same things. Sometimes it's like hearing my grandma talking about the war, you know. It's not that I don't think it's important in its place ... yes, I think that's it, in its place, and there are other things going on now, so why do some people have to focus on the bad things all the time?

I don't really call myself anything, define myself, as they say. I'm one of the queer girls if you like. That's what I'd say. I love it. The whole scene around it – how people act, the bars and the clubs, the clothes, the mixture of people, the drugs. I couldn't have done it when you had to be A Lesbian. I couldn't have done it because it was all too much like hard work, and for what? It isn't like I don't care about anything, although I've never been exactly political in my outlook, but the future looks so shit for most people my age. I'm OK, I work, but for most people it isn't like that. So I suppose the idea is to have as much of a good time as I can, while I can. Well maybe I could've done it, been a dyke and a feminist and that, but I wasn't around then anyway. I can't really see it though. My mum was big into feminism at one time, so that's probably what put me off too. She wasn't exactly overjoyed when I told her about my first girlfriend. But now it's like, this is what I'm doing at the moment, it's great and I'm having a wild time. But who knows what I'll be doing by next year. Labelling yourself one thing or another is just asking for trouble. It doesn't make sense to me to be all political about who you're going to bed with.

The Queer scene means you can be who you want and there's no one who can say you should or shouldn't be doing this. And if they do, fuck them. 'Lesbian' sounds like some ancient old lady to me, not that there's anything wrong in that, just it isn't me. Me and my friends call each other lesbian if one of us does something that the rest think is fogeyish or too serious. I suppose that says it all really. Dyke's all right I suppose but to me it sounds like it means someone very butch, and I'm not into that.

It's no odds to me if people think I look like a lesbian, whatever that means. And it's no odds either if people think I don't. I mean what does who I'm sleeping with have to do with what I look like anyway? I walk down the street in a dress and platform sandals and no one realizes what I was up to in bed last night. It's such a buzz, and there have been times when I could say that's better than the sex itself, whoops. It's all a game anyway isn't it, coming on a bit butch or being well femme for the night, nothing serious. I know some people take it to extremes, I just like messing around. The women I want to know, will know anyway, when they see me out, and the rest, I don't care. I don't want to look like a target either for people who can't deal with it or they're into violence or whatever. That's what I meant about not setting myself up.

Right now I've been going out with this woman for a few weeks. We met at Box and then I saw her everywhere I went. So we like the same places. We go out: we go home to fuck. That's what it's about for me, going out to places – after all they call it going out with someone don't they, not staying in. I can't imagine doing that: boring. Maybe when I'm old and tired and bored of it all. Usually what happens is I get bored with going out with the same person, and yes, the sex gets boring too, and then someone else catches my little eye. I'm not after anything serious, although who knows what would happen if the right woman came along. I don't know if there is a right woman, I can't really imagine. There certainly wasn't ever a right man.

I don't have the time or the inclination to find out what I want out of sex with people. I mean, if it's good, great, and if it isn't, there's no point is there? The scene's for fun and fucking, and that's what I want. I'm not interested in all this hand-wringing about what we do or don't do in bed. What's all this fuss about dildos anyway? Anyone who wants a real dick inside them knows where to go, right? I don't see the problem, you know, do it if you like it, simple. It doesn't hurt anyone.

A while ago, this woman I know asked me – I don't know if I should be telling you this, but no one's going to know it's me are they? – if I wanted to have a scene with her and this gay boyfriend of hers. And the thing was, I didn't like him. I didn't like how he looked or what he was like. I just didn't like him. So I said no. But if I had liked him, I dunno, I'm not against sleeping with men at all, I don't think they're the enemy or anything, but it made me feel a bit funny. A little bit queer. She kept trying to persuade me, go on, everybody's doing it now, she reckoned. It wasn't that it was a threesome, it was that I didn't like him, and as well, something to do with him being gay. That sounds awful, like I'm a homophobe. I don't mean it like that. But I did think about whether it would be safe – I do ask about safe sex when I meet someone new, but it's different with women. And I wanted to ask – not if he was safe himself, if the sex would be – but I felt stupid, even though I know it's more stupid not to ask. The whole thing made me uncomfortable really, in a way I didn't like at all.

I'm not sure if I change my behaviour or not. I change how I look if I'm going out or going to work, obviously, I have to. My boss would drop down dead if I turned up for work in some of my club gear, especially anything made out of plastic or leather. Anyone would think she's an OAP the way she carries on, and she's not even forty. I think the difference is, if I'm after someone or not, otherwise I don't think my behaviour changes. I'm not out to shock particularly, so there's nothing much to change. I don't think I look anything out of the ordinary. I think I look like what I am, a young woman who spends as much time as she can afford in clubs.

So when you ask what it means to me, that's it.

JULIA TANT IS A FIFTY-TWO-YEAR-OLD ARTIST.

Some lesbians want to be mainstream, to live entirely like the status quo, they want to fit in, they want to appear invisible in society, they want to come across as straight people even though they know they're not. Some of them want to keep their sexuality hidden, whereas others don't mind people knowing they're gay, but they don't want it to be obvious. It may be that they don't want to be dangerous, yes, but it's not dangerous to me, I just call it living a normal life.

For myself, I don't like the way society functions even if I was a straight woman, so I'm certainly not going to like it as a gay woman. At the same time I want to be a regular member of society. I wish I didn't have to go marching because I'm gay; I wish I didn't have to go marching so that women can have the right to have an abortion. I'm very political in that I want to take a stand in the world about things I feel should change, and that includes the whole situation about being a gay woman. Whenever I feel that women, men, gays, straights, pensioners, anyone who isn't getting a decent deal in society, I'm also supporting it in some way, whether it's writing a letter to the paper, writing to my MP, going out on a demonstration, just speaking up at a party when I hear somebody saying something. I could never be a mainstream lesbian in their sense of it.

My mum said to me the other day, and she's never been particularly one for how I am or how I look, that I look younger than both of my sisters of fifty and of forty-six. And I do, because they're both very traditional. I think homosexual women do, on the whole, look younger than heterosexuals. I think it lends itself to keeping you younger. You can make more choices, you go out and about more, you think more for yourself.

What it means to me to be a lesbian is to try to live differently, and to relate differently to this world. All my life I've known I was a lesbian, but I really knew the word for it when I was eleven. I knew I was a lesbian when I was about four or five but I didn't know there was a word for it. At the time I felt perfectly happy about it, I felt to be me. It was only later on that I discovered it wasn't OK to be that, then I found it scary, because I knew it wasn't considered normal. I can't quite sort out how much was my personality and how much was because I was gay, or whether it was both. You can't separate it out.

I wasn't actually out in the 1950s, I came out in the 1960s. In the 1950s when I was twenty-five, I did go to my first ever gay club, which was the Gateways. I ended up going there through a straight couple, funnily enough, who were friends of my auntie. My stomach nearly fell away when I saw what it was. I wasn't really necessarily expecting a gay person to look any different than me. I was wearing a dress and high heels but I was gay. It wasn't just that it was all these women together, it was how they were. I always say to people that when you come out, you're not just coming out as gay, you're coming out in all sorts of other ways as well as a person. So when I went down there, and saw all those women – half of them really really looking like men and behaving like men, and a lot of them obviously wanting to be men and the women looking very heterosexual, more so than a lot of heterosexuals I knew – I was almost sick. I didn't want to be part of that, although to them I would've looked as though I was already, because to the butches I would've looked like a feminine one.

As a child I always loved cricket and lived and breathed football: I was the best player, I got all the goals. So I used to be wanting to wear shorts and plimsolls all the time. So my mother was forced to let me do that because she didn't want my dresses getting ruined, but on the other hand she wanted me dressed girly. From a very early age I didn't understand the world, it didn't add up to me, and one of the ways it didn't add up was with clothes. I remember going shopping for shoes with my mum, when I was maybe eight or nine, and I was looking in the shop window, and she said, 'You shouldn't be looking at those ones, you should be looking at these ones.' And it didn't make any sense to me. Shoes were shoes. I didn't see them as having sex organs attached to them, pricks on the end of one and vaginas on the other. So it was my mother who started making me aware that I couldn't just wear what I liked.

I was seeing this woman and we were in bed once and all this fluid came out of her, and this had never happened before with anyone I'd been with. She got really embarrassed because she thought she'd wet herself. At the time I just went along with that, and told her not to be worried about it, it didn't worry me. Inside my head I was thinking it wasn't like she'd wet herself and anyway I quite liked it. So I was saying all the right things to keep her happy, but I was confused about it.

That relationship ended and about two years later I started seeing someone else, who was quite traditionally masculine in a way. She told me that no one had made love to her before, and if she was telling me the truth, I could believe it because she was such a butch sort of woman, but I wasn't going to have any of that. And it happened with her every single time. The only reason ejaculation got discussed at all was because the relationship became complicated, because she was living with this woman she'd been living with for many years. One relationship ended because sexually she couldn't or wouldn't do a damn thing. When she got into her next relationship I thought to myself, I already know what's going on sexually there. I finally got to meet up with this ex-girlfriend again, and I asked what went on with them sexually, and she asked what I meant, and I said, 'Let's put it this way, you didn't do anything, did you?' 'That was what was perfect about it, it was a relationship made in heaven,' and I said, 'Because she did everything and you did nothing.' And she said, 'Of course, what else?' And it's like they're almost proud of the fact. The one who does it all is proud of the fact that the other one doesn't do anything. Maybe it suits those people because it suits their present fantasies of each other.

There are a lot of younger lesbians who choose to be unpolitical now and perhaps in the short term that's all right, that they think that. But in the long term I don't think it's going to be OK to be unpolitical. There are younger lesbians who think the same way as I do, that it's OK to look like a lesbian. They believe that feminism or some of the values of feminism are very important and should be incorporated as part of your lesbian identity. Straight society's making it seem that it's suddenly OK to be a lesbian as long as you look the right way. There is this craze now for not looking like one. Even Madonna's part of this. I was thinking about this this morning when I was putting my lipstick on, and that is, nobody goes about calling heterosexual women, lipstick heterosexual, do they? No one would dream of talking about lipstick and non-lipstick heterosexuals, and yet suddenly that's exactly what's happening to us. When I wear lipstick, I don't do it to be girly, I wear it in the same way that men do, as an adornment, it's all part of dressing up. It's totally irrelevant to my identity, it means the same as wearing this chain.

I think the amount of fuss that's being made about it is totally connected with AIDS. I think straight women who are now being encouraged to go to bed with gay women want them to look the part and that means, in company, looking a bit like themselves. And I think gay men are promoting gay women to go to bed with them for the same reasons, they think it's a safer area. It could be very damaging and dangerous for gay women. Once you know what your sexuality is, you can't chop and change it like that. It's not dangerous for gay women who'll get off on it and use it as an opportunist moment: that's always happened. They're just going to have a good time at the expense of heterosexuals and they won't get hurt. The same I suppose will apply with gay men, although I can't imagine too many women being opportunistic in that area. It's presented as radical gay sexuality and so was free love in the 1960s, and look what free love did to a lot of women. Lesbians are being used as a convenience for the moment and some may benefit from it, and as many are going to get harmed.

I was always on the scene until the late 1980s, and on the Women's Liberation scene too. When I was at art school I was changing my lifestyle and

I found more and more that I didn't seem to have a lot in common with the lesbians I met. It wasn't to do with my age, because I knew other women the same age as me. So I decided I would just choose my friends from wherever; then I realized that once I got off the gay scene you don't meet many gay people, and all my friends started being straight and I began to feel isolated again. Once I went back to it I'd got much older and found there were hardly any women my age, and also I've given up drinking and smoking and that's a problem because everywhere is so smoky. And they cater for much younger women.

There's the Older Lesbian Network, but they were not where I'm at. I think they're very middle-class, a lot of them, and they've all got good jobs or they're retired, and they've got their own houses, so it's a very suburban life that I don't fit into. I'm very involved in class politics and they find that quite difficult, can't handle it.

The last Sappho meeting I went to, the woman I was sitting next to said to me, 'Do you know where you go if you want to meet a feminine dyke?' I know what she means, but at the same time it really annoys me. I cook, I sew, I clean my house, I wear make-up, OK I've got short hair. I already know she's not seeing me as one, and she's stereotyping me – you'd have to have long hair, dress in a certain way; would she have to have a handbag, I'm not sure, high heels?

I had my own disco for five years, from 1976, and in the same place there was another one that was very butch/femme and almost none of the feminists used to go to it, but I always did, because I'm interested in people. I remember standing at the bar one day and these two women came in looking very macho, 'boys out for the night' dykes. And I got chatting to them. So I said, 'Have you two got girlfriends, where are they tonight then?' And they said, 'Oh, this is our night off, we have to have our night out away from those two once a week.' Eventually I steered the conversation round to sex, and asked them if they made love to their girlfriends – 'Well we'd be in trouble if we didn't, wouldn't we?' And when I asked them if their girlfriends made love to them, it caused a complete uproar. 'Could you imagine her making love to me. What planet are you from?'

what do sm dykes wear to work?

fashion and behaviour

They know, in a rather uncanny way, who belongs to the fraternity and who does not. They sense the kindred soul and get the signal, even when the appearance of the other woman is perfectly 'normal'.

Charlotte Wolff[1]

I walk down the street in a dress and platform sandals and no one realises what I was up to in bed last night. It's such a buzz.   Lou

Even though I had had those feelings about other women, I wasn't able to recognise them when applied to me by a member of my own sex ... . Without images of lesbians in books and the media, or indeed anywhere, I had not learned to expect and interpret the signals from women. How blind we were made.

[Harriet]*What A Lesbian Looks Like.*[2]

Not in a million years, I'd never know you were. You probably have a dress scheme that would be recognised in your own peer group but it just goes over my head really.   Carol

During the interviews for this book, there was a process between myself and interviewees of a kind of coming out to each other, a sorting out of our various systems of recognition. I knew already that all the interviewees either were or had been lesbians, but not all of them knew I was. Some asked me during our initial meeting, prior to deciding if a full interview would take place, whether I was a lesbian, and I was either mildly surprised, resigned or slightly annoyed that they could not tell, depending on my mood. Since I do not subscribe to the view that first-hand knowledge is an essential requirement to writing I realise I am being slightly contrary here. There is no reason then why a straight woman should not have been doing this kind of research, although it does seem unlikely, and would have led to a different kind of book.

Other interviewees assumed I was a lesbian, and during the course of the meeting or interview it would become clear that I was. Some women, broadly speaking the ones who talked most about their commitment to feminism, asked me about my own politics, on one occasion to discover if I 'had feminist principles', and once to find out my opinions on SM. Sometimes interviewees assumed that my outlook was theirs.

As interviewer I was constantly looking for clues in what people said, so I could ask questions to draw them out on particular points, and they also asked me questions looking for clues as to my opinions and position, usually in a more oblique way than asking an outright question. And that begs the question, what could they have asked me that would firmly position me anywhere in particular? Why, for example, should my opinions about SM be seen to give enough clues about my politics? Women asked me if I went to certain clubs; if I knew 'those girls'; where I drank (not if); and all sorts of other questions that were ordinary conversational pleasantries on the one hand, but revealing markers at the same time. Establishing common ground – in terms of social networks, venues, politics – is an unremarkable social gambit in any circle; among lesbians, and presumably anyone who operates in any kind of minority community, the questions are different and more loaded.

At the time I had been reading a collection of oral history interviews based in Belfast, *May the Lord in His Mercy be Kind to Belfast*,[3] to give me some ideas and get me in the mood for my own interviewing. The parallels were there, people being at pains to locate what the author's background was – as they had all but one located themselves in terms of Catholic or Protestant – and therefore his opinions, and making sure that they told him of their own early in the conversation. One interviewee who did not, or would not, identify as Catholic or Protestant had been told, as were so many lesbians who declined to identify as butch or femme, 'You must be something'. The other similarity was in some interviewees choosing to use pseudonyms, although not for quite the same reasons, but personal safety could be said to be at the root of both.

It is always of considerable interest, and often perplexity, to straight people – and to gay men who do not seem to have developed the knack – how lesbians can recognize other lesbians. This chapter looks at some of the factors around lesbian image and behaviour: how we dress for recognition in different environments; what labels we use; how we look or behave differently in situations in and outside the lesbian scene. Often attracted to large cities for their twin attractions of anonymity and community life, lesbians and gays have always used clothes as one way to recognize each other, and even formulated and used a language, Polari. This is little used now, although the title of the shortlived boys' magazine, from the *Pink Paper* stable, *Bona*, is a Polari word meaning good. Polari was very current in the 1940s and 1950s, particularly among gay men, as a way in which secrets could be exchanged on the bus without any bother, and it also served as a means of recognition.

Elizabeth Wilson, talking about the use of fashion by lesbians and gays, says, 'Secrets are displayed yet masks worn,'[4] which seems to have a wider relevance than clothes. It serves as a more general comment on the attraction and attitudes to urban life for lesbians and gay men, including many aspects of the *demi-monde* lifestyle which we may have no choice but to accept: the exhibition and the disguise. Being observed and observing are major activities in any subcultural environment.

There's a whole system – and systems within systems for particular groups of lesbians – by which we recognize each other and our particular leanings. Style is a part of it, but style is not always worn as an information guide to the person's life, although it is still often talked about as though it were a mirror to the soul. There are so many 'going into the wrong bar' stories – you were in shorts, they were in silk; you were butch, they were in rainbow shoes – and there can be a certain amount of hostility in transgressing a venue's codes. You may not get past the door. But since we all know about packaging in these media-literate times, why are different values operated in relation to clothing?

There is more to lesbian style than the clothes you wear, it is also about your look, how you look at the world, and to the world, how you carry yourself, how you look at and behave to other women. Jokes about dyke-spotting abound; in some high streets in north-east London you can practically trip over them in the street. Eressos, the resort on Lesbos where lesbians go to get back to their Sapphic roots, has long been known as 'Hackney-on-Sea'. But not everyone behaves the same way about recognizing another lesbian: some women always smile, some – uncharacteristically friendly perhaps – say hello, some cruise if appropriate, some look frosty as if to say, 'Don't think I'm going to acknowledge you just because you're a dyke,' some only acknowledge you if you look like they do. Some women turn on the gaze automatically, at once open, sexual, hooded, clandestine, cold; from others there is no more of a flicker than from any other unknown person in the high street.

The choices we make about fashion are about peer pressure as much as personal taste, and, of course, market forces. We might not want to look all alike but, apart from the basic pleasure that many people experience in being part of a group, for lesbians there are other reasons why we want to be able to recognize each other. 'Fashion . . . is a means of expression on a mass scale of solidarity and group identity.'[5] Without visual identity, there is no presence, and that means no social or support networks, and no community. What you look like is, perhaps like your lesbianism, only one part of how you choose to display who you are. Over the years there have been many changes in display and self-representation, changes in what is classed as acceptable behaviour: the signs are culturally specific. These cannot be seen in isolation from those in the mainstream. There are twin choruses that on the one hand complain how boring most lesbians look, and on the other, how often the mainstream has first castigated lesbians for how they look and then co-opted their looks.

The fashion industry, adapting perhaps both to the recession and the influence of postmodernism, has changed its tack from producing a few basic looks for each season to a recognition and display of the variety of looks that women actually wear. The wheels of the fashion industry turn too quickly for any hard and fast signs to exist within it of sexual and social identities. Most people's wardrobes, however, do not have quite the same rate of turnover. The press, as we have seen, is overwhelmingly grateful that lesbians have, supposedly, begun to look as chic as the next woman, because that is enough to make them the same as the next woman. Only the *Sun* actually recognized the designer-dyke danger factor – 'now you can't tell who They are'. There may be different meanings attached to how you look depending on where you are. On a very basic level, what may be considered butch externally, may be at the least looked on as kiki within the lesbian context, or, a look which is seen in the office as slightly unusual but not lesbian-indicative, may be relished and accepted as a lesbian look in other places later on that night.

The images change over time.

Is it sick to be chic? Camping did someone wittily suggest? In Guernsey? A swarm of lesbians descending like locusts upon that innocent isle? And what will the well dressed butch wear then, poor thing? Khaki shorts, nice and baggy to just below the knee? A shiny green rayon shirt with a pocket to keep her biros in? Maroon socks, with clocks climbing up each ankle? Sturdy ginger sandals. And if it's really hot, a handkerchief knotted at four corners upon her head? Will she be really dashing and sport a monokini? Not unless she wears a string vest as well, you may be sure. It's not that she's afraid of being arrested, but those east winds can be very treacherous. And she doesn't give a fig for the long-suffering public image.[6]

The opening shots for Camille Paglia's *Without Walls*[7] featured models in The Suit, the monocle, and the SM gear. The SM look dates from the 1980s, while the suit and the monocle come from the 1940s and 1950s, both from butch-looking women, although the monocle is an upper-class affectation whereas the suit may feature, in different cuts and varying quality, throughout all classes.

The most visible lesbian looks, until the upsurge of media interest in lesbian chic, have necessarily been those which are considered butch – even if not butch in a lesbian sense – and macho. Lesbians who look and/ or behave butch are more recognizable as lesbians, between ourselves and also in the rest of the world. This is one of the factors that has probably led to a pervasive feeling over the years that the butch dyke is the real dyke – which takes us back to the attitude which comes across from Radclyffe Hall's Stephen and Mary, Stephen being the genuine article, and Mary having the 'choice' to return to heterosexuality. While the suit and the monocle may have continuing relevance and recognition value, the SM gear, embracing self-proclaimed outlaw status and flaunting the unacceptable, together with the allegedly ubiquitous designer dyke, who at once rejects and courts acceptance in the mainstream, must be the two most current images of lesbian looks. The twin polarities perhaps of defiance and assimilation.

With the widening of the pool of images which can be considered lesbian, it becomes less obvious who is and who is not, and perhaps the recognition is more in the gaze than the outfit: the sex in the stare. It has often been said that most lesbians look like anyone else, but there have been times, related to the historical strictures of dress, when lesbians who wanted to be recognized could achieve this easily through image alone. There was a time when the wearing of trousers or a particular haircut – a crewcut, a no.1 crop, a greased DA, a flat-top, a short back and sides – was all that was needed to advertise your sexuality. And, as plurality hits hairdos, we have seen a variety, encompassing femmes with big hair, obligatory short no-style feminist hair, urchin cuts, little plaits, locks, bobs from Louise Brooks onwards, henna, bleach, crazy colour, curly perms, wedges, french pleats, shaved heads and wigs. Lesbians who dressed as men; lesbians who wore clothes considered to be masculine or not quite feminine; lesbians in dungarees (although surely many dungaree wearers must have been straight feminists); lesbians in 501s and DMs before these were appropriated by the mainstream; short fingernails and short hair; lack of make-up; all these have had times as defining factors. For many lesbians who live in the anonymous safety of the urban sprawl and within the visible safety of the scene, it can be difficult to understand how serious it used to be not to wear mainstream women's clothes.

Fashion dictates have long since discovered the allure of women in men's clothes. Was it Tootal who years ago had a shirt advert with the slogan which ran something like, 'She looks even better in it than you do'? This was no early example of advertizing to the lesbian market, rather a realization of the possibilities of women wearing men's clothes, a precursor to power-dressing and the sexiness of cross-dressing. So evidently it is not just the attire, but also the attitude, the eye contact or lack of it, which proclaims lesbian. This is the inverse of the argument which is often raised about designer dykes: that in the 1990s lesbians are free to look feminine (whether one attributes that to the gains of the radicalism of the 1970s and 1980s, or believes that 1990s lesbians have finally thrown off the shackles of feminism). Proclaiming that the look is differentiated from mainstream femininity, precisely because it is lesbian, and also because it is femininity with attitude, some wearers of the designer look claim great advances. An opposing argument to this (as outlined in *Sexperts*) is that exhibiting femininity – no matter how it is undercut or who it is aimed at – has a very different meaning when you are in the middle of an anti-feminist backlash.[8] This is unhelpful because it leads quickly to the question, when are we not? And this takes us straight back to the inescapable double-bind of dressing for feminism which so concerned women during the 1970s and early 1980s: that wearing men's clothes, in a movement basically opposed to attributes of patriarchy, was not welcomed, but neither was wearing women's clothes, which were seen as objectifying and restrictive.

Lesbians in the 1970s and early 1980s – or more precisely lesbian feminists – used to generally take the approach of covering their bodies to remove them from the arena of heterosexual behaviour, or wore larger sized clothes which did not reveal outlines or breasts, in an attempt to avoid objectification, male or female. There were women who wore bright colours, rainbow colours, dangly earrings, but they were considered to be leftover hippies, women who were involved in the spiritual side of feminism. Later on this became the preserve of Greenham women and other peace protesters. In fact there were women who looked all sorts of ways, but the dominant, and only acceptable, image was of a sort of baggy androgyny. This was, mistakenly, seen as a more natural way of dressing for women, as distinct from the artificiality of fashion. Elizabeth Wilson makes a division in attitudes to wearing of clothes, between 'the authentic' (who uses clothes to demonstrate the discovery of the true self) and 'the modernist' (who creates an image through use of clothes). This is useful in looking at how women, and lesbians particularly, approach their own dressing.[9] In 1978, as reported by the *London Women's Liberation Newsletter*,[10] Top Shop was the site of a feminist action for which the slogan was, 'This shop sells rape gear.' The report did not elaborate, but the assumption can probably be made that 'rape gear' refers to unsuitable female clothing which could lead to sexual violence. This sounds disturbingly close to the 'contributory negligence' with which a judge accused a woman who had been raped, for having been out too late at night, and which caused an outcry, especially among feminists.

During the 1970s and 1980s, occasionally, at discos and parties, someone would take off their (probably baggy) top in a celebration of breasts and femaleness, but this was generally considered wild and probably drunken behaviour. Many lesbians are now much more inclined to display their bodies in all sorts of dressing-up modes, whether wearing harnesses at Pride or displaying their Wonder Bras or wearing lycra dresses. Makeup, high heels and long nails, which for decades were anathema to the right-thinking lesbian, and which were once seen as symbols of female slavery, are now more likely to be seen as liberating. Turning up with only your bra on is, in this post-Madonna age, hardly noteworthy. Camille Paglia, is not impressed either: 'The sheer tedium, I don't care if they put on all the fishnet stockings in the world.'[11]

Fetish clothes, leather, PVC and rubber, uniforms, harnesses and bondage gear are also ways of exhibiting the body. They are sometimes worn to advertise what the wearer wants to do with her body or have done to it. All these kinds of clothes have become more widely available, more mainstream, and so create less of an impact than they used to during the 1980s. The wearing of hankies in the back pocket offers another kind of serious and complicated guide to sexual desire, although one much derided as an imitation of gay men's habits, and, on a less critical note, as one which caused confusion and mirth among those not in the know. As US imports go, it never really took off in the lesbian world.

Tattooing, which has a history in the lesbian world going back to the 1940s when the women involved in the working-class community of lesbians in Buffalo had their arms tattooed with a blue star,[12] still retains, among its aficionados at least, a certain cachet as a slightly bad-girl body adornment. Apart from the usual array of dolphins, mandalas, snakes, stars and roses, lesbians who have been bikers or punks may display tattoos with different messages. And lesbians also use transfers which rub away after a few days, or a night in a club. Body piercing, though, looks set to be the 1990s dykey thing: pierced clits, tits, labias, noses, lips, belly buttons, eyebrows, have become part of the lesbian's rich tapestry of choice. In 1994 Channel 4's *First Sex* devoted half a programme to body piercing, interviewing a group of women who saw it as a sexual enhancement, and a self-affirming body decoration. One woman talked about how piercing had been a means for her to take back her body as her own, and as a site of pleasure, after the demands of pregnancy, and about the joys of breast-feeding with pierced nipples. Other lesbians see it simply as mutilation, using similar arguments to those once used against make-up and high heels. Some black women see white women with pierced noses as particularly inappropriate, as another example of western women ignoring its cultural importance in other parts of the world.

Gradually though – and at the sharp end of the lesbian scene there is quite a quick turnover – the shocking becomes the mundane, and new forms of sartorial outrage will come to the fore to replace that which has become boring and too common. 'It is the fate of all fashions to describe a trajectory from the outrageous to the banal'.[13] Fashion has a high turnover of looks, and even the trickle effect from the catwalk to the street has become not only much shorter, but also much more of a two-way process. If lesbians look like anyone else, this could mean we just blend into the mainstream. We may need to use other means to continue to know each other.

The ultimate badge of lesbianness, in the sense that no one could miss the clue, must be sexual. Which begs the question, is a lesbian finally only recognizable as a lesbian if she is involved in some kind of sexual activity with another woman?[14] One woman can leave room for doubt: two, holding hands, kissing at the bus stop, touching, does not. Knowing when and where you can, and when, for reasons of safety, you should not, is a quickly mastered art for lesbians, although some play safe and just do nothing and others believe it depends on what they look like – if one of them looks boyish and the other girly enough, then they can 'get away with it'. And there is always that edge of risk, of getting away with it. At other times of course, you are not trying to get away with anything at all, but just walking down the street, catching a train, shopping in Sainsbury's, and that in itself is enough to move some homophobes into action. This is why Pride is such a relief, if not also a reminder that you cannot be in a park with your significant other(s) and be affectionate, demonstrative, physical, the rest of the year without risk.

One interviewee mentioned that during the 1970s she wore so many badges enlightening the general public to her sexuality and politics that she clanked around like the ghost of Christmas past. In an interview in *Women's Voice* (the now-defunct women's magazine of the Socialist Workers Party)[15] in answer to the question of why 'gay' people wear badges, the interviewee replied, 'It may sound silly but gay men and women are invisible unless they wear badges.' It is difficult not to smile at this, and yet we are still doing it, except the signs are less often badges. We have been through the double women's symbol, the pink or black triangle, the labyris, and currently the rainbow flag is in vogue. An advert in *Arena3* from 1970 offers 'A subtle recognition in a modern idiom' to purchasers of rings, cufflinks, pendants and tie pins.[16] This is in stark contrast to the two-hands-making-a-cunt-shape and Women's Liberation symbol of feminist jewellery, and the clit and nipple rings of 1990s jewellery adverts. There is also the red ribbon symbol which denotes the wearer's solidarity with people with AIDS. And this fades in and out of fashion, perhaps with the tide of the de-gaying and re-gaying of AIDS. For some people the red ribbon has become debased as it has been identified with what is seen as a cynical and opportunistic Hollywood stance.

Not all women want to wear badges: not all women want to be or can be recognized. Visiting a Kenric monthly social disco night, the women who had obvious indicators of their sexuality – dress, manner and so on – were a small minority. Kenric is an avowedly non-political group for all women, for which, up until 1976, women had to have their husbands consent before joining. This must have necessitated some creative explanations but evidently was not a deterrent: Kenric has existed for nearly thirty years and has some 1,800 members nationally, who pay an annual subscription for the monthly newsletter. Women there were appreciative of the Kenric approach, 'It's for all women', and had made friends among the membership, finding it friendly and not 'stand-offish' like the rest of the scene. Some of the women there had travelled a good distance, from Kent and Sussex. Perhaps it is due to its non-political ethos, in the widest sense, and the fact that it is still quite low profile in contrast to the much more visible and upfront elements of the scene (although efforts are being made to change this), that Kenric attracts a different mixture of women than is to be found in other parts of the scene.

Apart from a handful of exceptional circumstances – which perhaps only cover separatists and those of such class background that they never have to consider how their behaviour might affect others – lesbians have lives to lead in the world and always have had. There are probably occasions when everyone has to make efforts, to look less dykey than they usually do, but this need not be seen as selling out. This has not always been the case. There was a time when the acceptable behaviour was to come out to everybody, on the bus, in the paper shop, and, if not actually telling people, then sporting a lesbian look which left nothing to the imagination. In many lesbians' lives there have been times when even the most unclued-up straight would have been hard pushed not to realize.

Passing as straight is an occupational hazard, but there are times when it would be foolish and dangerous not to do it. This depends very much on how you look. For some women, passing is not an option, whether that has been a conscious or political decision or not. Passing may be confined to particular situations, at work for instance, or the difference between what you wear on a Saturday night and on a Monday morning. This can be a matter of degree, casual against formal, or more extreme. Arena3 advises:

> What to wear to work depends enormously of course, on what you do. A professional or executive job, or one involving a lot of contact with the public, demands some concessions to convention ... The good plain suit, the classy overcoat – these may be expensive but they are always right and never let you down. In some jobs it just doesn't matter what you wear – but why look awful if you don't need to.[17]

Passing can be something you do to make sure you do not get passed over for promotion, or to save your children from homophobic bullying from teachers and schoolmates, or it may be, as it was for many women in the 1950s and 1960s, the only way of living with your girlfriend without exciting comment. 'Don't mind you wearing men's clothes, if only you'd wear high-heeled shoes so they could see you were a woman,' commented one woman about the freedoms offered in Brighton during the 1950s.[18] Joan Nestle talks in A Restricted Country about how you had to make sure that you wore three pieces of women's clothing so that you could not be arrested for transvestism.[19] You could of course be humiliated by having to display these items.

Passing is a ritual of survival, although one that is less frequently necessary than it once was, at least for those who do not have homophobic workplaces, do not have children, do not live in small towns and rural areas. Efforts to pass as straight, whatever their extent and occasion, are often recognizable as such by the rest of us, seeing the signs of women looking ill at ease in unaccustomed feminine trappings. Casual style, which allows many women to pass, is noted as the ultimate disguise for the closeted professional lesbian in Inge Blackman and Kathryn Perry's 'Skirting the Issue'. They suggest that 'getting away with it' might be experienced as excitingly subversive rather than closeted by the wearer.[20] Passing women are generally associated with the 1950s and earlier, when to pass as a man opened up the possibility of living with another woman, which was otherwise denied or fraught with danger. It also meant access to better-paid employment, social space and wider options than were available to women. Passing is not yet confined to history.

Jennifer Saunders did not get away with it – although 'it' looks likely to be lesbianism rather than trying to pass – but came in for criticism from feminists – who might have been expected to be sympathetic – pillorying from the press, and imprisonment from the legal system. She was jailed for six years in 1991, for dressing as a man and indecent assault. Although she asserted that the two girlfriends she was accused of assaulting had insisted she dress as a man so that their relationships would not be seen as lesbian, her girlfriend testified that she thought Jennifer was a man. This, in an affair which was supposed to have gone on for five months, is a little hard to credit. In her discussion of the case in *Queer Notions*, Cherry Smyth[21] also notes the muted response from lesbian groups (apart from LABIA) and puts forward two possible causes for it: disapproval of her use of a dildo, and of her macho image. Not the right sort of lesbian, apparently, despite the widespread embrace of butch and femme.

More recently, Billy Tipton, a trumpeter, whose fame was vastly magnified by the discovery of his gender, was discovered on his death to have been a woman, shortly before the release of the film *The Ballad of Little Jo*, about a woman who lived as a man in the nineteenth-century American West. His wife appeared on *The Oprah Winfrey Show* to tell a disbelieving audience that they had never consummated the marriage and were affectionate with each other to an extent that left it possible for her to have been unaware of her husband's gender. She said it was his desire to be a jazz musician which led him to live as a man, so it seems the old reasons of women seeking adventure and opportunity that they saw as otherwise unavailable may still be valid.

Many of the women I interviewed had stories of the women who dressed as men living down the road, who everyone talked about but more or less accepted. Often this was the first time they had been conscious of knowing what a lesbian was. Whether these women were passing women, or women trying to pass, or women who dressed differently and stood out because of this, is impossible to know. It is interesting that, often, the reported response to these women was that they were eccentric, rum old girls, rather than anything more critical. Again, we cannot know whether this was due to tolerance and acceptance within a community, or a sanitised version given to interviewees by adults who could not reveal the awful truth.

What you wear, how you wear it and your demeanour while wearing it may signal that you are a dyke to the world, or only to a small section of the lesbian world. Alternatively, you can hone your image into a sartorial mixed message, and there are a seemingly infinite number of ways to keep the public guessing. It is about indicating your membership in the club, on the team. Sometimes the markers are so specific that they are designed to indicate which section of the club, and received as such. For the most minutely attentive dyke scene spotters it can be possible to tell which clubs a given lesbian might go to.

So the question 'What do SM dykes wear to work?' becomes a variation on the theme of 'And what do lesbians eat for breakfast?' The world at large may only pick up your lesbian signals – whatever your intentions or your feelings about the desirability of sending them out – when you are locked into a passionate public embrace. While infinitely more possible, in more circumstances, in terms of safety than thirty or forty years ago, this can still lead to violence and harassment. And while the butch, always and ever the most visible dyke, is likely to be visited by more hostility on the street, it can also be the case that femmes and kikis, once clocked as lesbian, will unleash a bitter torrent informed by its perpetrators' confusion and disappointment. The plurality of styles which can be recognized as lesbian seems likely to keep expanding, and the codes by which we then recognize each other will become correspondingly more complex, ingenious and enticing – and perhaps irritating to those who cannot understand them. Finally, whatever we look like and however we behave, the embrace and the gaze are probably the two ultimate signs which mark us out.

NOTES

1. Charlotte Wolff, *Love Between Women*, Duckworth, 1971, p. 130.
2. National Lesbian and Gay Survey, *What a Lesbian Looks Like*, Routledge, 1992, p. 55.

3. Tony Palmer, *May the Lord in His Mercy Be Kind to Belfast*, Jonathan Cape, 1993.

4. Elizabeth Wilson, *Adorned in Dreams: Fashion and Modernity*, Virago, 1985, p. 201.

5. Ibid., p. 154.

6. Letter in *Artemis*, vol. 1 no. 8, August 1964.

7. *Without Walls*, Channel 4, 3 May 1994.

8. See Arlene Stein (ed.), *Sisters, Sexperts and Queers*, Plume, 1993.

9. Elizabeth Wilson, *Adorned in Dreams*, p. 231.

10. *London Women's Liberation Newsletter*, 1977.

11. *Without Walls*.

12. *Boots of Leather, Slippers of Gold – The History of a Lesbian Community*, Routledge (USA), 1993, p. 152.

13. Elizabeth Wilson, *Adorned in Dreams*, p. 152.

14. See Sonja Ruehl, 'Developing identities', in Tessa Boffin and Jean Fraser (eds), *Stolen Glances: Lesbians Take Photographs*, Pandora, 1991.

15. 'Lesbians fighting the wall of silence' *Women's Voice*, no. 35, November 1979.

16. *Arena3*, vol. 7, no. 4, April 1970.

17. *Arena3*, vol. 1, no. 6, June 1964.

18. Jo, in Brighton Ourstory Project, *Daring Hearts*, 1992, p. 25.

19. Joan Nestle, *A Restricted Country*, Sheba, 1987, p. 38.

20. Inge Blackman and Kathryn Perry, 'Skirting the issue', in 'Perverse Politics', *Feminist Review*, no. 34, 1990, p. 74.

21. Cherry Smyth, *Lesbians Talk ... Queer Notions*, Scarlet Press, 1992, pp. 23–4.

GLORIA HASWELL (NOT HER REAL NAME).

I never wanted to look like a lesbian, which meant boring. It wasn't about looking butch, there weren't many butch lesbians around then, in the 1980s, because they all hid in bars that I didn't go to – apart from Kane's – but I was always too drunk when I went there to really notice.

I think women growing up outside London in small towns beyond the reaches of radical feminism probably were butch and femme. A lot of older women were, and not in a bar dyke way. But it was outside my experience really, apart from a couple of teachers at school. They got a really hard time, including from me. I knew what it was about because I'd read *Portrait of a Marriage*. It was serialized in the *Sunday Times* when I was thirteen and I read every word of it. It was deeply influential, it was a very lucky combination of clothes, lesbians and writers. And I thought, that's for me. I know they're a bunch of anti-semitic shits, but you have to read more critical stuff to find that out. I thought it was incredibly romantic. I didn't know about butch dykes then, in Sittingbourne.

I remember going to the Carved Red Lion. And when we got there I was just horrified, people just looked so dull, like feminists. Those awful boots that are made in Wales and really bad haircuts. I had always considered myself quite a hip young thing, and I was fiercely insecure about my appearance and I compensated for that through my clothes.

I'm never recognized as a lesbian unless I'm in a lesbian place. I feel very ambivalent about passing. I know I can do it, and a lot of women can't, and I escape a lot of homophobia through that. I've had long hair for a long time. In the early 1980s I cut it short, and I think that was a bit of trying to belong, but I started growing it again in the mid 1980s. Gay men seem much more recognizable to each other and they cruise each other on the streets, and lesbians don't do that so much and I think it's a bit of a shame.

I think being a lesbian means that you exclusively have sexual relationships with women, and you do have sexual relationships, you don't just say you're a lesbian. I don't actually care why I'm a lesbian; I don't feel a need to find out, it's not important to me. I'm deeply distrustful of psychological and scientific theory anyway, and I think it would be impossible to reach any firm conclusions. I don't see myself as part of a particular group of lesbians except that I belong to a loose friendship network of women in their thirties of whom a significant number have started sleeping with men. And that's quite an issue for me. Some women can make choices about their sexuality and be incredibly opportunistic about sex. I feel that I just couldn't have a sexual relationship with a man and that is a very specific experience which should be recognized. I am not part of a continuum which gives me a wider range of sexual partners, or allows me to escape homophobia, or to reclaim heterosexual privilege, all sorts of things.

If I was eighteen I'd think Queer was really exciting and I'd be really into it, because it's much easier to be queer than it is to be lesbian. The women I've known, who've slept with men wouldn't call themselves queer because it's a generational thing. They call themselves lesbians, which I find very difficult. With women of a certain age, the reason why they've slept with men is that they've either had a very difficult lesbian relationship that's ended badly and/or they can't find a decent girlfriend. And that's why I think it's sexual opportunism. I am very sympathetic to both those things, and I think it's really difficult, if you're not on the scene, to find new relationships and find people to sleep with. Probably harder to find people to sleep with than have relationships with ...

There's been an added dimension because some of the women I know who've gone straight were some extremely visible and vocal radical lesbian feminists. I get this sense that they just used other women's issues. They could have been anarchists or libertarians or trotskyists or anything in a way. Obviously, a woman's right to choose and all that – I'm not being facetious, I would defend a woman's right to choose her sexuality to the ends of the earth. To the outside world, women who go straight prove what they already think, which is that they just need to find the right man, or it's just a political phase that you go through.

But it leaves me with the feeling that I'm part of a declining number. I feel very isolated from the lesbian community because it only makes itself visible in terms of club culture. It used to make itself visible in quite rigid political meeting culture and that is equally excluding. It should be both, and the politics are still there but in a different form. I think direct action is a really good thing, and I wish I did it. And I don't because I'm not very politically involved now, and I think that's a whole way of being and I was that way once. I'm lazy and I stay in my mortgaged flat with my girlfriend and say, 'Oh isn't that a good thing, but it's too cold to go out.'

Although there's been an increasing number of column inches in mainstream magazines over the last few years devoted to lesbians, the images are not mine. It's fickle, it's exotic, not a sign of any lasting acceptability. It's nothing more than the cynical media looking for another way to sell newspapers. The 1980s were about the individual who had no relationship to any other people, apart from the economic. And the 1990s has seen a complete reversal of that, far more introspective and relationship oriented, which is why everyone is obsessed with their relationships, pictures of babies, Eternity, etc.

Then lesbians got caught up in the designer consumer boom as well, as much as anyone; for those of us who had jobs, it was time to join in. I don't think it's about age, because young women were doing it too, coming into it without knowing that there had been this prescription around dress. They do still suffer from it in a way; if you go to the Duke of Wellington you'd think that was still happening. They look like baby bar dykes. Maybe it's just something we all have to go through, it's probably just a reaction to being teenage girls, which is fair enough.

In terms of behaviour, I don't feel I want to make a lot of statements about myself and my sexuality through my behaviour and interaction with other people, which some people do. In straight work situations it's actually quite difficult to create opportunities to come out. I think by coming out you're giving a lot of yourself away, and that's something you never have to do if you're straight. But I do try and do it whenever possible, because I don't like people making assumptions about me generally. I hate people assuming I'm a vegetarian, which they do a lot, because I ride a bike and they know I'm a lesbian and I don't smoke. They assume you're incredibly politically correct, like because you're a dyke you have to take the whole package. I suppose, compared to them, I am. I do think it's a part of my sexuality, although I don't think you have to be political to be a dyke.

I do think lesbians should be more like gay men, anyway. I think they should loosen up about sex. But it's very difficult because lesbians are women and the issue's more about women than lesbians. I do envy gay men in a way, not because I want to go out and have anonymous sex with people, because I don't know if I could. I have seen that gay men can sustain long-term relationships and have sex not necessarily with each other, and it isn't necessarily a problem.

I think the reasons lesbians aren't able to sustain sex in long-term relationships, are things I don't know anything about, psychoanalytical things, like associating sex with novelty, with danger. There is a place for the cosy side by side stuff, and that's one thing that gay men really envy lesbians for, that women are incredibly affectionate, which is an advantage in terms of maintaining relationships, but it kind of can knock out the other.

My lesbianism doesn't have much effect on the things I like doing. I've always liked music and literature and film, and, apart from a few examples in each of those genres, homosexuality, and specifically lesbianism, has very little place. But I enjoy those things for their own sake. This has to be possible for any member of a minority group, in order to be able to sustain yourself in the wider world, to be able to read what you want into things and to take what you can. I would hate to have to live for all my cultural enjoyment to be specifically lesbian; that said, I wish there was more of it. What lesbian content there is is usually very negative.

My experience is that I am not treated equally in this world. I think it's symptomatic of society being organized in a particular way, and that's also why I'm a socialist and I would be if I was straight. It was a problem having those politics in the 1980s when rad les fem politics were much more in the ascendant than they are now. I made a lot of mistakes around class and race, I was opposed to any sort of separate organization for any group of people. I was on the far left of the Labour Party in the late 1970s and early 1980s, and then the far left believed that, come the Great Day, all those inequalities would be ironed out, and that true socialism would lead people to treat each other equally.

Socialism then seemed to have no psychoanalytical handle on how oppression was internalized and all that, so people would automatically not be racist because they knew racism was wrong and not part of being socialist. Whereas we know now that socialists are quite capable of being racist, homophobic and everything else. Radical feminism was more analytical and looked much more at what living in this kind of society did to you internally, did to your psyche. Socialism has taken it on to some extent now, through dealing (or not) with the issue of black sections and looking at the issues that black MPs have raised, and also because they have learned through feminism.

So it did change my mind about separate organizations, and also I have to say that I was a victim of poor analysis because although I bought into the Left's theory around separate organizing and sections, it was very convenient to me as a white middle-class person to believe that. I wanted to share in other people's struggles. The way that lesbian politics developed through the 1980s really slapped me in the face with those things, and said, You're Wrong. I don't think I was as damaged by all that stuff as a lot of women have been. I do think that the political development of a lot of white middle-class women was stunted by that period.

At one point I was paid to be a lesbian as well. It was frightening because you really have to perform. The pressure's always there at work, but this was different because the world was a lot more casual around work then. Being a professional lesbian you just felt very visible. But you felt like you had to say the right things, and God help you if your project did anything off.

I worked for an organization that had an office in the London Lesbian and Gay Centre. It was on to a loser from the start because it couldn't deal with all the different needs and political sensitivities of what was an increasingly fragmented community, if you can call it that. It wrongly mixed political issues with simple service provision, and I think that was really symptomatic of a lot of lesbian and gay projects: people's personal agendas determined the sort of service that was being offered. People who thought they were not politically right-on didn't use them. This wasn't about white people feeling they couldn't use certain projects, I think if you were black also you could be made to feel that you didn't have the level of analysis that the workers had. When people came to use those services they were expected to be sorted out, for example around their sexual practice, and a lot of them weren't and still aren't.

I feel mortally embarrassed about the 'anti' stance I took on SM for a short time, because it's completely at odds with my supposed libertarianism. I know I'm allowed to change my mind, but I should never have done it in the first place, I was swept along. I do believe in censorship but only in terms of harm and I don't think that's a harm issue. We really got it wrong, who the real enemy is. Speaking as a white middle-class gentile woman, other women have relatively little power over me compared to men, and women whose sexual practice involves SM can do little more than offend me really, in terms of appearance. At the time, we thought it was the last battle, and if we lost this one we'd be swept away in a tide of bacchanalia, some sort of Weimar type thing.

It was like socialism then, I think people thought the right sort of politics would lead to a lessening of differences which would create a community of common purpose. And people don't think that any more, although there are a series of communities and they are linked inextricably, in terms of future and purpose, but in terms of subcultures they're very different, in the way they experience the world and other communities around them.

CAROL WILLIAMS (NOT HER REAL NAME) IS FORTY-THREE.

I didn't realize at the time, when I went into nursing, how much I would hide behind the uniform and how comfortable I felt in a traditional female role, where I could be totally hidden. Never mind that I used to walk with a bit of a sway or anything like that, I was in a dress with a little cap perched on my head. It wasn't really until I left the health service for another job that I realized I did not know how to dress, I did not know how I wanted to look. Or I did know how I wanted to look, but I might well be accused of being lesbian and that bothered me.

I want to be safe from labelling. I wanted to wear good clothes, well cut clothes, but basically trousers and shirts, but I am really horrified of being thought of as mannish. And yet there's no way I want to be, there's no way I can be, feminine and frilly, but at the same time I do not want to be labelled. But now I'm being quite upfront and open about my sexuality. When I'm with my friends in my social setting, I really don't care.

I told my mum that I was a lesbian when I was twenty-one. She was very good but at the same time it really worried her, and she said to me, quite categorically, 'Promise me you won't dress in suits and you'll always wear your earrings,' and I always, always wear earrings. Even if I'm dressed really tattily, helping someone move house or something, I always wear my earrings, always. Studs that is, never dangly earrings. I suppose it's to identify with the female gender, but now guys wear earrings as well, and I love all that, that kind of crossing over. I think the more of that that's done, the less people will feel polarized about what they have to wear.

I've just been invited to a launch thing to do with my job and I know I won't go because I don't know how to dress. I miss a lot of social occasions because of this. It is tied up with my sexuality, completely. Ever since I was a teenager, I remember once going to a party and a friend, Beryl, said to me, 'I like that dress,' and I felt ridiculous in it. She was perceiving me as a female friend and I was perceiving myself as this person who was forced into a dress where it wasn't right. My mum used to try to positively reinforce the idea that I should wear skirts.

But it just feels very uncomfortable, it wasn't on, and I tend, when I do wear a skirt, to take on this body language. I sometimes still catch myself smoothing down the back of my skirt when I sit down, which is a habit from when I was in nursing, because you wear these very wide skirts so you can hoik them up and run if necessary, lots of room to lean over beds and so on, very sensible. Also if I'm wearing a skirt I tend to cross my legs instead of sitting more relaxed like I usually do, and I'm very conscious of it at work. The more relaxed I am, the more open I tend to be.

Dress is a major issue, it's a real problem. My hair makes a statement, but it isn't all spiky and wild. One of the women where I work is a lesbian, she has hair like that and I really don't like it. That to me says, 'I am a lesbian.' I don't think she's particularly political. I guess it's just the way she chooses to wear her hair.

I would've preferred to be much more boyish, if I hadn't been forced into skirts, I would've lived and died in jeans, worn trousers. I did want to have a sex change when I was younger. As a teenager, even then I was quite tall, I found it difficult to get women's trousers. I would have been very happy wearing what people considered to be male clothes. Well cut trousers, good shirts, I'd love to wear a waistcoat, but I never would. I would love to wear really good lace-up shoes, but I never would. It is a major issue. Now, some thirty years on, I am so glad to be a woman. Thank goodness I did not change my sex.

I am quite threatened by other women who do dress as they are supposed to dress, who look like feminine women, because I feel very big, awkward, and dressing like I shouldn't be. It's obviously really bothering me tonight, because I don't feel great, because I haven't been well, it's really getting to me.

Other times, it's different. Like I'm going on this walking weekend and one of the women has actually said she's attracted to me. She's just separating from her husband and thinks she wants to have a relationship with a woman, and we've talked about it, and we're very close. Then there's Andrée, who's recently come out as a lesbian, and I know she really likes the contact with me, and she sees me as someone who's positive about her sexuality, and thinks, yeah it does work. I feel really safe and I feel like I belong and it doesn't matter what I wear. And there's me thinking, I'm the one who's got the hassle, I'm the one who's discriminated against, you're all safe with your husbands and your kids and your homes. And yet I get the feeling that some of them look at me thinking that they wish they were different.

The first images of lesbians that I can remember are the very images that today I don't like, very butch, short-haired, spiky-haired, swaggering, beer-drinking women who walk in an exaggerated male way. I do not ever want to be seen as a woman who wants to be a man. Today it's different, there's a lot of different ways you can be, but when I was younger all lesbians were like that. Not in a million years, I'd never know you were, unless you had some sort of jewellery on, not just looking at you, I wouldn't know. You probably have a dress scheme that would be recognized in your own peer group culture but it just goes over my head really.

When I was younger it was very much butch and femme. There was no feminist identity as such, it was all very covert. I can remember one woman, she wore pin-striped suits, ties, the lot, and I was told that when she went to work she had her hair down and she wore tight skirts. And I really found that quite disconcerting. We used to go to a club called the Vortex, people used to dance and so on. Certainly you didn't hold hands when you left this place. Then in Essex there was a group of women, we used to meet in the pub sometimes and we used to meet round each others' houses. The same women came to all the parties. Sometimes we'd come into London, but I wasn't a great clubber. And then when I got together with this second relationship, we never went anywhere. She wanted nothing to do with the scene at all, nothing at all.

Feminism didn't hit me until very late. I chose at a very early age not to share my life, or have relationships, with men. Therefore the only men in my life were my father and my brother, and they were enough to put you off men for life. I think to myself, lots of these feminine issues ought to be left to the heterosexual women, they're the ones that deal with it on a daily basis. I've made my political choices and I've chosen to opt out of it completely. I don't want women going on at me, saying you shouldn't be thinking this, you shouldn't be thinking that. You know, I might comment about something of a sexual nature, I don't want one of my friends turning round and saying 'You think just like a man, you do.'

I was talking to my upstairs neighbour recently. She does actually have quite mannish features, not that I'm saying she isn't attractive, and she said, 'Oh yes, I'm a lipstick dyke.' I actually did not know what she meant. 'I like to put my lipstick and heels on.' I mentioned something about relationships and she asked me if I was a lesbian. I knew by her body language what was going on. I said, 'Yes, are you?' And she said, 'No, not yet.' And I thought, 'Are you planning to be?'

I think it's a cop-out to say gay. It's very much in terms of men, so I wouldn't use it for myself. I don't particularly like dyke, I've not got hold of that. I tend to say lesbian woman, which makes people laugh because you can't get a lesbian man. The thing that draws me towards gay men is that they can actually look like men, they're lucky. They often look how I would like to look. Their clothes are not the boring kind of men's clothes and they do tend to look more interesting.

JO, TWENTY-FIVE, ALISON, TWENTY-SIX, AND JACQUI, TWENTY, MET AT THE NORTH LONDON LINE PROJECT FOR YOUNG LESBIANS AND GAY MEN.

JO: I knew lesbians existed before I came out but they were much older, middle-class, it was the Greenham Common stereotype. I was a punk and there was a lot of anarchist and feminist music at the time, and that was when it all started to become acceptable, with the shaved head and everything. I really liked that image. It was only when I found an image that I liked that I actually felt settled about being a lesbian myself. It really surprises me when people say 'I came out in 1987', or whatever, because I can't actually find a date anywhere in my own history when I can say, 'Yeah, I came out then.'

JACQUI: I knew that there were gay people and I imagined them as small, short, with spiky hair, and a bike parked outside. A motorbike, not a pushbike. And gay men, they were all limp wrists and fairy-like, how they're portrayed on telly sometimes. The first serious girlfriend I had was my mum's best friend's sister. I knew that there were lesbians but they were all into Greenpeace and demonstrations and stuff, and I knew I didn't want to be like them. And if they weren't like that they were the total opposite, leathers, tattoos and everything. When I first started seeing Tracey, she was a butch type and I found myself dressing like her, trainers and jeans, not really caring about my appearance. But a few years before I was never out of skirts. So it was this dramatic change, and now I'm in another sort of change where I split up with my last girlfriend and I'm trying to find myself again, how I actually like dressing.

And it was the same with music, to be gay you had to like a certain kind of music. Country was big, and I hate that. I think people think to be gay you have to be certain things: Greenpeace, butch, listening to certain music. Even the speech patterns.

ALISON: I always say 'partner', because when I meet up with people, I don't want them to be insulted, or to think they're necessarily heterosexual. So I say partner, and they can say girlfriend or boyfriend. 'Dyke' I think is really wonderful, so positive, no negative connotations at all. I didn't hear the word when I was younger.

At college the women were just weird. They are very weird, lesbians, aren't they? And I thought, God, I'm not one of those. They were all either really, really skinny or really, really fat and they all had tattoos. I didn't know one lesbian who wore a scrap of make-up.

JACQUI: To me 'queer' is used by the people who are straight, talking about gay people, not so much abusive, but mimicking those words. I think the word dyke is used more by younger women. I don't like to use the word lesbian, because it brings up facial hair and hairy armpits and stuff [all giggle], it's too much of a category of people and I don't class myself in that sort of category. I just say gay or dyke. It's like something you add on to your list, when you describe yourself to people, I'm this, this and this, and I'm gay. A straight person wouldn't even consider telling you they were straight would they? It feels like there's a barrier to cross every time, whether it's with straight or gay people. Politically I have to give myself a label. In an ideal world I wouldn't need to. It's not an issue for me politically, it's just something that I happen to have been born with, and I'm just going to try and make the best of it. Whoever disagrees, I don't want to know them.

JO: Well, they do tell you they're straight, I've found that. Women especially, they'll say my boyfriend or my husband.

ALISON: I thought I couldn't be a lesbian, because they all had short hair and I had long hair and they all wore dungarees. It changed and now I've found a place which is comfortable for me. It's like uniforms, so you know what people are into. I got accused of being a fag hag, because of how I look!

I don't talk about sexuality very much, I just go for nice people. I don't think it's that odd just to go for nice people. I go out with men every now and again. Just to try it out, keep the family happy for a while. I still call myself a lesbian.

JACQUI: A friend that I used to go to school with rang me at my mum's and said 'I hear you're the biggest dyke in Camden. Are you coming out, where do you go?' I said I didn't go out to many places, here and there. And she said, 'Oh God, you can't be out that much, I go everywhere,' and I thought, well that's up to you, and it'll be different with the next person as well. I think you do have to be on the scene a lot to be classed as a true dyke. If you're not on the scene there's questions asked, where are you hanging out, who with?

JO: I think there's a lot of pressure to follow gay men. There used to be this Greenham Common thing, and that's gone, it's like, we're not doing that now, we're behaving like gay men. Like setting up that cruising ground for women. Encouraging women to be walking around at night. . . .

ALISON: Well I've been told that Safeways in Stamford Hill on a Sunday is the best cruising ground for single women . . .

Jo: ... and there's supposed to be particular places where you stand, you know, the meat counter, dairy products, depending what you're into.

Jacqui: I'm more on the scene now, because of splitting up with my partner, and I didn't go out very much anyway, because I had all that I wanted there. The scene's good, but it's very hard to make friends without people thinking, does she want to know, or the girlfriend getting jealous. So many places are mixed you don't know who you're talking to any more. Then there's this thing that a lot of gay people are turning to other gay people to pose as partners, for some reason or other....

Alison: I think the best thing is to be independent. If you're a lesbian you maintain your independence no matter what. You can still be with someone and be in a loving relationship. Nothing's taken away from you, it's more added to you. And yes, that is part of the attraction. Everything's equal, there's no power struggle. They understand your periods as well, I mean it's a major part of a woman's life. It's not just, 'Oh, no sex for a week.'

Jo: The first place I went was Venus Rising, back in the days when it was Eve's Revenge. I didn't see it as a place where lesbians went, just where women went. It was only afterwards I realized. I thought it was a real mixture. I started going to mainly male places, with gay men. There'd be a drag act, and I thought, this can't be what it's about. I don't go out that much, but I've certainly noticed it changing in the last few years. More women being out, more women being visible.

Jacqui: I haven't really thought much about SM. I've tried it out, but not to that extreme, and it was good but I wouldn't go, you know, right into it. Too much pain involved, from the stories I've heard. I think it can overpower some people. You can get lost and it can also be quite dangerous. You've got to know what you're doing, you've got to have trust, a safety net, a secret password or something. I think I'd be embarrassed as well, as much as anything.

Jo: Being a woman is political, being working-class is political. When somebody oppresses you, I think there has to be a political reaction to that, and so I think a lot of the decisions I make are political. In a perfect world I wouldn't need to identify as a lesbian, I'd be a person and I'd sleep with whoever I chose. Coming out is a political decision as well. I've worked in places where it hasn't felt safe to come out, and then I'd feel guilty about that, because I think I should be saying, look I'm here, I'm a lesbian. So yeah, politics plays quite a big part for me.

Somewhere along the line I've decided that I'm a lesbian, so I'm not even going to look at men, because I'm bored with that and it doesn't do much for me. And I think that's a political decision. I didn't have this overwhelming incredible sex drive to go and sleep with women, but I did, I happened to sleep with women, and I happened to find it much better sleeping with women. I don't want to share my life and get close to men. I could, I just don't want to.

7 lesbian looks

butch, femme, kiki

They went in the pub where me mum and dad drank, they used to play pool, and my dad liked them, strangely enough. He hates women playing pool. They drank pints with him. I realized that they were women and they were actually sleeping together.   Lorraine

Hey you big girl's blouse
Wanna ride on my handlebar moustache?!
Drag king   Sister George[1]

I went through a stage of looking extremely girly when I was about nineteen and I was very aware then that I looked butch ... but it only lasted about six months and then I thought, what are you doing? You look like a real bimbo. I think I'd rather look like a boy than a bimbo, thank you.   Lorraine

U-G-L-Y she ain't got no alibi.   Go Fish

There have been cultures which have revered those who take on the dress and attributes of the other sex, in the sense that they are people unbound by convention and so have been attributed with a certain visionary power beyond the ordinary. But there are more tales, from the 'hunters and gatherers' style of anthropology, to the exceptional and rule-proving Amazon and other matriarchal and matrilineal cultures, which let us know how long societies have been organized along strictly gendered lines, involving notions around dress, behaviour, work, pursuits, brainpower, and biology. Since stereotyped gendered behaviour is general in society in the twentieth century, this is obviously going to have some influence on lesbians.

For straight society, lesbian is synonymous with butch. A woman who looks in any way less than conventionally feminine runs the risk of attracting abuse, over and above the use of lesbian as a term of abuse which all women risk if they raise the male ire in any way. Lesbian chic has not shown any convincing evidence of bringing about changes in these attitudes, and it will be interesting to see if it proves able to achieve this, and thus become invested with an importance far greater than its current media favour promises. Dress can be used as a means of displaying your age, your political allegiances, your race, your religious beliefs, your employment, your gender, your culture, your class, your feelings, your wealth, your rank, and yes, your sexuality. This is not a new thing, although different cultures and communities vary considerably in how far this kind of expression of personality is encouraged, and what level of conformity is expected.

Where this differs for lesbians, and for other groups who are not necessarily immediately identifiable, is that, given the continuing invisibility of many aspects of lesbian life, lesbians have had to find ways to find and recognize each other. Many lesbians have also used clothes to differentiate themselves from straight women, and refused the limitations of straight women's dress as part of their visible lesbian identity. Straight women's clothes have often been less comfortable, less hard-wearing, less roomy and more constricting than men's, ensuring that women are wearing the clothes for the job. So there are a host of reasons why lesbians have looked and chosen to look butch.

Until the 1960s, men had short hair, women long, men wore trousers and women skirts and dresses. Wartime was liberating for some women because it removed, if only temporarily, some of the constraints of female life, and allowed women to focus on more than homemaking, mothering and femininity. 'It was obvious from their clothes and by the way they took to the masculine role with great gusto that they were really enjoying the war.'[2] Trousers and short hair became more feasible during this time, purely for practicality's sake of course. But this must have made lesbians' lives somewhat easier, given how unusual it was for most women to wear trousers, at least in public. (And there are still many employers who expect women to wear skirts.) But the postwar period saw women kicked out of the factories and back in the home, and the launch of Christian Dior's New Look, full skirts and nipped-in waists, decidedly feminine, and certainly not a look for working women, since even getting that amount of material for one dress was a problem with clothes rationing. There were other more surprising sources of criticism of women for wearing trousers: *Artemis* magazine, which appeared in the 1970s, saw it as a co-option into masculinity. Influences from different cultures have become standard since the 1960s embrace of what was known as the ethnic look, from the high street to the catwalk, with varying degrees of sensitivity about what is being worn and by whom. Up until then, there had been fewer styles to choose from, and far less communication transnationally, with no multinationals recreating the world – the capitalist western world, that is – in their chosen image. With the opening up of world markets in the late twentieth century has come the international imposition of sameness.

A feeling of alienation from the dominant image can discourage women from being lesbians. Several interviewees confirmed this, saying that the images of lesbian life they encountered put them off, until they met likeminded or like-looking lesbians. Younger women mentioned Greenham and feminism in this way; older women talked about role-playing. But not everybody finds the same things off-putting:

> Role playing heterosexual parts perhaps made their relationships more real and understandable to me and the other girls who knew about them. I never felt this knowledge was negative ... I remember being fascinated by their behaviour and interaction, how we knew and they knew but it was never openly expressed or discussed.[3]

Outside major urban areas, lesbians may not have access to meeting places, magazines, films and other literature that would alert them to the myriad possibilities. Or they may have been (or thought they were) the only goth lesbian in their town, and the other lesbians may have all been into listening to Cris Williamson and gardening.

Within lesbian culture, butch and femme have whole clusters of meaning attached to them. They are, as Sue O'Sullivan and Susan Ardill have pointed out, overburdened as terms due to the underdevelopment of lesbian language.[4] Butch and femme are used to discuss: appearance; sexual behaviour; role-playing and playing with roles. Role-playing is generally seen as historical, taken to relate to a bar dyke style of living, while playing with roles is a more modern, Queer perhaps, reinterpretation, a lifestyle item. Butch and femme suffers from the general confusion and conflation between playing at something and being it, which I have already touched on in terms of lesbian style, only more so because of its historical usage in sexology. As Lillian Faderman points out, despite

Radclyffe Hall's adherence to the 'incurable invert' ideas of Havelock Ellis – which differed substantially from Freud's psychoanalytical perpective which allowed the prospect of a 'cure' – both Hall and Freud attributed butch and femme roles to lesbians. For Freud there was the 'active' lesbian who sought and pursued a feminine love object; Hall's terms were different, the invert (the natural) and the mate of the invert. The work of both, given its ubiquity, served to further the notions of butch and femme as models for behaviour for lesbian couples.

While fashion could be said, increasingly since the 1960s at least, to be fluid in its images and interpretations of masculinity and femininity, lesbians have accumulated a set of time-specific and fixed ideas around butch and femme. Altogether far too much meaning invested in two words. There is the butch and femme wherein the clothes were followed through by the behaviour: heavily stereotyped in terms of clothes, butches flattening breasts and cutting hair and femmes emphasizing their female-ness by the standards of the day; butches behaving in a macho/gallant way towards their femmes, lighting their cigarettes, protecting them from the advances of other butches; femmes in big hair and big dresses, keeping house. Sexually there are as many tales about stone butches, who gave sexual pleasure and orgasms but would not or could not accept it themselves because it was considered too female or too threatening to reveal themselves as female, as there are contrary stories of how roles ended at the front or bedroom door. To dress butch and act otherwise – which now would have an erotic trajectory of its own – was considered unacceptably confusing: two butches dancing together, 'would be like homosexual and heterosexual at the same time'.[5]

In an extremely hostile climate, butch and femme let you know where you were, gave signals about safety, and markers about how to behave, socially and sexually. There were no other role models. Butch/femme in the 1950s made lesbians visible (although at the same time there were lesbians who tried, and succeeded, to pass this way). This was frightening for lesbians, who then had an even greater need for the safety, consistency and reliability of role-playing, and also for lesbians who were more concerned about passing as straight and moving towards assimilation.

A good many members who have attended the first two MRG (Minority Rights Group) meetings have been somewhat piqued by the exhibitionist tendency of one or two others, and want to know if it is really absolutely necessary to turn up to these meetings dressed in what is popularly known as 'full drag'. As the majority of women homosexuals are not transvestites we shall be glad if at future meetings there will be no further cause for wounded sensibilities.[6]

This was one of the answers:

I find it extremely difficult to believe that my dress could have wounded anybody; on the contrary I have been wounded by certain members of a Group that was to be my hopes and dreams. Also I disagree that the majority of women homosexuals are not transvestites. At least fifty percent are or would like to be.[7]

Organizations for lesbians which existed in the 1960s were very concerned about how they appeared in the mainstream: one of the objectives of MRG was 'to seek ways of improving the public image of the lesbian'. And from the USA, *The Ladder* commented, 'Our organization has converted a few to remembering that they are women first and a butch or femme secondly.' Pages of their journals were given over to discussions about how lesbians should dress, and gripes and fears about how they did dress.

There is also a general fear of the lesbian sterotypes which do exist ... it sounds snobbish to say so but in all honesty it seems to me that many of the stereotypes are women who do men's jobs – bus drivers, garage hands, and through their vulgarity and displays of drunkenness and physical violence they antagonise gay and straight people alike.[8]

And it wasn't only feminism that had its criteria for the 'right' sort of lesbian:

It seems to me that it is the lesbian for kicks rather than the true lesbian who would be more inclined to go in for 'full drag'. Flashing full drag in public places merely cheapens us and our aims by inviting derision from the public whose acceptance and support we badly need. One can only conclude that the wearers of full drag just do not wish to be ultimately accepted as an integral part of human society.[9]

Volume 8 of *Arena3* carried a series of articles on 'The Butch – examination of a stereotype'. One of the articles cites as the 'cause' of butchness, lack of female conditioning and traumatic sexual experience stunting emotional growth, and further, sees the butch as existing on the 'fringes of the pseudo-criminal scene in the larger cities'. She is described thus:

> The necessary swagger and stance; the exaggerated masculine attentions to
> the girlfriend – sometimes referred to as the 'wife' – when out and about in
> the group; the near-ritualistic behaviour over trivialities like opening doors,
> lighting cigarettes, buying drinks and, especially, dancing with other people's
> femmes. . . . Promiscuity is possibly far less prevalent among ultrabutches and
> their femmes than among the more feminine 'fifty–fifty' girls.

And this a portrait from a supposedly sympathetic organization, if one that
now appears conservative.

We may think now that gender-fucking is an entirely new thing and that
fashion has always been an anathema to the right-thinking lesbian until
the advent of the designer dyke. Read on then, through these extracts from
*Arena*3 ('non-extemist outlook and refreshing lack of aggressiveness'):

> For most lesbians, the problem is a little bit trickier than for other women.
> Some simply don't care – and look awful . . . others spurn feminine clothes
> altogether. . . . The rest effect an unhappy compromise which does nothing
> for their morale, while giving the impression that they get their clothes at
> jumble sales (and rather late in the afternoon at that).[10]
>
> Quite seriously I'd say to any gay girl – be yourself. If the unisex clothes and
> scene is for you, get out the loon pants and the tank top – or, if you want to
> feel completely a male and want to dress like one – good luck to you. Plenty
> of fem girls like me think you're the greatest. . . . For two years I've been trying
> to replace her, and I've a stack of time tables and AA maps for any lonely fella
> who feels like a-travellin' my way.[11]

It was also threatening for the rest of the public to see visible lesbians and
begin to realize that lesbians were their relatives and neighbours and
workmates. There were exceptions to this, some lesbians are less frightening than others: Nancy Spain, a society woman who moved in exalted
circles and featured in newspaper society columns, was considered
unfrightening enough to appear on *Juke Box Jury* in her hacking jacket and
cravat. Alison Hennegan, who also mentions this in her piece 'On becoming a lesbian reader',[12] notes that her mother's reaction to her desire to
buy lesbian paperbacks, of the 'twilight women from Hell variety', was that
it was 'not nice, rather sordid' – which is very possibly different from her
reaction to Nancy Spain.

What followed the singularity of the 1950s image of the female was an
all-too-neat turnaround. After the constraints of looking feminine came

the feminist strictures of rejecting male-defined images of women, which included most things remotely feminine or, to some observers, female. Dress was not supposed to reflect much more than your politics. There was a very narrow range of alternatives. Make-up was out, so were skirts and dresses; jewellery was only acceptable as women's symbols or labyrises. In general, dress was functional, dowdy in shape if not in colour, and big.

To many feminists in the 1970s, butch and femme was a crystallization of everything that feminism opposed. There is still much debate about how far butch/femme is a lesbian-developed cultural behaviour, and how far based on or differentiated from heterosexual behaviour and style.

> I had seen women dressed like this before, back when we were just beginning to talk about ourselves with excitement, in bars where women who knew nothing of this talk still dressed in ways that were a sign of the past we were trying to destroy. In an odd and embarrassing fashion they had excited me, these women that bound their breasts to hide the fact that they were women, these women that would not let you touch them 'down there' because they could not admit they were not men, and I had often wondered what it would be like to go home with one of them. But they were too butch for me to come on to them, and I was not femme enough for them to come on to me.[13]

Seen as aping the worst stereotypical aspects of both masculinity and femininity, of giving lesbianism a bad name and a bad image, of rejecting feminism's preferred androgynous and supposedly neutral and natural look, butch and femme was roundly rejected as self-hating and unreconstructed. 'She hung out at Gianni's, where the serious bulldykes went, the ones who were into cross-dressing. At least that's what they used to call it, before the style seeped into the upper classes and got renamed the "androgynous look".'[14]

Although feminism's androgyny was ultimately also seen and experienced as butch itself, in the 1960s the blurring of gender boundaries around dress was unimaginably radical; GLF brought a politics of dress firmly centre stage, and dressing became political. Androgyny was then a rejection of limitation and gender circumscription, whereas it came to signify through feminism a denial of difference, and an attempt to level and bland out desire.[15] Lesbians who came out into the atmosphere of change of the late 1960s considered those whom they saw living a closeted existence as both ashamed (of their own sexuality) and shaming (to themselves), and this history was rejected wholesale as irredeemably backward.

As lesbian feminism waned in the late 1980s, things changed again: although butch had never been entirely out of favour – in terms of how people actually looked if not politically – femme enjoyed a certain reclamation into the fold. Through this, Joan Nestle's description[16] of butch/femme as part of lesbians' erotic heritage became an accepted truth for many. To have a butch/femme past, for so long unmentionable, became a boastable, sexy item, at least on the level of dress anyway. To actually behave in a seriously macho way is probably only considered sexy in the outer reaches of gender-fucking and SM scenes, and unwelcome elsewhere. Although it had long been acceptable on certain occasions for dykes to wear tuxs, big frocks became wearable again; but despite a lot of talk, to be femme is still not considered as strong and true a lesbian look and identity as butch. Faderman notes that how the words used carry with them judgements about the inherent values of each: butch/stud, femme/ fish.[17] (Fish, although somewhat reclaimed, used to be a term used pejoratively by anti-lesbian gay men.) I have already pointed out the conundrum that, while lesbians reject Havelock Ellis's and Freud's construction of the true, mannish lesbian, among ourselves we uphold something similar, against her more 'feminine' mate, who has been consistently downgraded. One answer to this – not entirely convincing – is that it is a lesbian rejection of society's negative construction of femaleness. While lesbians may fight against this elsewhere, the idea of the butch being somehow more really lesbian prevails.

There is the so-called post-feminist butch who chooses that look and those codes of behaviour to live her life by, or merely to enhance her desire and operate as she cruises. Her counterpart, apart from her fellow butches, is maybe not so much a femme, as a girly girl. Times and terms change, just as different eras have different fashions or uniforms. But a butchy femme seems similar to a kiki. And there seems little difference between butches and daddy dykes, androgynes and lesbian boys.

Role-playing has come to be seen as a stimulus to sexual appetite, beyond the limitations of female conditioning, and although there is still resistance to this, the tide has certainly turned. Lesbians into drag, self-styled dyke drag kings and queens, once unthinkable, are a force of their own. (Stormé DeLarverié, who was a bouncer at the Cubby Hole, a now closed bar in New York, perfected the art of illusion and took the idea of gender-fuck to dizzying heights even before the term was invented, by performing as a male impersonator.) Dyke drag queens and kings now feature regularly in lesbian images which is often an early step towards hipness and visibility in the lesbian mainstream. Androgyny, although still the norm (in a butch kind of way) has been discredited through its association with what was seen as bland, no sex feminism. A more accurate definition of androgyny has increased in popularity with the rise and rise of the androgyne of the day, kd, so this may remove the non-sexual tag.

The outlook on the post-feminist, postmodernist butch is that by and large she is playing with it, rather than being it. In this way, butch and femme are seen as performance, and style is not synonymous with identity. There is the danger that this is merely a pseudo-theoretical way of saying butch on the streets, femme in the sheets. But the huge changes in the ways in which lesbians display themselves and their sexuality, and the photographic and written work on lesbians and representation which are fairly pouring off the presses, suggest that there is room for optimism here.

Some butches have wanted to be boys and some have become boys; some were tomboys (but then so were some femmes); some drag up or cross-dress for nights out, for fun; some, like Jennifer Saunders, have become butch to try to assuage their girlfriends' problems about being lesbian. No post-feminist butch, her situation and experience does point out some of the variables and some of the pitfalls about being and playing lesbian and butch. If the sanctions against lesbianism were not so high, there would have been no question of dressing as a man for any other reason than that she wanted to, nor would she have been imprisoned for it, nor would she have been largely forgotten about in the lesbian press.

... And in the third corner we have kiki, more or less acceptable at different times. Although kiki has never been a term, or a category, with such currency as butch and femme, and is still far more recognized in the USA than in Britain, it now means someone who is deliberately both, rather than the 'neither fish nor fowl' connotation it used to have. Despite the long-term rejection of serious role-playing, there is still resistance to the idea of women being kiki, along the lines of being not quite a real lesbian, and it is often still tainted with middle-classness. Lillian Faderman also comes up with 'bluff', a somewhat pejorative combination of butch and fluff, and says that kiki was also used of (largely middle-class) couples who were both butch or both femme.[18] It seems as though gender-fucking could go some way to take over where kiki has never taken off, and certainly it is more fashionable in the 1990s than kiki has ever been. Kiki will probably continue to be used by a generation of women for whom gender-fucking means youth, in a similar way that many women of a certain age have rejected the queer label.

In November 1994 the Victoria & Albert Museum opened an exhibition called 'Street Style', using clothed mannequins, exhibition panels, photographs and text panels to explore the vast array of styles from the street from the 1940s to the present day. Included in this were six mannequins dressed in different manifestations of specifically lesbian and gay style, including: a man's suit made for a woman; pink dungarees; a Biba dress which belonged to Elizabeth Wilson and was then worn by a man into radical drag; the jeans, plaid shirt and work boots clone uniform; fetish gear.

Shaun Cole, a curator at the V & A working on the exhibition, was keen to find ways of representing relatively hidden aspects of lesbian and gay dress history. A photograph of a pinky ring, for instance, pictures of gallery girls (a largely 1940s manifestation of the lesbian fan, swooning over the likes of Tallulah Bankhead) who advertised their allegiances through the slightest suggestion of deviation from women's usual dress codes, a hat tilted just so, the cut of a coat. He was also anxious to avoid what might be seen as stereotyping by the public or lesbians and gays. It is easy to shout stereotype, but, like clichés, stereotypes are often based in truth, and distilled down until they reach a point of reductionist parody of the original. Nobody would suggest that the diversity of lesbian styles over the fifty years of the exhibition's range can be demonstrated within the limits of six mannequins; rather the six and the attendant text and other items of clothing and photographs were used to say these are some of the styles that you might have found being worn within this time. Where no examples could be found, this was pointed out as evidence of the clandestine nature of many lesbian and gay lives. Similarly there was ample opportunity to demonstrate to the viewing public that most lesbians and gay men look no different to themselves.

What is interesting, as if the V & A including such a substantial lesbian and gay input were not enough, is the amount of cross-over from minority to mainstream straight wear: what was once clone uniform is now everybody's workwear uniform; the Biba dress speaks for itself; the kilt look and fetish gear have both become high-street looks. The influence of the mainstream has often been overlooked in discussions of lesbian dress, as if lesbians really are strangers to fashion, whereas in reality the influence works both ways. The liberalization of dress codes for women in the 1960s with the advent of trousers, the miniskirt, and the hippy era (although we may not actually believe in these as sites of any real liberation for lesbians or women in general), and the wearing of DMs and 501s in the 1980s which became mainstream fashion, are examples which have clearly crossed over from opposite directions.

Lesbian style has always been a nexus of choice – in terms of style and finances and safety/visibility issues. Until the late 1960s, gender roles and the clothing that went with them were far more ingrained than they are today, when their transgression is *de rigeur* in some circles for trendy young things. Before the sartorial liberation of the 1960s it was very hard to show your sexuality in your dress unless you were prepared to attract heavy reactions against you. Even more than in the present day, most lesbians and gay men must have looked like everyone else, because the penalties for doing otherwise were too much to contemplate. At the same time, looking different was not experienced as a choice for some women, either because that was just how they looked, or because of their need to fit into the lesbian world of the time.

Upper-class women, who could afford to dismiss those kinds of consideration, had more leeway to look butch. Femmes were only recognizable if they had a butch on their arm. Pinky rings, different hairstyles and make-up were, in public at least, often the extent to which most women felt able to go. Working-class women, in the main, could not afford the same extravagances, and we are often therefore left without images of working-class lesbians, relying instead on those of upper-class women from the Bloomsbury Group, Radclyffe Hall, and so on. This means that not only are most people's images of lesbians founded on the Radclyffe Hall look, but that many women are put off by this, in terms of dress and of class. This has had other adverse affects: the lack of images to the contrary reaffirms the prejudices of those people who refuse to believe that homosexuality is something which happens in their class, in their country, in their culture.

Women who look, and who choose to look and behave butch now are still likely to attract more hassle and homophobia than a less visible lesbian. They may also attract censure from some of those lesbians who want to choose when and where they are out, or who see butches as an assault on their own credibility, both on the scene and outside it. Femmes are likely to cause confusion in straight places, and may still be treated as second class dykes in certain circles. There's no certainty about the value of butch and femme for lesbians – it can be freedom or limitation, a boon or a bind, at particular times for some women. In any case, as examples have shown, butch and femme codes vary across the axes of race and class and age, and are received and named differently. Some women who choose to be butch or femme feel they are following gender identifications within themselves. At the same time, it is possible to see butch and femme as a method of lesbian categorization which has evolved for many reasons – some imposed on us, and some of our own choosing – and become a sexualized index of behaviour.

NOTES

1. Sister George, Handlebar, Catcall Records.
2. Myrtle Solomon, in Hall Carpenter Archives Lesbian Oral History Group, Inventing Ourselves, Routledge, 1989, p. 18.
3. Morag, in National Lesbian and Gay Survey, What a Lesbian Looks Like, Routledge, 1992, p. 37.
4. Sue O'Sullivan and Susan Ardill, 'Butch/Femme Obsessions', 'Perverse Politics', Feminist Review, no. 34, Spring 1990, p. 80.
5. Rene Sawyer, Hall Carpenter Archives Lesbian Oral History Group, taped interviews at National Sound Archives, London.
6. Arena3, vol. 1, no. 6, June 1964.
7. Arena3, vol. 1, no. 7, July 1964.
8. 'Personal Texts', Sequel, no. 3, Gay Pride issue, March 1970.
9. Arena3, vol. 9, no. 3, September 1972.
10. Arena3, vol. 1 no. 6, June 1964.
11. Arena3, vol. 9 no. 3, September 1972.
12. Alison Hennegan, 'On becoming a lesbian reader', in Susannah Radstine (ed.), Sweet Dreams – Sexuality, Gender and Popular Fiction, Lawrence and Wishart, 1988, p. 165.
13. Jane De Lynn, Don Juan in the Village, Serpent's Tail, 1990, p. 23.
14. Ibid., p. 225.
15. E. Wilson, in Tessa Boffin and Jean Fraser (eds), Stolen Glances: Lesbians Take Photographs, Pandora, 1991, p. 57.
16. Joan Nestle, A Restricted Country, Sheba, 1987, p. 100.
17. Lillian Faderman, Odd Girls and Twilight Lovers, Penguin, 1992, p. 172.
18. Ibid., p. 168.

SALLY MUNT IS THIRTY-THREE AND WORKS AS A SENIOR LECTURER IN CULTURAL STUDIES.

To begin with I had a relationship with a woman which was not named as such. It was never ever stated: homosexuality or lesbianism was never said. It went on for quite a while, so retrospectively it's quite interesting. We just did it in the middle of the night and never referred to it in daylight. She was a woman, who is now a priest, who I was living with in a religious community, not just that but a celibate community, so there was no such thing as a gay or lesbian culture around us to identify with.

After that I spent a couple of years being what I would call bisexual in the sense that I still had no gay or lesbian identity. I was living in Weymouth and I only knew three women who slept with women, so we didn't really constitute a community, and I think that's quite important in terms of an identification. I think bisexual was a less frightening term to describe myself.

It was incredibly clandestine. It was a community of single and married people, so the married people were having sex, one presumes, but probably not. It kind of grew out of the fact that I did something called primal therapy with my counsellor which was about rebirthing. She did it at the same time, and this had a levelling effect, so in some respects what we did for each other was to enact the mother. I think that kind of eroticization is deeply linked to nurturance and all that sort of thing. Sexual feelings came out because of that. Emotional feelings were already there. I think it tipped the balance.

But the thing was that out of this bisexual experience, or this bisexual identity that I'd had, I definitely became a feminist at that point, and I decided that I'd move to Brighton, because I was going to do a post-graduate course and I'd heard there were lots of dykes. There was an awful lot of longing to be part of that. Almost immediately I got here I became a lesbian. And that was because there was something to identify with.

What I did for the first couple of years was be a bar dyke; I was down at the Long Branch every Friday night for the women's disco. At that point I was much more of a lesbian feminist than I am now. I think that was partly a reflection of the time, partly a reflection of the hegemony of the Brighton lesbian scene then, which was in a very predominant way lesbian feminist, bordering on separatism. At that point there wasn't any butch/femme to speak of, or, if there was, they went to the rougher pubs and it was obviously a class difference going on. The culture that I belonged to was strongly lesbian feminist, it was check shirts, jeans, flat-tops and Doc Martens. I don't know if it's possible for me to say that I identified as a butch then, because, although

I'd heard of the terms, it wasn't a real identity for me because I didn't see anybody doing that. But you know, the old joke about lesbian feminists was that they were all butches. I think that to begin with, those first couple of years in Brighton was just like this erotic adventure because I'd discovered this whole culture of available women. It wasn't that I was particularly promiscuous (not that there's anything wrong with that of course), but it was more that I was just dazzled by all these out dykes, and that was really exciting.

I'd say I was fairly securely placed as a lesbian by then because of this previous experience in Weymouth. Also, during this period my mother died, and so I think it was even more important to me to have a secure community to come back to, because I was nursing her in Huddersfield. While she died, and also for a long time afterwards, it was very important to me to feel like I had emotional roots in a community, and therefore I think I was very within the particular culture I needed to be.

In fact, the uncomfortable aspects of that community for me was actually more of an issue about class, and this wasn't a new feeling to me, because I'd lived in the south since I was eighteen and I'd lived in totally middle-class environments. I think the lesbian feminist community was quite bourgeois, and although in some ways that's something that I've always aspired to, in other ways it's still a world that makes me very uncomfortable. I think there was a sense of my own alienation that came not from a dyke identity but from a working-class identity. I'd say that what happened was that if I ever mentioned the subject [there] was a total defensiveness on the part of other dykes, along the lines of, 'I really don't want to talk about that, it's just destructive. I've seen so many people being destroyed by that conversation, I really don't want to have it', which is a totally effective silencing technique.

I only knew one other working-class dyke in the scene here, in the student scene, and she's still my friend, and we still have conversations about what it's like to be a working-class dyke, and she's still the only person I have that conversation with. I will say things to other people but no one ever volunteers. I, for my own health, will say things but I always feel mixed about saying it, because I feel like people think I'm trying to make them feel guilty, which is not the case. I'm just trying to say, 'Hello, I'm different,' and even that is a source of confusion, because I'm a university lecturer. Many middle-class women have told me I'm not working-class anyway because I'm a university lecturer. But it's about how you grew up, and what kind of culture you come from, it's about relation to capital, relation to money, relation to home, relation to space; it's all about very intangible yet strong things which I'm going to think about more for this book I'm going to write about butch and femme.

My teaching and my job description is I'm a lecturer in cultural studies, and this is the way I get a job. If I was to say, I'm a senior lecturer in lesbian and gay studies, people would just laugh. I've had so many times where I haven't got the job because my c.v.'s too dykey, or when I turn up, I'm too butch for them to cope with. What they usually say is that the other candidate's area was closer to what we wanted or what we needed, with our established courses.

I made a decision about lots of different aspects, how closet I was going to be. At the moment I still have one vestige of closetry left which is that I'm not out to my father. Although I can't imagine that he doesn't know. [See postscript on page 162.] But you know, my mum's dead, he's the only parent I've got, and, even though we have such a crap relationship really, there's just this little piece of me that hopes that one day he and I will be reconciled, and I'm sure that my reluctance to tell him is about that.

The other thing that's happened to me a lot, five times, is I've been passed over for a black candidate because of what the panel perceive to be their equal opportunities policy. And I have a lot of problems with that, because it pitches me in competition with black candidates who I actually feel the opposite towards. Poverty of resources over equal opportunities means that they'll appoint one Other. And almost inevitably, that's a black Other (assumed to be straight); they don't 'see' class or sexuality, which is a racist thing in itself. Basically, in humanities in higher education you have, by and large, senior people in their forties who are appointing. They have this politics from, you know, 1968, which has been flavoured by Thatcherism, and it's this peculiar blend of a bit of socialism, a bit of liberalism, a bit of unreconstructed masculinity, and a bit of unreconstructed racism and sexism and homophobia. They have a certain amount of consciousness and it's about as much as they can cope with to appoint a black candidate. Also because I teach lesbian and gay studies, people expect me to know everything about race. So it works both ways.

How I approach my job is I try and distance myself. I do change my behaviour, I just don't change how I look. I see a difference between teaching lesbian and gay studies as an intellectual discipline and being a dyke. You can't get stuck into this thing where, for example, only black people can teach about race. I have to separate my personal, emotional lesbian identity from my professional, lesbian and gay studies identity. At work I'm more distant than other colleagues; more unapproachable, very formal. I use all that stuff to protect myself, because there's so much homophobia amongst students for a start. In a few weeks I've got to give this lecture on lesbian and gay liberation to 180 eighteen-year-olds. That has a cost. I'm so excited that I can do that, because for some of those kids it's the first time they've ever had to think about it. I don't mean they've not called each other fairies. I mean they've never had to really use their minds to think about it, and so to me I have this dual thing going on, self-protection and vulnerability.

One side is this total excitement in that I can use the academy to be an activist, because education is the key to changing people's prejudices, so it's terrific to have that opportunity. It also lays myself on the line very definitely and that's a dangerous thing to have to do. And so in order to avoid potentially harmful situations I have this great sense of distance and I think that has its difficulties. For example last year, I have this lecture on lesbian and gay bar culture from 1960s. Last year two students' parents rang the Dean and complained that their daughters were being corrupted, basically, by having to put up with this kind of filth masquerading as academic work. I don't know what the Dean said, whether she backed me up or not. I imagine in some ways she had to, because it was an attack on her faculty as much as on me. Last year, too, I taught on this course with a gay lecturer, in which there was a very small amount of lesbian and gay studies in our course in US popular culture. And there were six lads who used to sit at the back of the class every week and never take a note, sit with their arms crossed and stare hostilely at me solidly for two hours. That's the sort of crap I have to put up with all the time really, and also the way in which my ideas are dismissed, because I'm seen as some kind of weird extremist pervert. There's a genial support amongst the immediate colleagues I work with, but they have a complete lack of understanding about the issues. They don't know anything about lesbian and gay studies, they just go, 'Oh well, listen, Sally, you can do that, it's your kind of thing.' So there's support in the sense that they respect me and they'll let me get on with it, which is important. There's another step, which is to positively engage, and that's what they don't do.

There are a small minority of dykes and slightly more gay men who will come to tutorials, and I have my own little equal opps policy, so with all non-white, non-middle-class, non-young, non-straight students, I will give them extra time. I do get some support from them but I also have the opposite problem sometimes with dykes which is that they tend to have much more conservative politics than I do. They tend to be very lesbian feminist and anti-pornography and all that. I think they have an expectation that I will support them and I don't always agree with them.

My politics are, well I'd say that I was a feminist lesbian, but not a lesbian feminist as such. I'd say that my intellectual position is totally informed by feminist theory, but I'd say that my politics were lesbian and gay. In other words, I'm not into censorship or, I don't mind women having their own spaces as long as the end product is not separation. I think that, whereas it may have been more beneficial to feminism to go temporarily through a separatist phase during the 1980s and explore that more, I think because of AIDS we can't afford to do that, because AIDS is a catastrophe which affects women too because of homophobia. I had lots of arguments with dykes about this. What it does is that it completely puts people into fixed categories and that's the very thing we should be working against.

But I don't want to be too unkind about lesbian feminism, because I think it was very necessary and very exciting. I think it achieved a lot of things in terms of how we value women and how we understand how political institutions oppress us and affect us. Like the growing consciousness about breast cancer, it's like, would we have thought in those terms if we hadn't had feminism? Would we have tried to analyse the resources scientifically and medically going on around breast cancer if we hadn't had AIDS, you see? These things don't operate in isolation, they have knock-on effects. To paint it as though it was an anti-sex, moralistic movement is the same anti-feminist rhetoric that the Right uses. There's also now this 'oh weren't they naïve' response to 1970s feminism. No, they fucking weren't naïve. You think of what they achieved in those ten years between 1968 and 1978. A huge amount of political education was achieved, and I think I really am suspicious about this because it's how we as dykes undermine our own history all the time. The pressure on us is so much that we want to be perfect in everything we do and there's no tolerance. Tolerance is like this terrible liberal word, and I think no, actually I'm all for tolerance. It's like a struggle for empathy.

You have to look at people's intentions as well as their effects; and people judge on the effects alone, and they say, 'You did that wrong and now we're never going to speak to you again.' Well, hell, what kind of critical agenda is that? To look at lesbian culture in the 1960s and to say that it was pre-political is an insult. Bollocks, those women were really putting their lives on the line for what they believed in, and their desire, and I think it's very patronizing. I think the Queer agenda was sometimes the same thing. They've said, 'Oh let's trash that, we're not homosexuals or heterosexuals any more, we're just Queer; perversion's wonderful and whatever you want to do you can do.' It's this kind of Reichian 'however I fuck, somehow this is liberating'.

One of the good things about Queer was the reintegration of transsexuality and transvestism and gender-bending, and possibly bisexuality as well, into that general alternative sexualities agenda. I'm very excited about the 1990s, there are new forms appearing. I'm very hopeful really, because I think that as a community, or as a set of communities, lesbians and gays are incredibly dynamic, incredibly intelligent, and we form and reform our agendas so quickly.

I was involved in Section 28 quite a lot, there wasn't a lot going on in Brighton for a couple of years after that, and now I'm in Nottingham and there's not very much going on there either. I feel like my everyday is a political struggle, and therefore I don't feel like I rest, because every time I go out I get homophobic hassle 'cos of the way I look. So I don't have a break from being a dyke, and I'm an activist all the time because of what I do. I identify as a butch, and I identify as a butch not in a post-modern sense, this is not a role that I put on and put off and go partying. There's nothing wrong with that, if it gives them a bit of fun, I don't mind. I think it's fine for some people to be like that, but I'm not like that. I identify as a butch, I think, in a kind of historical sense, in that the thing that really fills my heart is walking into a bar and there are some old butches in their fifties and sixties. I don't want to romanticize butch/femme too much, because I think it has lots of downsides as well, but it's important for me to identify with a historical tradition of lesbianism specifically, and I think that I'm not clear about my gender really. I know I've got a woman's body, I've been told, but I've never felt like a woman. The only time I feel like a woman is when men behave to me as though I am a woman, and that forces me into a position of femininity that I feel entirely uncomfortable with, and I demur because at some level I must have been brought up to be a woman and that programme still exists. I feel much more at a deep level 'butch', although I don't want to essentialize this as a 'true' identity. I don't think I'm a butch in a cosmically true sense or anything, but it feels the energy that's the most real to me at the moment, and has done for the past few years. What butch is, though, I don't know, I don't know. I think it's a gender position which is not masculinity and is not femininity, and it's not particularly bound to heterosexual paradigms, although it's obviously influenced by them. I think it's something which is genuinely and specifically erotic to lesbian culture, and it's very much an erotic identification for me, I mean I get a thrill out of it.

At the moment it's quite interesting for me, too, because after being involved with femme women, bisexual women, or women who are more femme than me for years, I now find myself involved with somebody who is probably more butch than I am, although she doesn't hold to definitions as rigidly as I do. I said to her last night – true confessions – that what's erotic between her and I is this sameness, which is a real shock to me, because I've always been attracted to the difference. I can't decide whether I want to be the butch or fuck the butch or be fucked by the butch. It's a really complex thing that I don't understand, and I think it's to do with unconscious as well as conscious desires, and a sense of deliberate play but also of deep seriousness. I'm not sure where I am with it at all, I mean I'm definitely attracted to women.

I'd like to understand what gender identity is and how it's related to sex and the body. This woman I'm seeing at the moment, on the night we picked each other up (I'd like to say I picked her up but . . .) she was wearing a dress. And she said to me, 'Would you have picked me up if I was wearing my butch gear?' I said, 'No, probably not. I'd have approached you as a butch buddy and had a kind of whaaay hey chat with you.' It's not about clothes, it's about a whole attitude, stance, erotic signal, all sorts. This is what I'm saying, that it's an erotic configuration more than the clothes you're wearing.

What I wear is very important to me and I love dressing up. I now don't wear any women's clothing at all. Ever. Very occasionally I wear a sports bra if I'm wearing a white shirt. I feel like I'm transgressing something, definitely. I find my clothes erotic to myself and give me a great sense of being strong. I do get taken for Sir a lot, awright mate, all that. I hate it. Toilet traumas, every time I use a public toilet, especially motorway service stations, they're the worst. I got thrown out of one recently, because I wouldn't say if I was a man or a woman. Public space is strongly gendered: public space belongs to either men or women, it's not neutral. People really don't like you transgressing those boundaries at all.

The knickers were the last thing to go. Right until the end I was still wearing Marks and Spencers women's knickers, and then I discovered men's briefs and they're just like knickers but much better. Buying clothes is always a trauma. I shop at Gap a lot, they have mixed changing rooms and you can buy men's clothes in there, no problem.

*Postscript: I told my dad recently, to which he responded, 'Oh I guessed that anyway.'

JANET GREEN IS FORTY-SIX. SHE USED TO WORK FOR THE TERRENCE HIGGINS TRUST (THT) AND IS NOW IN SOCIAL WORK.

When I was about seventeen, I used to go to this big dance hall in Tottenham called the Royal. I went there three, four, or even five times a week, with my best friend Sue. And part of the ritual of going dancing was spending at least half an hour in the ladies loo, doing our hair and make-up. One night we were there, backcombing our hair like you do, and as I put my arm up to brush my hair, my arm brushed her breast. It was electric, it was just stunning. I'd slept with boys before then and never felt anything like this, completely gobsmacked. So I started thinking about it at that point. My sister confided to me that she was going to swinging parties, which were basically orgies. I asked if women ever went with other women. And she said, 'Oh yes, anything goes.' So I started going to parties, and sure enough, women did. On the down side, there was also the expectation that the women there would sleep with the men, so, you know, there's no such thing as a free lunch, basically.

Then I met a man who was older, wealthy, and I was impressed. I said to him I might be bisexual, and he said he had another girlfriend who's bisexual. We got on like a house on fire, we really gelled from the moment we met. We went on having threesomes for about four months, and eventually Carol and I ended up having the affair and dropped the boyfriend. And I had a relationship with Carol for about seven years after that. I've always been aware that, for a lot of women, when they come out is a time of confusion and angst, but I really never felt that. I think it was because of the hedonism of the parties – it was very much sex is fun, that was the message. Couldn't do it now of course, with HIV and AIDS, but the worst you could get then was a dose of the clap, which was dealable with.

Carol had had a taster of the scene with another girlfriend. In effect Gateways was the scene, so it felt like she was the woman of the world and I was the *ingénue*. She took me down there. I'm sure everyone says this about the first time they went down there. I walked down those stairs after all the palaver of getting in, because you had to knock on the door with a password practically. My mouth just dropped open. I'm sure my chin hit the floor.

First of all it was wall-to-wall women. It was a tiny room, and packed. Very electric atmosphere, very exciting. And of course I went through the whole bit about gawping at the butches and trying to decide were they really men or women, because they were so so butch. I loved it. There was another club we went to called the Rehearsal, because the Gateways closed at eleven, pub hours. We used to go after, it was in Windmill Street. That was a mixed club, but very mixed and it felt OK to be there.

With the butch and femme stuff, it was made clear that you had to be one or the other. Carol had very long hair right down her back, but she also used to wear shirt and tie. I remember, down the Gateways one night, some butchy type looking at her and saying in a really hostile way 'Huh, she ought to make her mind up what she is.' The group of women we used to hang round with down there, a lot of them were in the army, or had been and had been found out and kicked out. Within that group were women who had been privates, and women who had been officers who were often very well-educated, middle-class women, and inevitably very butch.

Because I liked clothes and dressing up and enjoyed putting on make-up, it seemed obvious to me that I should be femme. I didn't even think about it really. But in my sexual relationships it was very kind of equal. Being a femme, I found myself very popular. Yeah. Oh yeah, oh yeah. There was none of the derision – not so much now but a few years ago – that women got for wearing dresses and make-up and things like that. You were valued and cherished. I don't think I ever bought myself a drink down the Gateways. I milked the situation really, like you would when you were nineteen or twenty.

One or two of the women I went to bed with did carry it through into their behaviour, it wasn't just about dress. One woman in particular I can remember who frightened me, as she was making love to me. She didn't want me to touch her at all, but she was also saying, 'I want to fuck you, I want to put my prick in you.' It freaked me out. I've wondered if that was what women really wanted, or if it was what they thought they were supposed to want.

When I went to do my degree I fell in love with another student. At the same time I discovered feminism. Occasionally, because we were doing social work placements, we would be in London and we'd go to clubs and pubs, and that was quite a treat. I think I told you about one incident when I'd gone straight from my placement, and we'd gone to a club and I was in a dress. I was the only woman in the place in a dress. I felt very awkward and out of place. There was a lot of looking and 'has she come to the wrong disco' sort of stuff. There was a uniform really: jeans, and either shirts with ties, with the tie loose at the neck, or collarless shirts and waistcoats. The Annie Hall look. And everyone had short hair of course. There was a real feeling that you had to conform. You had to be very careful not to say the wrong thing: about feminist politics, not to talk about girls, only to talk about women or womyn or whatever it was. All sorts of things, there was so many of them I can barely remember them now. There was so much about language; around appearance, it was very unsound to wear make-up, high heels, shave your legs. I'd always shaved my legs since I was twelve. Just about everything I did actually was unsound. Some of the things became habit and that felt OK.

But there were other things I felt uncomfortable about. I'm not sure how much to tell you. One of the things I enjoy sexually is dressing up – I like silk, satin, that kind of material, and stockings and suspenders and that sort of thing. That was something you could never talk about with anyone else, you really couldn't. So yes, there were things that were done in secret and not talked about. I remember the dyke who said, 'I'd never trust a dyke in a dress,' and that really summed up the feeling of the times. I remember getting to a point where I was thinking, first of all it was my family telling me what to do and say, then it was men, and now it's women doing it, and I'm not having it. I remember feeling very rebellious, thinking, I've had enough of this, I want to be myself and I don't want to be policed all the time.

It was during the time I was at Lesbian Line that I started to feel like this. I think it came to a head for me when it was decided that any new volunteers must either be black or working-class. It was when all that working-class stuff was coming to a head, and working-class women were demanding that middle-class women gave them their cheque cards or Access cards or whatever it was. And they were doing it. Silly girls [uproarious laughter]. I remember one very middle-class woman who had a lot of money talking to me, because I was a working-class woman, about whether she should hand over her Access card. I said, don't be ridiculous, don't do it, unless you're going to give it to me of course.

So yes, disenchantment set in. I mentioned to you about the last Lesbian Strength I went on, and how angry I felt at the end of that – this isn't about strength at all. It was about war and hostility. People wouldn't go to the LLGC because that was where the SM dykes met, or something like that. There were other women who felt like me. It's very strange because, as you say, it is the same language that people use when they're coming out. Very similar feelings about owning up and being secretive. So it was a time of revelation; again, going back to when I was seventeen and wondering whether I was really a lesbian. Similarities about feeling I was the one and only feminist who wasn't right on. I remember hearing the expression 'the thought police' for the first time and thinking, yes that's right.

This is a contradiction in terms maybe, but it was so liberating to be able to have a bitch about it all and how awful it had been. It was quite a big portion of my life; when I was on Lesbian Line I was putting in a lot of hours, not just on the phone lines, on the organizational side as well, and there were so many meetings to go to, so many demos to attend. Keep the GLC alive, pro-abortion, Reclaim the Night, you know, you name it really. That was a lot of time to be feeling I was walking on eggs, and it constituted my social scene too. And sexual scene. At one time at Lesbian Line during one of our regular meetings, every woman in the room was having a relationship with another woman there.

Moving on from there, when you actually got to bed with someone, it was still like treading on eggs, you had to find out what was acceptable – was penetration all right? Very difficult. And the language for it all as well: what do we call our genitals – 'Is the term pussy all right with you or must we call it vagina?' – do you know what I mean? All of it! It's amazing that we ever got to bed with each other.

When I went to work for the Terrence Higgins Trust in 1985, [someone] said, 'Why are you going to work with men? And actually what does it matter if they all die?', or something deeply unpleasant like that. There was only one woman who said it, but I think more thought it. I suppose by the time I went to THT I was disenchanted with feminism, and I had been on Gay Pride quite a few years running. I was coming more and more to the feeling that we're stronger together, lesbians and gay men are stronger together. So it did affect me going for that job, it felt like my community. It was the most amazing time, frustrating and stimulating, and angering and saddening and joyful. I can't begin to tell you. The media was going mad, the phone never stopped and the letters poured in. And I was going out and doing talks and health education. Oh, and I wrote the first women's HIV leaflet in the country. It's one of the bits of work at the Trust I'm proudest of. So yes, it was part and parcel, it was not separate from my sexuality.

I use the words lesbian, dyke, gay. I feel fine about reclaiming dyke but less so about reclaiming queer. It has been used as a derogatory term within my family, something I grew up with. So I find it very difficult to be positive about it, and I try and be terribly liberal about the people who are using queer, like on Pride or something when loads of people are wearing 'queer as fuck' t-shirts. Gay is a term I will use as a compromise if I feel people will be more comfortable with it.

I keep saying, 'I'm forty-six now, this really isn't a phase that I'm going through.' The family still see me as the rebel really, and I get a certain amount of enjoyment out of that. I suppose it's a bit adolescent really, sticking two fingers in the air. I'm actually not sure at the moment whether I will have any more sexual relationships. It isn't necessarily about sex for me any more, it is about more than who I sleep with, and it is about having women friends who I identify closely with and feel very close to, about having a community. I suppose too it's about having been sexually active and having had the most satisfying sexual relationships with women, and also having had the most satisfying emotional relationships with women – and the most fraught ones as well. As I said earlier, there's no such thing as a free lunch. And it represents change for me – I mean periods of change, growth, development – so I suppose it's quite symbolic for me in lots of ways. I feel very good about identifying myself as a lesbian. So there you go.

FARIDA IS THIRTY-SEVEN, AND A MOTHER.

I felt frustrated when I came to this country, the way women come up to you. Where I come from, if you go to a club, if you walk in on your own you don't feel lonely, you're not in a corner. The same with gay men and women, they are more together in France than in England. I was really surprised when I see 'women only' – we're all gay, you know what I mean? We're all happy with it at the end of the day, because that's what gay means isn't it [laughs]?

Sexually, there's a difference between here and France. Maybe I just find the wrong women; every relationship I have in France, we talk, we are not shamed of talking about likes and dislikes. It's coming like that now in England, slowly. I think it's changing because of AIDS.

Like I look butch, I'm not a butch. I'm a woman. If I was going to the club, I was the butch one, because of the way I walk and the way I dressed up. I'm quite feminine, I wasn't taken as a man in France, but here, yes.

When I first come to this country [1981] I didn't go out for three years, and then when I did, there was this woman, and she smiled all night at me. I thought, she's really nice. I'm quite shy to go and ask somebody to dance, embarrassed, so I sort of smile, and when I went to the toilet she said to me, 'Come on babe, I'm going to screw you tonight.' Seriously . . . so I said, 'Oh, I have to go home, I've got children to go to.' And I ran out of the club. That shocked me, I can't look at that person no more. I have to get to know someone to talk like that, you know, to me it's like being used if someone talks to you like that the first time. It's like a man behaves, exactly, this is what I thought about the gay scene here.

My hairstyle, I've always had my hair short, and when I come to England it's a lesbian hairstyle. The same with SM, I love the clothes, because the colour I like is black – black and silver. So I've got Moroccan trousers, big army boots and my jacket. If I wear that, I've got all the SM women after me, and I don't understand, because I don't call myself SM. In France they call that New Romantic, New Wave, which is about dress, and the English mix that up.

I get attracted to a woman emotionally and for security. The security is very hard to get but the sex is what I like best with a woman. To me, if I go out with a woman, I expect, love, affection, friendship. Here they're like, 'Come on babe bang bang bang sleep.' I could live with a man, easy, but don't come up and rub me and things like that because I don't like it. I did that when I was married. I sleep at least twice with my husband, that's all.

In the gay clubs in England I always get aggravated. They say karaoke; they don't give women a chance, instead who do they choose? Four men. One man was singing about killing his mother-in-law. If you want to be a woman, do it properly. Don't try to be a woman dressed up like a nun and have a beard and a moustache. I've got one friend, he's a star in Brussels, Mrs Grogantine, that's his name, he's got breasts, he came to England to have a sex change. He's lovely, he done it properly. I've got a few friends like that, and I fancied a woman and she was a sex change.

I left home when I was seventeen and a half. It was strange because I heard the word lesbian, I knew it was women going out with women, but I didn't know what exactly you had to do. I ended up in a hostel run by nuns, and this nun said I had to change my name, because you could not stay in that place if you were mixed-race. So she said, 'What's the translation of your name, Farida?' And I said 'It's Françoise.' And she said 'OK. By the way, I've put you in this room with this girl called Yasmina, but we call her Mina, same mixed-race as you but her mum was French.' Mina told me she was a lesbian, and I got paranoid, and so I went to sleep in another girl's bed, and we end up doing something in that girl's bed.

My first relationship was when I was about twenty-one, and that was Christine. She brought me a cup of coffee afterwards and she said to me, 'You liar, you have slept with women before,' and I said, 'No I never have, your body is my body, this is our scene, my need is your need, maybe sometimes you need something different.' I knew I was a lesbian from when I was thirteen. It was really strange because I notice there was something wrong – at that time I thought it was wrong – I thought there was something wrong with me. I went to the doctor, I told my husband about it, and he said, 'Yes it's normal, a lot goes on.' The doctor said, 'Is that all?', and then said if it lasted more than ten years it's because I'd come to what I wanted. Some lesbians have been lesbian for ten years and they then change, but I think that's something to do with insecurity. It's very hard in women's relationships to be secure because there's more jealousy between women. We're the same, and we both want to be the best. I think it's something like that.

I didn't go out with anyone for a few years because I had a drug problem, and because the last woman I was with lied to me. I don't believe you live with someone for three years and they never tell you a lie and suddenly they do. To me it was like three years down the drain.

When Tracey met me she knew I was a junkie, and after three years she said that she needed a break, and that was fair enough. And my son went down the road and saw her with another woman. I told Carol I'd prefer her to come up to me and tell me that she fancied someone else, to be honest and tell me, and then you take it from there. I ended up in hospital: I had a nervous breakdown because I didn't believe what was going on.

I was working in BrassTacks as a carpenter once, and this woman come up to me and said, 'Farida, you're gay aren't you. How do you cope with your children?' She was asking how did I break it to my kids. So I said that with some kids you have to wait for them to ask you, other kids you have to tell them because they don't ask. For me it was when my son says, 'Mum, . . . ' He was about four, and then he grow up with it and it's OK because he never see any men after that.

'All the lesbians here want to know everything and sleep on their own' – it's an Italian expression. It's all, 'Oh Farida's got a girlfriend.' I counsel people with AIDS and HIV. I was an ex-junkie myself so I know this guy, and I stayed in his house for four days, and someone goes to Carol and said I was doing this and doing that. This woman came up and I could see what she was going to say, and she said, 'Oh I see you've got a boyfriend, and he's HIV isn't he?'

I think there's lot of jealousy in gay relationships. I notice that, and that makes me very aggravated, when you go to the club and you want to go and have a quiet drink with your girlfriend, and people cannot leave a couple alone. They cannot see a relationship but they have to stick needles in it. When I see couples, I go, 'Look aren't they sweet,' and it's true, you don't often see people in long life relationships.

I put Carol on guard, because I told her if you go to the club you've got women who'll chat and chat to you, and keep you talking and talking, when they know your girlfriend is waiting there, and that causes arguments. I explain to her the gay scene because I've been there longer than her. When we go home at Christmas I will take her to this club in Belgium and she'll see the difference. I used to have my own bar, a women's bar, and it was good because it was half women and gay men were welcome.

Me being mixed race, I'm not black, I'm not white, but I consider myself black because of my dad. If I go to 'black women only' things, I get the impression that I'm rejected. If I go to 'white women only', I am rejected as well. And when you say you're French you get 'ooh la la and voulez-vous coucher avec moi ce soir' and all that. I argue with people when I say I am not French. I've got French nationality and I'm not proud of it, because all my life, from when I started at school to when I left at seventeen, I suffered racism. The French never consider me as a French person. I was a *boulyoume* and that's like dirty black, nigger.

People said 'Would you go out with an English woman?' I said, I don't care what you are, I don't look at a woman like that. I look at the way she stands, I expect a woman to be open and natural, how she stands.

In England there is a lot of women who don't have that conversation about how there are two sorts of lesbian – there are clitoral lesbians and vaginal lesbians. And here I've never read anything about women who are *clitorienne* and women who are *vaginale*, because we call them *guime* and lesbian in France, two different words for it.

I was going out with this girl for six months and I never had an orgasm. So I said, 'Right Cathy, I'm not giving you an orgasm if you won't give me one, it's selfish.' I notice that if you go to bed with a woman here it's 'me first'. You can't do that: you've got a tongue, you've got hands, you've got feet, you've got knees, use them.

When I went to SM clubs, all the women thought about sharing, sharing your lover. I'm not doing that – what's mine is mine. It's the same as if I told my son to go and share his mother with someone else.

I met this woman who was calling herself SM. SM always intrigues me and scares me, because as a child I got beaten and things at home. They do say SM women often have that. I came home from the pub one night and there was this woman in my bed, and I said, 'Hey, it's not Christmas, is it?' She'd been bullied as a kid and she told me all about that, and we ended up in bed. It turned out I was more SM than she was. You know when you get into it and you hug the person really hard? Well I don't call that SM. But she did.

work and leisure

living the life and making a living

I walked down those stairs after all the palaver of getting in, because you had to knock on the door with a password practically. My mouth just dropped open.   Janet

So we like the same places. We go out; we go home to fuck. That's what it's about for me, going out to places – after all they call it going out with someone don't they, not staying in.   Lou

From sixteen to twenty I lived and died for the Gateways. It was a dive of a place. It had nothing to offer you, but it was there. The first time I went there, I lived on the memory of it for about two months.   Ria

It's Pride that does that to you. It gives you so much confidence you can do anything.   Lorraine

I do think that a lot of useful networking goes on down the pub or whatever, that's mainly a straight set. I think that's something that makes a difference. And it also means you're not going to be married to a useful man; you might be married to a useful woman...   Reina

The demolition of the assumption that lesbians, like gay men, exist only at night in smoky, seedy basement bars is long overdue, even though for a long time they may have seemed to. Leisure time for lesbians, for the most part, is spent in remarkably similar ways to the population as a whole: television, music, watching videos, reading, drinking, eating, dancing, playing board games and sports and so on. Staying in and going out. The difference may be largely in where these pleasures take place. Lesbian culture, and lesbians in culture, have remained marginal in a way that gay men's has not been; mixed and lesbian-only events and venues and their respective visibility, acceptability, and cash backing has long been an issue. Against the background of the burgeoning level of specifically lesbian culture, another important difference – and one that is being increasingly explored – is lesbians' relation to the cultural mainstream.[1] This chapter also looks at how lesbians earn the money to be able to afford to go out or buy videos, books and music to enjoy when they stay in.

Even subcultures have institutions, in the senses of customs, rituals and establishments, albeit on a different scale to mainstream ones, and this is one way of countering marginalization. And we have also devised systems for finding out about them, from information services like Switchboard and the shortlived Rainbow, to listings magazines. Lisa Power says of the early days at Gay Switchboard, 'We probably carried more information than about social and campaigning organizations – a myriad world of Chipping Norton GLF and Llandridnod Wells CHEs that no longer exists, replaced with a few regional commercial meccas and a London explosion of hotels, plumbers, shops and other services.'

A subculture can be nourishing and affirming; it can also be claustrophobic, limited and limiting. The scale, which may look small in relation to the mainstream, in no way diminishes their importance to lesbians who use them, and probably, due to their nature as minority concerns, increases it. Subcultures also have their own icons, who may be internal, like Martina, or reappraisals of mainstream iconic figures, like Dusty Springfield or Madonna, or, most recently, cross-over figures like kd lang.

The enforced low-profile nature of lesbian social events has had, and continues to have, effects on what is available and how it is received and enjoyed. Until feminism in the 1970s, bars were the only lesbian places to socialize publicly, and in many places this is still true. In the past, the need for secrecy played a part in heightening the status of lesbian pursuits and venues. Gateways was one such institution to the generation of lesbians who frequented it. Gateways is remembered, by women who went there when there were no or few alternatives, with a mixture of fondness and horror; and by women who arrived on the scene later, when entry through that hallowed door was supposedly only gained through impossible membership, with a certain amount of awe.

More recently, the Carved Red Lion, in Islington, London, has taken on a certain status (mainly due to its wild Artex ceiling, perhaps) with its generation of early 1980s lesbians. It can never have the same significance because the sanctions were far greater during Gateways times. In 1993 a Gateways reunion was held, apparently full to bursting. The Ace of Clubs, the Duke of Wellington, and Eve's Revenge/Venus Rising, long-running London venues, are all institutions, love 'em or hate 'em, but the fact that they have all existed during the same period means they can have no special meaning beyond the personal.

Kenric, which has existed for twenty-eight years, inspires incredible loyalty from some of its members. As a national organization, it is seen as a lifeline by women in some parts of the country where there is no other lesbian organization, or none in which they feel comfortable. Women I spoke to at a Kenric club disco valued it for its non-sectarian appeal to all women. 'I think it's lasted so long because it isn't political,' commented one member. Recently Kenric has started to try to widen its appeal, and shake off its old image of being largely for closeted rural women, mainly at the upper ends of the class spectrum (although this was certainly not true the night I visited). The example newsletter which is provided for journalists and researchers shows an enormous range of activities, and organizers stress that Kenric is 'for its members' in the sense that it is the members themselves who organize activities according to their own preferences, apart from regular events such as the monthly disco. Skittles in Somerset, afternoon tea at the Angel, Guildford Discussion Group, a night at the music-hall, are only a few examples. These are followed, in the newsletter, by a (very short) round-up of the gay press, and then the usual adverts for accommodation, therapy and contact ads, plus phone-a-friend and a correspondence circle for aspiring pen friends.

The range of activities and services available through Kenric membership is reminiscent of those offered in other, older publications, such as *Arena3* and *Gay Girl* (which it became). These included folk evenings, wine and dine, playreading, library evenings, tennis party, which sound as if they are from some forgotten twilight zone of old England and lesbian existence instead of being merely thirty years ago. The US version of what Sappho and Kenric offered, as advertised in *The Ladder*, was remarkably similar, save for the language differences: picnics, bowling (alleys not greens) Koffee Klatch, Gab 'n' Java, informal bull (!) session.

Sappho began in the 1970s when 'apart from the Gateways Club and Kenric, there were fewer meeting places, discos or conferences for lesbians'.[2] Its purpose was to encourage lesbians to set up activities and groups in their own areas. Sappho also had the reputation of catering for the more upper-class lesbian. Apart from the monthly magazine and discos at the Sols Arms, to which CHE men were invited 'because we didn't know enough lesbians to fill the Euston Tavern',[3] Sappho was also responsible for starting Action for Lesbian Parents, and organizing the first lesbian and gay teachers' conference in 1973. The magazine, written by readers, was intended as 'an authentic record both personal and political, of lesbianism in all its diversity'.[4] Alternative and feminist bookshops barely existed then, and Sappho was distributed through sex bookshops. It ceased publication when it 'was no longer the only once a month contact with other lesbians. We had served our purpose. It was time to go.'[5]

Artemis, 'for women who love women', took over when Sappho ceased in 1981, promising to speak to 'all lesbians, or more broadly, for all women who love women ... we want Artemis to be daring, controversial, danger-ous, stylish, witty, homely and friendly. Quite a mix but then Artemis is here to reflect a whole world. Your world.'[6] The cover graphics showed a svelte, short-skirted, viking-hatted, sylph-like amazon, which reflected the matriarchal, nostalgic, somewhat schoolgirly style and politics of the content.

Other lesbian publications which disappeared in the 1980s included Sequel, Square Peg and the London Women's Liberation Newsletter. Sequel adver-tised itself thus: 'A lesbian feminist publication for isolated lesbians ... reflects our support of ecology and animal welfare groups and we encour-age vegetarianism and veganism.' In response to a complaint that the magazine did not have enough which was directly concerned with lesbian-ism, Sequel wrote: 'Let's face it, as lesbians, we often have very little in common – except the obvious sexual/emotional and social aspects of our lives.'[7] This was fairly ground-breaking stuff at the time – lesbian sister-hood, social, sexual, emotional and political, was more than enough in common, in a climate when many lesbians were reinventing themselves, starting afresh with feminism.

Square Peg called itself 'the journal for contemporary perverts'. It was alternative, upfront, sexual, mixed, arty, offering fiction and plenty of art work. At the time, Square Peg was decidedly innovative, and it led the way for journals with stronger design input, higher production quality and higher prices.

The London Women's Liberation Newsletter also died a death during the 1980s, once no one came forward to provide the free labour to continue to produce it. The LWLN probably provided the best view of the London lesbian feminist scene, and often one which could make you feel glad it was a long-distance view, given that it came only by post. Apart from invaluable listings of events social and political, including courses, meetings, films, theatre, pets, messages, jumbles, benefits, music, petitions (and even those were often highly contentious), there were constant battles waged on its smudgy xeroxed pages. Diatribes against other people's politics, behaviour – and just other people – leapt from it, and the following week there would be counterblasts from those maligned. As soap opera it could not be beaten, but it could also be politically tortuous.

Magazines for lesbians appeared with an almost bewildering frequency in the early 1990s. *Shebang*, *Lip*, *Quim*, *Diva*, *Lesbian London*, *Phase* (not to mention *Attitude*, which, although ostensibly for gay men, will undoubtedly be read by many lesbians), all appeared from the late 1980s, four of them during a single twelve-month period. It's probably too early in their lives on the newsagents' shelves to forecast how things will pan out: how many of them will continue (*Shebang*, *Quim*, *Phase* and *Lesbian London* have not), given what some see as market saturation. Will we have time to be lesbians once we have finished reading the magazines? One wonders how the magazines' publicists are forecasting the future developments of their market. Certainly *Shebang*, *Lip* and *Phase* were largely targeted at a young lipsticky market, while *Diva* pitched itself slightly outside that. *Quim* was decidedly and refreshingly anti-lesbian chic, lasted the longest so far, and, whatever one's views on its content, it had far and away the most interesting layout and best design, but then it did not have to deal with all that boring text which the others have.

Lesbian London located itself in the political market, rather than the sex, lifestyle 'n' fashion segment which all the others inhabit, with varying emphases. it was free, as is *Shebang*, but was independent, not from the *Pink Paper* stable, and apparently editorless, which *Lesbian London* may have seen as a way of allowing a diversity of viewpoints, but which some of its readership saw as a clue to its failure. *Spare Rib* and *Outwrite*, both feminist rather than exclusively lesbian, failed financially, as did Sisterwrite Bookshop in Islington in 1993, and their demise spoke volumes about changing patterns, priorities and politics during the last decade. In common with many things feminist, there was a veritable queue to kick *Spare Rib* when it was already in the hole (see Chapter 4). Some of the *Spare Rib* bashers came in the form of the usual anti-feminist diatribes, but also from erstwhile collective members who had become – along with many of the magazine's subscribers and purchasers, presumably – disenchanted with the magazine, which after a long history of being produced mainly by white women, had been run and changed by a group of black women.

Outwrite, itself launched as an internationalist paper before *Spare Rib* had taken on this perspective, was helped by GLC grant funding, and fell victim to the twin losses of finances and optimism which GLC abolition brought about.

The climate of grant funding gave rise to the prospect of a very different kind of institution: The Lesbian and Gay Centre in central London (LLGC), the Camden Lesbian Centre/Black Lesbian Group, Black Lesbian and Gay Centre in Haringey, Manchester Gay Centre, and the forthcoming Greenwich Lesbian and Gay Centre. All but the first of these still exist in one form or another. The LLGC began funded by the GLC and went down as an (unsuccessful) profit-making venture. In its time it hosted a range of groups from a housing association to theatre groups and a counselling service. It saw the SM wars and attempts to deny entrance to bisexuals, transsexuals and transvestites. It also saw Lesbian Strength fall apart, literally outside its doors, in a welter of recrimination between pro- and anti-SM factions, and with the LLGC charging women an entrance fee, on the day of the Lesbian Strength celebration in 1988.

Lesbian Strength, that annual highlight in everydyke's summer calendar, used always to be held on the week before Gay Pride, which was itself a much smaller affair than it has now become. Some women would go on both, others stuck firmly with Strength. Lesbian autonomy was seen as paramount in a way which it no longer is – if it were, someone would organize Strength. Gay Pride was always much more visible, and more visibly fun, although every year much criticism (and thanks) is levelled at the Pride Committee, just as it was at Lesbian Strength. Every so often, articles and letters appear in the gay press about resurrecting Lesbian Strength. Megan Radclyffe raises the spectre: on the positive side, 'It heightened our visibility. We celebrated our existence without apologising . . . . While the media are courting us, it would be a crying shame to waste this ceasefire by the tabloids when the publicity could be turned to our advantage.' On the unlikely side, however: 'The march would probably have to culminate with kd lang, Lea De Laria and Martina performing death defying acts of cunnilingus before most dykes would even consider yomping across the city.'[8] And then there would be the dykes who would leave town for the weekend rather than risk coming across such an appalling vista, whether they objected to kd et al or cunnilingus.

Some people had trouble with the whole gay centre ethos, just as some women did not believe the way to liberation was paved with grant-aided women's centres in every borough. Community centres have to appeal to widely diverse constituencies of people. Lesbian and gay centres try to provide day and evening activities which will satisfy the needs of all men and women who call themselves lesbian or gay (or bisexual or transsexual in some centres), a huge and often thankless task. The London Lesbian and Gay Centre tried to straddle the concerns of the commercial and community scenes, and discovered ultimately that even to please some of the people some of the time, and get them to pay for it, was too daunting.

A parallel movement could be seen within the expectations of the LLGC's users, who, from being seen as outside commercial concerns, became identified as a growth market with a sizeable disposable income, at a time in the 1980s when markets were shrinking rapidly: a new niche to conquer. The increased visibility of lesbians and gays persuaded the mainstream that there were commercially viable opportunities to be taken up and also that lesbian and gay initiatives could survive and prosper. The men's scene, which had already taken on business status, grew massively as the pink pound was recognized as a growth currency, and the women's scene moved to a large extent from the community centre to the business sector. Lesbians stopped going to meetings, which for a lot of women had been a social life in itself, and instead started going out clubbing, just like everyone else was doing. The London Women's Centre – relaunched as a more commercially focused venture, The Wheel, in 1994 – has attempted to bridge this gap.

Early in 1993 the London Women's Centre hosted a kd lang convention – something of a turnaround in a venue more usually associated with political meetings and benefits. The LWC was also the venue for a conference in November 1993, 'A Lesbian Agenda for the 90s', itself a highly unusual event in these times. It spanned lesbian adoption, survivors of violence in lesbian relationships, the politics of desire, kd lang, and lesbian PE teachers, so work, leisure and politics were all represented. Some workshops had restricted entry: for lesbians, black women, working-class women. Confusion about this policy, in pre-conference information relating to the welcome accorded or not to bisexual women, accounted for the only printed criticism I saw. The conference was sold out, as was the kd convention.

The same tide which brought in funding for gay centres led to a few progressive councils setting up separate lesbian and gay equality units. Others included the issues on their equal opportunities agenda, during the mid-1980s, when local authorities had a wider brief than they currently do. The GLC, in particular, produced several publications specifically about lesbian and gay issues.[9] Although many publications prefaced their recommendations with an assertion of 'lesbian difference', that lesbians were not all the same, the recommendations tended to sound as if we were. Or, if not all the same, then all wanting the same things.

Extending the principles of equal opportunities into service provision, some councils also sought to provide entertainment services specifically for lesbians. Pink September, North London Pride, and so on, were welcome on some levels, but often caused resentment and hostility from the rest of the population and loud criticism from those they were meant to serve. Similar responses are often forthcoming in relation to TV programmes made for and by lesbians, like OUT, which often attracted the sort of in-house censure which only a minority group can muster.

Until the 1980s, when coverage of Section 28 and the Sue Lawley abseiling incident turned things around slightly, lesbians made only very occasional appearances on TV, and then pathologized as sad and bad girls. It was in this climate that *Out on Tuesday* (later renamed OUT) appeared, and this timing surely had effects on both production and audience reception. That it was the first TV series made by lesbians and gay men also inevitably influenced its attitudes and outputs. 'It was not an objective anthropology of lesbian and gay life,' as Penny Ashbrook, a producer from *Out on Tuesday* notes.[10] In 1994, while watching the fifth and final series of OUT, I learned that the first lesbian kiss on TV appeared in 1977. Great strides.

Its detractors aside, OUT has had a great impact on lesbian and gay culture, and concerns about ghettoization appear to have been unfounded: 'The fact that there was a lesbian and gay series made everyone else sit up and take notice and start to deal with lesbian and gay issues. It had the effect of increasing coverage everywhere rather than ghettoizing it.'[11] Coverage has indeed increased significantly in the last five years or so; and OUT has played its part in that, giving a new group of people television experience which has then been taken on to other channels and programmes. The popularity of the gay club scene and, yes, lesbian chic, have all led to phenomena such as youth programmes like *Passengers* having a high lesbian and gay content. Despite initial fears about the effects of queer TV on advertising revenue, ratings were high enough to show that it is popular rather than minority viewing.

At Christmas 1993, Channel 4 made an effort to live up to its remit of serving television fit for 'minority' audiences by transmitting a whole two and a half hours of programming for lesbians and gays. *Camp Christmas* was panned, provoking hopes that no straight people had watched it. (It also brought forth the most incredible stream of homophobic filth from the public, the press, MPs and clerics.) Meant as a 'gentle parody' of the Andy Williams or Val Doonican-style shows, complete with the jumpers, the almost universal response from lesbians and gays was that it managed to be more embarrassing than either of those, and that most of the participants acted as though they felt the same. As with the gay press, gay TV is generally looked on very critically, in an 'I-don't-know-what-I-want-but-it-isn't-this' manner. Now that OUT has finished, it will be interesting to see whether there will be continued efforts to include lesbian and gay TV across the programming board, or whether viewers will have to continue to obsess over characters in soaps and be content with an occasional 'special'.

The need which lesbians have to find a place in, and partake of, straight culture becomes clear when looking at films, videos and TV programmes enjoyed by lesbians. Apart from the current crop of sex videos, including *Well Sexy Women* (which interestingly or disturbingly quickly rose up the HMV video chart – pink pound aside, one has to suspect the straight porn brigade), *Lesbian Lycra Shorts* and *Lesbian Leather Shorts*, there are certain 'classic' lesbian stars and films. These include: *Go Fish*, *November Moon*, *Clare of the Moon*, Whoopi Goldberg, *Salmonberries* and kd lang videos, Madonna films, *The Color Purple*, *Desert Hearts*, *Coup de Foudre*, *Lianna*, *The Children's Hour*, *The Killing of Sister George*, Katherine Hepburn, Joan Crawford in *Johnny Guitar*, Garbo, especially in *Queen Christina*, *Olivia*, *Madchen in Uniform*, Bette Davis, Tina Turner.

A Question of Silence was the 1980s acme of lesbian feminist film before *Desert Hearts* appeared. It was screened so often at events that it lost its attraction, and its message, once taken on such a surface level, became politically old-fashioned and outdated. In 1993, Dangerous to Know was set up, a film club for lesbians in London, and *A Question of Silence* is again being viewed, by a new generation, in a different light. *Desert Hearts*, although widely enjoyed, was also criticized for its conventional narrative structure, as though dyke interest had been slotted into a regular Hollywood format. *She Must Be Seeing Things*, which appeared in 1987, and was probably the next major dyke feature, was refreshingly groundbreaking in both style and content, although picketed by anti-SM dykes and, famously, causing ructions at a London women and film summer school for a fantasy sequence perceived as anti-woman.

Occasional lesbian characters, strong women characters and a highly developed sense of camp are the distinguishing factors in many of these choices. Similar choices are made in relation to television viewing. Those programmes which are seen as required lesbian viewing – *Cagney and Lacey*,

Absolutely Fabulous, Rides, Blind Date, Golden Girls – qualify by the same sort of criteria. The films, plots and characters to which lesbian viewers are attracted range from the overt lesbian nature of some of the 1990s output, to the strong friendships between women which can be seen as lesbian-informed, but not entirely positive in terms of lesbian representation. There are still only a handful of films in which overtly lesbian characters do not meet a sad and bad end – suicide, murder, loneliness. *Go Fish* was particularly welcome, in that lesbianism was not presented as an issue (or a difficulty), it just was, with plain tales of everyday lesbian folk.

Gay radio programmes have advanced in similar strides to those made on TV, since 1957 when *Woman's Hour* first mentioned homosexuality on air, in relation to the Wolfenden Report. Programmes have been launched on several major stations, including GLR, Radio 1, Radio 4 and Radio 5. As radio coverage has grown, it has moved away from the club culture and music scene items, which have previously dominated many programmes, effectively limiting their appeal to younger people. As with TV broad-casting, the laudable desire to cover as many bases as possible, and thereby maximize appeal, often leads to the magazine format, which can mean that nothing is covered in enough detail. If there were more programmes which covered or included issues of interest, there would be no need for the use of this outmoded and often badly used format.

Loud and Proud on Radio 1 ran for six weeks during 1993. It attracted a certain amount of censure because the DJ, Paulette, is straight. One of the producers, Mark Ovenden, commented, 'We asked Paulette to do the show because she epitomises everything about the way we want to make lesbian and gay issues more acceptable to the straight community.'[12] Radio 5's *Out This Week* was broadcast as a thirteen-week series in 1994, was made by the same team who put together the one-off *A Sunday Outing* for Radio 4 in 1993. The editorial brief covers news and current events, with features including the legality of same-sex marriage, homophobia in the black community and the difficulties of being an out politician. *The Big O*, which deserves a prize for not using the words 'out' or 'pink' in its title, was a one-off show for lesbians in March 1994, from London's Brazen FM, a two-week station staffed by women and making programmes aimed at women. In the midst of all this short termism is GLR's *Gay and Lesbian London*, which marked its first anniversary in March 1994. Listening figures for the Saturday-night programme are about 500,000.

The 1980s took their toll in the publishing world as well as in every other business dimension. Sisterwrite bookshop was a casualty here, as dis-tribution of women's presses improved, and the women's and lesbian markets became coveted. Books for which women used to travel to the shop became more easily available elsewhere. The collective stated:

> Many will attempt to right-off [sic] the closure of Sisterwrite as a political indicator of the failure of any but the most commercial apects of feminism. However in 1991 Sisterwrite had a turnover more than three times as high as that in the mid 80s. [The] seemingly never-ending recession, high interest rates, council tax, mainstream competition and a Red Route outside our front door have all combined to force our cooperative-run bookshop out of business. (*Pink Paper*, 23 July 1993).

At one time Sisterwrite also featured Sisterbite, a café upstairs, and, later on, mixed books with gifts on the sales floor. The huge noticeboard upstairs on which women advertised accommodation, holidays, events, groups, services – a sort of subcultural *Exchange and Mart* – was another reason for women to drop by and hang out in the bookshop or café, apart from the other women there, of course. Silver Moon, another independent bookshop in central London, has probably taken over this important function of lesbian information and hanging-out space.

But in the lesbian and gay imprint sections of major publishers, the trend has been firmly in the other direction. Women's presses – Virago, Sheba, Onlywomen, The Women's Press – who were the main publishers of lesbian books in the UK, all survived the 1980s, more or less intact, (although Sheba sadly folded in 1994)some owned by different companies to those they had been under at the beginning of the decade. They were joined in the independent section by Scarlet, whose list showed a strong commitment to lesbian writing, including the Lesbians Talk Issues series, which has so far produced booklets on Queer, Safer Sex, Black Lesbians in the UK and Lesbian Domestic Violence. In the 1980s Onlywomen Press, the radical feminist publishers, initiated a series of meetings titled 'Lesbian Ethics', covering subjects such as sex and sexual practice, violence between women, monogamy and non-exclusive relationships. Nearly a decade further on, an interviewee talked about the Lesbian Response group, which is seeking to explore very similar issues. Onlywomen launched *Gossip* in 1986, a quarterly bound journal to provide 'a forum for the statements, analyses, theories needed to create a lesbian civilization', but after a few issues *Gossip* faded.

A tide of experiential, coming out stories emanated from women's presses in the 1970s and early 1980s, seeking to fulfil the demand for literary depictions of lesbian lives and characters who were heroes, not psychos. Lesbianism was always centre-stage, but not as the problem which was firmly located within the hetero/homophobe society in which our hero moved. Seeking recognition through literature describing the experience of an oppressed or minority group is a common demand in the early stage of any political awakening: the truth about us. I can remember the intense excitement which accompanied every book that appeared from lesbian or lesbian-friendly presses: each one had to be bought. Naiad Press, purveyor of lesbian fiction since 1973, was literally a lifeline for some women before other outlets and products mushroomed later in that decade. There came a point when critical faculties reaffirmed themselves over this identification-hungry impulse, and the numbers of books published started to be greater than those that could possibly be read.

Vampire books retain a special place in the lesbian heart, having gone through a certain reclamation themselves (see Chapter 2), such as the Anne Rice books and Jewelle Gomez's *The Gilda Stories*, which dykes devour voraciously, as they once queued to watch *The Hunger* featuring lesbian chic vampires, Catherine Deneuve and Susan Sarandon. It is difficult to say whether, for instance in the case of Anne Rice, publishers have recognized this market, and to what extent they are reviving and revising 'old classics', thematically speaking. Virago, purveyor of old classics themselves, launched a Lesbian Landmarks series in 1994, featuring work by Maureen Duffy and Nancy Spain among others.

Lesbian detective fiction is another genre which has taken off massively since the 1980s, although the gritty realism and strong hardbitten women characters of mainstream detective fiction always made them popular among dykes, much in the same way as *film noir* has always attracted lesbian interest. Publishers – women's and mainstream, hungry for new markets – have rushed to supply work featuring lesbians who, often, eat gourmet, lack sex (at least until the end), have tragic histories and drink too much, as well as uncovering dastardly deeds and exposing the guilty.

'Lesbian detective Hollis Carpenter, blunt-talking, gin-slinging, with Marlene Dietrich's cool looks, gives twice as good as she gets. . . . Can she still find the time to show Dalacroix's lovely wife Lily just what's been missing in her life?'[13] So reads the blurb for one. Sally Munt locates the attraction of the lesbian crimebuster as an outlaw and a crusader, good (lesbian) deeds on the edge of society.[14] She charts a history of trends in women's/dyke fiction: from self-discovery and narratives of self-development, through science fiction and utopian worlds to the crime novel. And beyond ... Jane DeLynn's much-heralded and derided cult classic, *Don Juan in the Village*, can be seen as an example of what followed crime fiction – with its explicitly sexual PoMo-style confused outlaw in a grown-up, hard lesbian scene in a post-AIDS world. In 1994 lesbian fiction truly hit the mainstream with Joanna Briscoe's Betty Trask Prize-winning *Mothers and Other Lovers*.

Drinking has long been a hallmark of lesbian culture, from the days when the only social venues were small, secret clubs – and clubs, for upper-class dykes, at least, have existed since the 1920s – and when lesbians were supposedly so self-hating and so damaged by homophobia that they took refuge in alcohol. There may now be more clubs, more visibility and more choice, but lesbians and alcoholism is no less of an issue. A section of the population which socializes as a group largely in clubs and bars is not unlikely to have such a problem. The growth in the number of pubs and bars where tea, coffee, non-alcoholic wines and beers, and soft drinks are an ordinary part of the fare is to be welcomed.

Lesbian detractors are not slow to point out that they do not find themselves as welcome in some gay cafés as they had been led to expect. This gay café explosion is recent; lesbians, with less choice of other venues, have been into this for longer, even if efforts at lesbian cafés and restaurants have usually been short-lived. In London alone there was Tabbies Café, also a sauna, in south London, and Kitty's Wine Bar in Stoke Newington. Increasingly in the last ten years there have been places where one would often find other lesbians eating, but that is probably more to do with location, housing and word of mouth than any indication that a restaurant is lesbo-friendly. Further, there is the complaint that straight women are more welcome than lesbians in some gay establishments, and the counter-complaint that lesbians moan about everything but never get it together themselves. The Lavender Pound has long been subsumed by the Pink one, and it never had the same clout in the first place. The development of gay café culture in London's West End, and Soho in particular, seems to be using gay in the now passé sense – we hoped – of gay male, rather than as the shortened form of lesbian and gay. The Freedom Café is outstanding for its exhibition of its priorities as white and male, young and beautiful, on its walls.

Whether lesbians want lesbian-only social spaces is another discussion: but many lesbians find it galling that there are so many men's places, even if the hallowed doors of Heaven did finally open to the lesbian horde. Since the late 1980s there has been a trend, with the attractions of Queer culture, towards clubs mixed along the lines of sexuality as well as gender.

On one level this appears very modern, but gay culture has, at different times, had a certain attraction to straights – in the 1960s, for instance.

Lesbians, meanwhile, had the backroom of The Duke of Wellington (north-east London), which used to be decorated to look like a womb, and is now sporting a garden shed/Guide hut look, and The Duke of Clarence (north London) which is like somebody's sitting-room. Why can't lesbians have beautiful but uncomfortable chairs and ragrolled walls too? Other bars are only available once a week, like the Wow Bar and The Box in Covent Garden, Shug's in Brixton and Tattoo at First Out. But it is not only homophobia which limits dyke nights – this has been a feature of the club scene for some time, as club has come to mean a movable feast rather than bricks and mortar. Now that there is more than a handful of options, there is some niche marketing, catering to different musical tastes, ages, dance styles and sexual practices. The choices in London have included the upmarket uptown Wow Bar; Asia, which played a wider selection of musics worldwide; bhangra sound Shakti; the sceney house and techno Substation; Sadie Maisie for SM; Rumpus, which caters for an older market who prefer music played with real instruments; a singles night at A Circle of One; A Truly Western Experience for those into line dancing and country music; The Bell for goths and indie kids; and the perennially popular tea dancing. On a different commercial level, there has always been something of a blues party scene organized around black lesbian circles.

Along with the rise of body beautiful culture among lesbians has been the cult of women joining gyms, and not just to cruise, but to train. Football, softball, squash and swimming are the other main favourites. There are lesbian football teams, softball teams, squash ladders, and swimming clubs to join, just as there are gyms which have, shiftingly at least, the reputation for being lesbian habitats.[15] The Gay Games, while not such an attraction in the UK as it is in the USA, gets a lot of publicity around fundraising events, although some lesbians have stated their intention to withhold donations since they discovered that aerobics was one of the non-competitive events being held. Non-competitiveness is something for which lesbians have never displayed a particular talent.

Not a few women reported that they went to the gym until they found a girlfriend, and then their attendance slackened off; others that they kept it in mind in case they needed to firm up their loosening muscles to attract new interest. As a group of people historically critical of image, it is unsurprising that some lesbians despise the whole gym mentality as feeding into the body beautiful culture, or body fascism. Dyke's Delight, the sauna in Covent Garden which so impressed the *Evening Standard*, quickly closed due to falling numbers. But other saunas/steam baths have also always attracted a high proportion of dykes, and seem to provide a venue where straight women and dykes can mix comfortably, attracting women across class and race divides in a way which rarely happens in leisure venues. For example, York Hall in Bethnal Green, a traditionally working-class area, has a large West Indian clientele, as well as the local dyke contingent from Hackney; and Porchester Row in Westbourne Grove, highly refurbished (perhaps to attract The Sanctuary crowd with its lower prices) has a catchment area which includes upmarket Holland Park and Kensington as well as the more seedy Paddington and Edgware Road.

Unsurprisingly, given the media's love affair with lesbian chic, there has been a flurry of interest and column inches given over to the 'phenomenon' of lesbians in modelling. They look butch in a very female and designer kind of way. The fuss is partly caused by surprise that lesbians can be attractive and interested in clothes. It is also because modelling, or any kind of supposedly glamorous and 'feminine' work, is not where the average dyke is expected to draw her pay. Mechanics and PE teachers, yes; glamour puss, no. Stereotypes abound at every level, from the dyke on the dole, to the school marm, to the manual trader, to the sex worker, to the concerned dyke in housing or social work, to the (closeted) executive in business, government and the forces. Huffty, who began 1993 on the dole and ended it with a job as a presenter on *The Word*, demonstrates both the extent of the stereotypes and their mobility. But it was not always so – many women had no choice but to live two lives: 'What would the other social workers have made of my forays to the Gateways Club? What would the women there have made of the Freudian world I lived in by day?'[16] And for other lesbians, job choices and career development were severely curtailed.

Many occupations which put a girl in uniform acted as a magnet for dykes: all branches of the forces, including the Land Girls, nursing, ambulance driving, and so on. The appeal for lesbians is obvious: a job – and a non-traditionally female one at that – a chance to leave home when few women had the necessary resources, and a lot of women. At the time of the 1939–45 War, opportunities for these kinds of freedoms and an all-women environment were scarce. They did not last long, as with the end of the war came a push to re-limit women's sphere back to the domestic. Young dykes in the 1990s, with employment prospects ever receding, still join up and face the threats which loom over their service careers, of exposure and discharge. For lesbians who object to the forces on a political basis, it is easy to be critical, especially when they have better job propects and ones which allow them greater latitude in their lifestyles.

The prison service and police force have similarly had a high percentage of lesbians within their ranks. Pat Arrowsmith talks about how prison, for a dyke in the 1950s and 1960s, could be strangely liberating, given the greater ease of opportunities for lesbian encounters than on the outside, although she is talking about it from the perspective of a short-term inmate, rather than an officer.[17] Recent press coverage about the rampant sexism of the police force at all levels makes the prison service look a more attractive career. The issue of homosexuality in the forces is only beginning to be taken up in this country, in contrast to the USA where there was a major (broken) election promise from Clinton to tackle discrimination. Many lesbians still find it a difficult issue to support, feeling no allegiance with anyone in the forces, whatever their sexuality.

The efforts in many local authorities in the 1980s to take on equal opportunities policies in terms of employment practice, as well as service provision, meant that jobs which had previously not been open to women now became good options. Equal opportunities recruitment policies in local government and the voluntary sector also encouraged lesbians into those areas, where the conditions were quite good and there were, on paper at least, no barriers. Manual trades became the career for the right-on butch dyke in the 1970s and 1980s, partly out of a desire for independence, and also as an equal opportunities initiative, since construction had always been such a male preserve, and a relatively well-paid one at that. Internally though, there were other pressures: 'I felt so much stricture and censorship from lesbians. I was supposed to be a carpenter to prove I was a real dyke. My differences were sloughed over.'[18]

There have always been women who, against huge opposition, trained in what were seen as male trades and professions: carpentry, plumbing, medicine, law, engineering, architecture. The sexual discrimination which all women faced in such areas has another dimension for lesbians, who could not afford to put themselves in the firing line. Being at risk of child custody proceedings; being married; not wanting to come out or not feeling able to come out in such a hostile environment – these can all be factors which influence career moves. Discrimination can take the form of perpetuating an employment culture in which lesbians are not welcome and cannot feel comfortable, and so will avoid, in addition to deliberate non-employment.

As more projects were set up in the 1980s specifically to deal with lesbian and gay issues (housing, employment, policing, therapy, health, parenting and custody, or general centres) there was a flurry of employment opportunities specifically for lesbians, the like of which had never been seen before. Lesbians were employed in greater numbers in more senior positions in councils and bodies like the GLC, the London Strategic Policy Unit which followed it, and the Association of London Authorities. There was, understandably, a certain amount of cynicism about this, around issues of co-option and tokenism (which proved in many cases to be justified). Many women were hostile to the women who were so employed, and the term 'professional lesbian' was often said with a sneer. These women often had to bear enormous pressure to perform well and manage highly charged situations, and were caught between the opposing priorities of their employers and the community (at a time when the community, such as it ever was, was disintegrating).

Other lesbians at work were at risk of harassment and, in some cases, sacking, if they came out or were forced out. Teachers, social workers or youth workers have been particularly at risk, with internal disputes often focusing on lesbianism. Two lesbian childcare workers were sacked from a Hackney nursery during the 1980s over disagreements about childcare practice and equal opportunities. And, if the climate changed briefly in the 1980s, the signs now point backwards, as legislation around employment rights is systematically dismantled. In 1993 two lesbians, Maria O'Rourke and Simone Wallace, were sacked from their jobs at a computer packaging factory in Scotland. This case could have important legal implications, as an industrial tribunal ruled that they could claim unfair dismissal under the Sex Discrimination Act, the first time this has been applied to lesbians.

Although lesbians remain vulnerable to intimidation and harassment in areas such as youth work and teaching, the situation has improved to the point where there is at least policy against this kind of anti-lesbianism. But policy is not always followed. Jane Brown, a headmistress in Hackney, became a national hate figure overnight, apparently through not taking up an offer of tickets for her school to see a ballet production of *Romeo and Juliet* because, among other reasons, it was heterosexual. Depite support from the school governors, the local authority, supposedly under pressure from central government (an interesting departure from their much-vaunted local control), wanted her sacked. It was then suggested that there had been impropriety in Jane Brown's original appointment, as her lover was on the governing board, although this pre-dated their relationship. Their address was leaked and so the two have been forced to move.

Some twenty years earlier, Maureen Colquhoun, then a Labour MP, suffered a similar press bashing and was also done over locally and nationally by the Labour Party. Susan Hemmings, commenting on the case, makes a point which encapsulates the response of many lesbians to this kind of harassment: 'And it harmed all other lesbians who were not in the direct line of fire, but knew how to read the smoke.'[19]

In response to the personal growth trend, thirtysomething lesbians are training as therapists, counsellors and other complementary medicine practitioners. This can be seen as a natural progression from areas of work like teaching and social work, which involve some use of counselling skills. Burn-out has become a familiar and recognized phenomenon, and moving on to less stressful pastures, in these health conscious times, is looked upon charitably. Lesbians are no less likely than the rest of the population to change careers, and be affected by the changing work patterns and recession which have lessened the expectation that a career is for life. Self-employment, with its measure of autonomy, can be an attractive prospect. The growth in lesbian and gay businesses and institutions is another factor: providing services for 'the community' in an area which is considered to be useful and lucrative.

As a group of mainly single women, less likely than heterosexuals to have children, lesbians in some ways have greater independence than straight women. This can mean more career options through greater access to training, even while suffering from discrimination, harassment or just discomfort in a straight workplace. While women still only earn an average of about 70 per cent of the male wage (and this twenty years after supposedly winning the right to equal pay), studies show that lesbians earn more on average than straight women, and have greater disposable incomes (although this could change if the tide of self-insemination continues to grow at its present rate).

This double-edged independence is also in operation in the social lives which employment allows us to lead. Unencumbered, usually, by the demands of husband and family, lesbians have more free time but suffer from limitations on where to spend it. The threats of exposure, ostracism and violence weighed very heavily on lesbian lives until recently, and for many women still do. This has always influenced the 'public' sphere of our social scene as well as the private. (How many lesbians do you know who will kiss their girlfriends goodbye in the mornings on their way to work outside the house, like any other couple?) In practice, the public sphere meant the bar scene – variously experienced as revelatory, claustrophobic, wonderful, terrifying – until first GLF and then the women's movement opened up their own social worlds, such as they were. In the final decade of the twentieth century, lesbians' social choices in urban areas have grown. Elsewhere change is less obvious, but often happening. It also looks as though lesbians may be moving towards the production of a less marginal culture than has ever been possible before, as lesbians themselves become less marginal in some ways. Whether these forays into the mainstream are simply an indication of exhaustion of all other possible subjects, or an indication of anything more substantial, it is impossible, as yet, to say.

NOTES

1. See Belinda Budge and Diane Hamer (eds), *The Good, the Bad and the Gorgeous: Popular Culture's Romance with Lesbianism*, Pandora, 1994.
2. Jackie Forster, 'Sappho: History now – a pioneer in its day', in GLC *Women's Committee Bulletin, Special Lesbian Issue*, no. 17, June 1984.
3. *Ibid.*
4. *Ibid.*
5. *Ibid.*
6. *Artemis* (n.d.).
7. *Sequel*, no. 18, March/April 1981.
8. Megan Radclyffe, *Diva*, no. 1, April 1994.
9. GLC/GLC Gay Working Party, *Changing the World – A London Charter for Gay and Lesbian Rights*, (n.d.); GLC Women's Committee, *Tackling Heterosexism: A Handbook of Lesbian Rights*, (n.d.); GLC *Women's Committee Bulletin, Special Lesbian Issue*, issue 17, June 1984.
10. Diane Hamer with Penny Ashbrook, 'OUT: Reflections on British television's first lesbian and gay magazine series', *The Good, the Bad and the Gorgeous*, p. 166.
11. *Ibid.*, p. 170.
12. *Pink Paper*, 13 August 1993.
13. Deborah Powell, *Bayou City Secrets*, The Women's Press, 1992.
14. Sally Munt, 'The inverstigators: Lesbian crime fiction', in Susannah Radstone (ed.), *Sweet Dreams: Sexuality, Gender and Popular Fiction*, Lawrence & Wishart, 1988, p. 93.

15. Jubilee Hall, in central London, has many lesbian employees as well as users. The Women's Gym in Islington, north London, has a similar reputation.
16. Elizabeth Wilson, *Hallucinations: Life in the Post Modern City*, Radius, 1989, p. 4.
17. Pat Arrowsmith, Hall Carpenter Archive taped interviews, National Sound Archive.
18. Cherie Moraga, and Gloria Anzaldua (eds), *This Bridge Called My Back*, Kitchen Table Press, 1984, p. 69.
19. Susan Hemmings, 'Horrific practices: how lesbians were presented in the newspapers of 1978', in Gay Left Collective (ed.), *Homosexuality, Power and Politics*, Allison & Busby, 1980, p. 157.

'ELLYOT DRAGON IS MY PSEUDONYM. MY BIRTH NAME IS NOT VERY PRONOUNCEABLE TO ENGLISH PEOPLE. I'M TWENTY-SEVEN.'

In interviews they usually write that Sister George are twenty, working-class and on the dole. I'm neither really, but I don't bother correcting them. I'm a masseuse, I do holistic massage. I work with people living with HIV and AIDS. I had to find something I could do apart from music. I make about the same amount of money as I would on the dole, but I keep my body moving and I do something for people I care about.

I first heard the term Queercore when a dyke band from San Francisco called Tribe8 came over, but not as a movement or anything, just that was what they called what they did. Finally, a band with energy. The audience really didn't like them, they were all screaming, 'Punk died in '79,' and they had no idea of this whole hardcore thing. In Israel I was in a punk band, the only one in the country, it was more of a hardcore band. It was a bit of an ambiguous band – you could never understand if they wanted to rape all women or save them, or whether they wanted to kill all the Arabs or kill all the Jews. It wasn't like they were stupid, they were totally weird, ambiguous beyond belief. After that I started my solo stuff, which was with my ex-girlfriend, and we just did guitar and bass and we could hardly play. We had all these songs about the Israeli macho and quotes from Valerie Solanas from SCUM. That was 1986/87, we were a Riot Grrl band most definitely. We were twenty-one.

So when the whole Riot Grrl thing started, I thought, yeah, this is back to what I know, what I feel I want to do. Sister George got together because of Riot Grrl, because the door was opening, something was happening and all of us saw Tribe8 a few months before. The music that kicked us into beginning was Tribe8, Hole, Bikini Kill. We went to see Bikini Kill at this Riot Grrl gig, with Huggy Bear.

We had a few ideas for the name, but Sister George stuck, because we wanted something that sounded Queer. We all liked the movie a lot, although it's stereotypical and obviously written by a man and everything. Beryl Reid is such a dyke heroine really, drunk and abusive to nuns, the acting is amazing. So this is how Sister George happened.

I don't think we have one shared idea about what Queercore is, but there's a definition that I really like: 'Queercore is an attitude problem.' It's not necessarily just a matter of sexuality. It's people who're fucked off with the gay scene and people who're fucked off with the indie scene, they want something new and kicking, and maybe something that Riot Grrl had. It's queers making hardcore music.

We have nothing to do with the Queer as in Old Compton Street. I'm not going to fight over the term with them. I would like us to aim for a big exposure and I don't want to get caught up in little definitions. People will have no idea what you're arguing about anyway. It's like who's true Jew and all that, it's like, pulleeze give us a break. There's a difference for me between saying that Queercore is not a question of sexuality, and not being too naïve. I know there will be straight bands who will play with the whole queer imagery, and rip us off.

It used to really bother me, all that stuff. Sinead O'Connor used to totally get on my nerves, because one album she was all shaved head, Doctor Martens, leather jacket, and the next one she was wearing this raving outfit. All the dykes were buying her records – maybe she's a dyke because she dresses like one. It's just like Madonna with that shit. I think dykes are stupid, they buy anything because it's dyke. I used to be like that: you're young, you're looking for icons.

We played Heaven, that's the only gay gig we've ever done. Tribe8 were coming over on tour, and they arranged the Heaven gig. They like very much doing gay gigs, queer gigs, lesbian gigs, anything. Actually it was one of the better gigs we've done, and we brought a lot of straight people with us, a lot of Queercore fans, and people who never come to Heaven otherwise. They were all at the front going crazy, it was brilliant to walk on a stage and everyone going wild. It was a move from little pubs to a gig. But all the people standing around were going, 'What the fuck is this noise, get them off,' and the DJ was one of those people, and so when Tribe8 tried to play she sabotaged them and tried to play music over them. So we weren't at all happy about that, and we don't want to do any more gay and lesbian gigs.

You know how it goes, when you're a rebel nobody likes you, when you're a famous rebel everybody wants you. I can just feel it coming, and they'll take us to their bosoms, and we'll go, 'fuck you'. We're just getting more and more radical in our hatred about what's happening in the gay community. A year ago, we were all saying that we were bored with the scene, let's do something new. Now we say we hate it. A lot of things have happened recently that's brought it all into a very clear focus. Capitalism, Pink Pound stuff, has just grown in the last year to such a massive extent. It's nothing to do with my lifestyle really, I don't want to know about it. Or the whole take-over of Queer Street, Old Compton Street. People that were involved in Chain Reaction are in Freedom Cars now – that shows you everything for me. All some people want is to get in the mainstream, and if they're not in it, they're bitter, and once they get a chance to join, they're off. The moment there starts being a flag, the rainbow flag, all the alarms in my head go off. You know, I'm Jewish, what more can I say? Look what happened when the Jews got a flag, and they got the country and then they found another people to kill. Next they'll find some country which is supposed to be the gay country. They'll take over some island .... People have often asked me what I'd do if there was a gay country, and right now I think it's the most horrific idea that anybody could ever come up with. The scene here is getting very American and the difference between poor and rich is just immense.

There was an AIDS march that UK Coalition for People Living with Aids organized. OutRage! showed up, about thirty of them with their crew cuts, matching t-shirts, whistles, pink flags and drums. And if that's not the Hitler Jugend, I don't know who I am. I was terrified. I could not march next to them. And if they feel good enough about comparing a Jewish Rabbi to Himmler, I feel great about comparing them to the Hitler Jugend. They look like them: they're all white, strong-jawed, crew cuts, massive flags, drums.

OutRage! annoy me a lot more than Stonewall because they're obviously white and male and middle-class, and they scare me and enrage me. Stonewall can fight the Age of Consent thing, and let them. But they're not what I'm involved in, it's not what I'm busy with. If they decide to ally with Edwina, Saint Edwina... they got what they deserved. First thing she said when they lost the vote was, 'I blame the demonstration outside.' I was involved in ACT UP but I didn't want to become an AIDS activist. I think they take over and tell PWAs what to do. And it happened there again: the gay community thing, all the power fights.

When I was a part of the gay scene, I was in the Chain Reaction gang so it was never inside the gay community anyway, because we were [whisper] sexually radical. We were not allowed in other clubs and we were attacked in Chain Reaction by feminists. It's always easier when it's 'us and them' of course, so it was a really strong group, and we had a brilliant club and we met every week, and everybody was sniffing and smoking and fucking in the toilets. It was great fun for a while. *Quim* started from there. The moment the dyke scene turned round and said, 'Oh, actually we want some of that too', we kind of left it. All the new squeaky leather dykes, it was fashion. The SM scene got taken over by the mainstream dyke scene and a lot of the girls were taken over with it. I stopped going to clubs very early on. Chain Reaction was the only club I'd go to, just about, and then I stopped going about four or five years ago. I hated the music, for me that was the first thing.

It's rubbish, it's so racist to say that Jewish girls and black girls shouldn't be involved in SM. Jewish girls and black girls don't want to be outlaws? Don't want to do dangerous things? Don't want to do exciting sex? Don't want to deal with their biggest fears through sex? Some do, some don't. There was a big debate once at Wesley House: hundreds of women, microphones, video cameras and a panel. Everybody was getting very dramatic and emotional and I got up, shaved head and this Chain Reaction t-shirt, little skirt and fishnet stockings, I think. I went up to the microphone and said, 'I come from a family of Holocaust survivors and if I want to play around with swastikas, I will. I won't see any of you tell me that I'm not allowed to: Who am I hurting? I want to deal with my own shit my own way.' I felt it was important for me to do it then. I was proud of myself, it was very hard for me to get up and do that. I really liked it, because a lot of Jewish women did say stuff like, 'How dare you SM dykes play with that when none of you are Jewish and you don't know what Jews feel like?' So it was just to say fuck off.

It was part of the 1980s right-on thing; everybody wanted to protect the minorities and the victims and they didn't know about it themselves. If a Jewish woman came up to me and said, 'The fact that I know you might play at home with swastikas in an SM scene upsets me,' by no means would I change my life for her, but I would definitely sit down with her and listen.

You couldn't get into a club in a leather jacket at the time. I was called 'fascist' loads, for wearing a leather jacket. Excuse me, I'm Jewish, do you mind? It doesn't mean I can't be racist but to call me Nazi is a bit much. They didn't make soap out of my family for you to call me fascist because I wear a leather jacket, sorry. Of course it doesn't make me immune to being racist. I do think that growing up in Israel does make you cheeky, too sure of yourself. Because we were raised on this, 'you are not going to be like diaspora Jews, you are not going to be like lamb to the slaughter, you are going to be strong'. It's very hard to kick out of your system.

I wouldn't want to be sixteen again, that's for sure. I had great friends who said, 'Oh well, you're gay then,' and that changed everything, otherwise I would probably be completely guilt-ridden. The whole fight was about just being a lesbian and even saying it. Coming out, telling your parents, and being out in the army, which was a hassle. Of course there are lots of dykes in the army because they take all the girls in, but out, no. I was in a base where I went home everyday. I lived with my girlfriend. I met my first girlfriend in basic training. There was a few more gay boys that we knew about, and we hung round together and got each other through it. It wasn't easy to be out at all; she was sent to an army psychiatrist.

Then I moved out of Israel and found all these girls who called themselves feminists, but weren't so bothered with feminist theory, but were getting into the SM thing. So already I was kicking feminism in the butt. I realized music was the most important thing in my life, and that stands between me and the gay and lesbian scene. It became more and more Pink Pound, so now I'm even out of that.

I call myself a dyke. One day that word will become too soft. Queer as well I use, lesbian sounds totally wishy-washy. In Israel it's still a dynamite word. And they don't know what dyke means anyway, so I wouldn't use it over there. *Lesbith* is lesbian in Hebrew, gay men call themselves homo, homosexual, and they say gay, the English word. It's like gay over there is what queer means over here. It also has a bit of a yuppy smell to it because it's English.

I don't have a day job where I have to tone down being a dyke; I used to flaunt it, but now it's not the first thing I say. I'm happy with who I am, I'm mad about things in the world, not just about being queer, so . . .

Postscript: Sister George has now split up.

REINA LEWIS IS THIRTY-ONE, AND TEACHES LITERATURE AND CULTURAL STUDIES.

The first thing I should say is that I do identify as lesbian generally, not as queer. My work is that I teach literature and cultural studies, and then I have various different research projects, and there's my day-to-day work at the university. I have done some performance work as a compère, I do this thing called 'Out of the closet and into the wardrobe'. I don't know if you went to the Jewish Lesbian and Gay Conference in London last year? I compèred the Saturday night entertainment. I do different outfits, what to wear to meet your girlfriend's mother, and the country dyke and all those things. Part of it is just outrageous clothes, because I'm supposed to be a comic, and part of it is this quite serious but send-up discussion about what people wear. Then there's this whole thing about being a lesbian fashion adviser, you know, you can call me up and I'll solve your problems.

My main research area has been looking at how nineteenth-century women writers and artists interact with imperial culture. I've done some work around lesbian culture because that's something I get asked to do. It's assumed that if you write something about lesbian this that and the other, that you are lesbian, and it also means if someone knows you are lesbian you're likely to be asked if you want to do such and such. I'm also doing a book with Peter Horne on lesbian and gay visual culture.

I'm out at work in a haphazard way. As a rule I'm not out to my students, but it wouldn't be that hard for them to look at me and what I do and work it out. Lesbian and gay students cotton on to it, so to them I'll say 'we', 'my girlfriend', whatever, whereas to other students – who may be gay or queer, I don't know – I'm not. I like it to come out in conversation with colleagues rather than, 'Hello, I'm Reina and I'm a lesbian.'

If you're working with relatively OK, liberalish, straight people, they have no qualms about saying, 'I've never met a lesbian before,' and they want to ask you things. If I think they're basically OK then I will answer. Usually they want to know things like what kind of relationship you have, do your family know, how do they respond, were you always a lesbian, when did you know? As it happens, in my case, I did have straight relationships. I had boyfriends from when I was sixteen to about twenty-five. I make a point of owning up to that, I wasn't a born-in-the-blood lesbian. I don't agree with that idea, and I felt oppressed by not being a 'real lesbian' for long enough to not be interested in perpetuating that for anyone else.

Again, I do think that if I was cruising the clubs and getting off with loads of women, I might not want to be so forthcoming. But before I was involved with

Sue and I was single and having affairs, I talked about it. Sometimes I find myself saying, 'Sue and I', in a way that overemphasizes it. I think one of the things I do is talk about my relationship as a way of asserting my lesbianism. But I also wonder if it's a way of normalizing it. It also sounds grown-up and settled and also that's in the context of me becoming a professional lady, having a proper job, turning up for work on time and not being hungover, and it's all just generally respectable.

I can't believe that I'm a senior lecturer. I don't come from an educated Jewish family. I've had the education my parents didn't have, and they're incredibly proud of me. In a way I'm still quite pleased to have arrived, and I still feel quite insecure about some areas of that.

There is a lot of anti-intellectualism and I suppose I would have to think of myself now as an intellectual, it's one of the things I'm paid to do. That's a very difficult thing for me to accept, not just because of popular anti-intellectualism, but because it's seen as a high thing to achieve because it's better, more special, than being a welder or something. I feel guilty that I can do that, and that's a very complicated thing.

I got this boyfriend when I was seventeen, a bit older than me. We went out for years and years and I loved him, and he was prepared to be different from the nice Jewish boy he'd been brought up to be, and I certainly wasn't the nice Jewish girl his mother wanted him to go out with, and so I got to be the gutsy independent feminist girl.

I was in Leeds in the era of the Leeds Rev/Rad les fem – well the aftermath was still rumbling – and I had many lesbian friends crying on my shoulder about straight women who had done them wrong. There was no way I was ever going to be able to do anything about fancying women until I got shot of the boyfriend, and that didn't happen until I was about twenty-five. By which time we decided to be non-monogamous and both went out and slept with other women. I'd decided there might be lesbians who didn't mind the fact I had a boyfriend. Well, yes there were, one.

I think if there'd been a discourse of Queer then, that's what I would have been. I might have ended up being lesbian but I would've been able to sleep with women earlier. For me that was this huge emotional and political leap I could not make. I knew lots of nominally straight women – I often talk about people being nominally straight, because they might have been sleeping with men but I knew they weren't only straight – who also felt like that, and there were also lots of women being celibate. The old lesbian law about never get involved with straight women is not based on nothing. I found myself on the receiving end of that and it was as horrible as everyone ever told me. And I was thinking, hang on a minute, I'm the one who believes that sexuality is diverse and don't guilt-trip straight women, and now I'm being positioned as a dumped-on wounded lesbian. It just felt qualitatively different. I think it is to do with power structures in society, and individuals cannot avoid them, only try to redress them.

I have my doubts about Queer. I veer between thinking, it's good in that it means people feel they can have a sexuality that is changing. That's much much healthier. If Queer reactivates the concept of bisexuality to the point where it becomes useable, I think that's really good. I think it's not very thought out positioning, a sort of celebratory 'everything to everyone' liberalism that doesn't really take on race, that doesn't deal with gender. And a lot of real feminist-bashing. It just pisses me off. If feminists made mistakes, it was because we were trying to overturn hundreds of years of oppression and exploitation. Politics is a process: you do things, you find out if they're good or not and you change them. It's not static.

I wonder if Queer is by and large a gay formation, in that it's largely lesbian and gay people who are now exploring sexual diversity, rather than nominally straight people who are. I've seen more women who have been lesbians having relationships with men, than women who have been straight having relationships with women. I don't know how two-way the exchange has been. I'm still thinking about Queer in terms of crossing gender barriers, whereas actually Queer is straight women who assfuck their men with dildos. It is still to do with exploring sexuality, but it's a different matrix. So it is a multi-faceted discourse, and that's what could be very liberating about it. Because once you problematize heterosexuality, then we're on a winner. The other thing that really interests me, is who are the men that lesbians are sleeping with? There's a lot of talk about lesbians and gays fucking each other, and that's Queer, but what about the lesbians who're sleeping with straight men? And what sort of straight men are they?

I started looking different before I actually slept with women; partly it was to do with lesbians, and partly it was to do with moving from Leeds to Brighton. This woman that I shared the house with was always involved in thousands of romances and scandals and traumas, and who she could and couldn't talk to at the disco. We'd be getting ready to go out and she'd say, 'What shall I wear? This, or this?' And I'd say, 'Look, it's a vest.' She'd say, 'But this one's got buttons and ribbing, and this one's got no ribbing but two buttons.' I learnt the intricacies of this detailed dressing, and then I had my hair cut short, which started as an accident.

And I cut my nails. Some lesbians have nails now. This woman in the house used to tease me, and say I'd have to cut my nails, and I used to say, 'I'm not doing it. I can masturbate without cutting myself to shreds so why can't I make love to a woman?' And of course off they came. I suppose when you're not having a relationship you could have a manicure. Grow your nails, it's something to do.

I never looked butch. I sometimes aspire to it, but everyone says I can't walk right. Sometimes I get pissed off because butch is better than being femme, it's more lesbian, and that pisses me off. I remember I reached a point a few years ago, I was shopping with my dad and he said, 'Do you want to go in here?' – some shop that I used to always go into – and I said, 'No, I need grown-up lady clothes now.' When I was in Brighton, I think I looked pretty obviously a lesbian, and since I've got more sophisticated it's harder for people to tell. It would bother me if other lesbians couldn't tell. If straight people can't tell, it doesn't bother me, because I've known straight people work incredibly hard to not think that incredibly lesbian-looking people were lesbian.

I have long talks with my friends about what the small things are that make those differentiations. I think it's a lot to do with how you handle yourself, how you speak and present yourself and the space you take up. I'm not exactly sure. I don't shave my legs, although I do shave my armpits a bit now. I go for designer stubble, I don't like to be completely nude, but I find I get a bit smelly if I don't do it at all, so I just shave it badly. That just stands out as feminist. I used to say it was shoes; whatever I was wearing, if I had a pair of big shoes on then it was all right, but now I wear heels sometimes. I have a lot of problems with postmodernism, but I do think the notion of pleasure's important, and playing with things, so I wear make-up. I'll tell you what I do with wearing make-up though: I don't wear foundation, I wear lipstick and eyeliner and eyebrow pencil and blusher. Women our age wear red lipstick, we haven't gone for this baby pink. We think we're Joan Crawford. Straight women our age do it too. We wear frightening make-up, we're not going for soft and pretty.

I don't think that lesbians never did talk about sex, but I do think they might not talk much about it publicly, and I do think that the SM debate has made women talk about what they do in a different way. But overall, the real problem for me about lesbian SM is it poses as something that is transgressive activity, and the problem with that is the boundaries keep changing. Della Grace takes pictures of women wearing sparkly bras in 1988 – by 1990 we've had Madonna, and it looks like last year's Top Shop.

One of the things that worries me about this whole discourse about SM, is that it has in effect colonized areas of sexual activity and named them as SM. What if I'm lying on top of my lover and holding her hands down and we're play-fighting, is that SM? I don't think that is, but SM [women] would say it is.

There's the sort of maternalistic anxiety that young women will think that this is the only way to talk about sex, and they'll end up doing it when they don't want to.

I do think the notion of consensual violence is really problematic; I defy anyone to put their hands on their heart and tell me they have never engaged in some form of sexual activity that they didn't want to do. You know, you let someone kiss you when you didn't feel like it. If it's SM activity, that just ups the stakes. I don't think talking about power makes it invisible, I really don't. Then you see *Coming to Power*, and the hankerchief coding, and one of them is going down on a menstruating woman. In any case this is pre-AIDS, but this is something feminists spent a long time trying to normalize, and now they're saying it is deviant.

I think that SM is rebelling against an authority that is maternal rather than paternal, and that the enemy for a lot of lesbian SM practitioners is feminism and other women, not patriarchy and men. That's when you get this, feminists don't do sex, feminists don't talk about sex. Then there's the whole Nazi thing – you might want to play with images but they're going to mean different things to different people. It's stupid if you think you can wear a swastika to a Gay Pride march.

Some people like being spanked, some people like being burnt, so? That's just what human sexuality is. It's about see and be seen, going to parties, going to clubs. I suppose I get cross that it sets itself up as the only way to have hot sex. It's available, it's public, it's a consumer durable, it's big business etc., etc., and they're trendy images. To some extent it's also about market forces. We don't have enough lesbian and gay images, they get over-exposed and then we get cross because they're not doing it good or right or new enough, and that's really hard. The problem is to signify an act of sexuality in a way that is not SM. I think that's what people who aren't into SM have to find a way of doing.

At the Fridge last summer, one night there was this sign saying, until 11 p.m. leather only upstairs. A woman who works there said it was because they feel they want their own space. And I was like, but they're not about women as victim, they're not about wanting their own space. That's what they criticized feminists for. I wanted to go to the loo and of course there was a massive queue downstairs, so I marched up the stairs. The woman stopped me, and I said, 'There's all these women here waiting to go to the toilet, they're going to wait until eleven o'clock because the queue's so big. I'm wearing leather shoes, does that count?' I complained to one of the managers, who was brilliant about it. I went to the toilet and of course there was nothing going on upstairs; I was a bit disappointed there was no major thing. I was wearing this outfit, I'm not really sure if it works, but anyway, it was this Edwardian slip thing, white cotton, A-line, I was wearing it like a shift dress with black platform sandals. For all they know I could've been into some coy virgin thing with my majorly butch dyke bike dyke lover. It's like you're only into SM if you look like you're into SM in certain ways.

LINDSAY SMITH RUNS ABOUTTIME PRODUCTIONS, A MUSIC STUDIO. SHE IS THIRTY-SIX.

Being a lesbian in music is fairly rare if you're talking mainstream. When I struck out properly on the music scene, I very much had to rely on these guys that I'd met up with and their expertise. They could get studios and I had no idea where to start. That's how I got involved in it. They offered me a support slot. This was in the punk 1980s when you didn't have to explain yourself so much, you could be and behave how you wanted probably a little more easily than you can now, in terms of sexuality. With the dawning of the 1980s, gay life took off for me in a great sort of way. I think punk had a lot to do with it, and being more political.

All the clothes were very wild, it was OK to kiss a woman in public if you wanted to. I think it was OK because it was an outrageous thing to do, I don't think it was deep down accepted. I think nobody would have batted an eyelid, if you were a dyke onstage being dykish, that was part of it all then, the exciting neo-revolutionary neo-renaissance.

What did happen was that after the first gig I did as support, the people there actually liked my band more than theirs, and we got this interest from a guy who told us to come back next week. And he got Cherry Red [record label] and all those people came down from Rough Trade and Blanco y Negro. I didn't say I was a lesbian – I didn't say I wasn't. I only did four songs; one song had some very direct lyrics about 'she' and 'her', but they liked the music and that was OK. I think money was his main priority. That really inspired me and gave me a lot of energy, but I didn't take it any further because I was in this disastrous relationship at the time. I didn't know any other lesbians in music, and I had a full time radiographic job.

One of the songs I wrote years ago had quite a specific sexual verse in it, and lots of lesbians didn't like what I was singing because they thought it was too upfront sexually. And to that I responded, who else is singing it? You've got all these other songs that are like 'It's a lovely day and I'm so in lurve and my heart is broken,' but no one's actually singing about lesbian sex. It was nothing compared to what you can hear now.

I used to take the songs along to companies and they'd go, 'yeah, yeah, like the songs,' and as soon as they'd sussed what they were actually about I'd never hear anything from them again. So as years went on I directed myself more to the lesbian alternative output. Unashamedly I'd say I'd love to be a superstar, all the fame and the money and all the things that go with it, and being a lesbian too.

What I've really enjoyed in the last years, I think there are more dykes out on the streets, more visible dykes. Confident, young lesbians. TV, and we all watch our programmes whether we like them or not, and I think it's great. And even Radio 1. I don't know if you'll ever see a lesbian band in the top ten, but what self-respecting lesbian band would want to be in the top ten? Because what you have to do to get there, we don't live our lives like that.

You do evolve, you meet more people, and start to shake down your own stuff, you read more. There are more things to see, things to do. I think you tend to gravitate towards people who think similarly, because you enjoy certain activities together, you want to watch *Tales of the City* and *Absolutely Fabulous* together, and you get a supportive network around you. And we have active discussions – my friends don't agree with each other at all.

Being a lesbian is a complete way of life, a way of thinking and being. Lesbianism is political, all-functional. It does mean putting up with a lot of pettiness and working your way through it; it also makes you very sensitized to other people when they encounter sexist issues, racist issues. It's great living an alternative life, I love it. If there are limitations, it's when you want to be in the straight world, say the music scene, then I do find being a dyke a disadvantage.

Lesbianism is a political statement, it has to be. Because you don't settle for the straight politics, you don't believe in the traditional male breadwinner, the woman at home washing up and looking after the kids, and that is what this country's politics is a lot about and I don't believe in that. And I love it when I hear people have abseiled through the House of Commons, I think it's so brave. And chaining yourself to railings, it's so brave. And that's political, and, even though I'm not the one that's chaining myself, I'm very much there in spirit.

You look at the lesbian scene, how wide it is, how deep it is, but we're very untogether as a body of people. I think the more choices and different types of people the better. It's the diversity that's great, but I wish there was more solidarity. What I was always upset about was people like Joan Armatrading when I used to go and see her in concert: she used male musicians. And I used to think, you silly cow, you have such an ability to appoint women musicians. k.d. lang, the same. I do feel that lesbians keep lesbians down.

I'd certainly heard the word lesbian when I was young. I'd met two lesbians in Scotland on holiday, and I was actively discouraged by my parents from spending any time with them. I just thought they were great friends. It didn't ever cross my mind why Jean wore men's pyjamas. I mean, I still think if someone wants to put on men's pyjamas it's because they're more comfortable. In fact they were role-playing. I did go and see them again years afterwards, about five or six years later, so I would've been eighteen or nineteen, and I drove up to Scotland. I went and confessed my own lesbianism, and Jean said she didn't know what I was talking about. I was so upset. She just blanked the whole thing.

I don't really understand role-playing though. I think you should wear what you want and what you feel comfy in, dress up in a suit if you want to go out in drag, if you're going off to the Too Too Glamorous Ball that we went to the other week. There were outfits galore, people dressed as Orlando. I went as Judy Garland, I know you'll find that difficult to believe. At the age of consent do at The Palladium there was no black contingent in any way at all, performers or audience.

A lot of dressing up then. The older dykes were all butch and femme when I used to go to Gateways, when I hit London. I wasn't really an out lesbian to the rest of the world but I was an out lesbian in the lesbian scene. The Gates was the most depressing place, very cliquey, very butch and femme. I would have called myself on the butch side, because I wore jeans and jean jackets and cowboy boots when they came out. I wasn't a role player although I was fairly butch at the time because I copied other people.

I knew in my head that there had to be somewhere to go in London. As luck would have it, the first-year student accommodation was just around the block from Sappho's Chepstow offices, where they used to have a meeting every Tuesday night. Before I could say knife I was down there pacing up and down outside. It was very unfriendly, nobody really spoke. Jackie Forster was fabulous to me and I love her till this day. She was there with a bunch of her friends drinking gin and tonics, and she said, 'Oh darling, you must be for us.' People were very very cliquey. It was social, and, as so often, it did revolve around bars and drinking and that sort of stuff. The only club I knew of then, back in 1975, was the Gates.

There's a lot of abuse and violence in lesbian relationships: it's not exclusive to men and heterosexual relationships. I was beaten up very badly by this woman for a couple of years until I realized, 'Hang on a minute I don't have to do this.' One day she smacked me in the face. Of course, knowing now, I should have just said, end of story. But I didn't quite believe what had happened. Eventually, after threatening solicitors, getting the police around and all the rest of it, I left. I became mortgageable and I bought a flat, as my way to get out of it.

I'm also adopted, and I've met other lesbians and gays who've been adopted, and there is actually quite a thread that runs through us in the rejection lark. We feel rejection, I think, very very strongly, because of that initial rejection, if anyone dumps us ...

9

lust **h**orizons
romantic **f**riendships
to **s**exual **o**utlaws

Loving's better than fucking and it's great to be a dyke.
Popular song from 1970s/80s.

SM Dykes – Fucking Brilliant and Brilliant Fucking.
SM Dykes Leaflet, c. 1985, Hall Carpenter Archive

For I had taken the promise of our liberation seriously, and thought that, with the right attitude, anybody could be perceived as the most desirable in the world – at least for one night.
Don Juan in the Village[1]

Going down on a woman is like looking into the face of God.
Lea De Laria, in performance at the Drill Hall, London, 1993

Sex is part of being a lesbian, but it is certainly not all, or the most important thing, about what being a lesbian is.
Sheila Jeffreys, interviewed by Veronica Groocock, *Gay Times*,
August 1993

The sexual power of the gay male stereotype is not something which lesbians have shared. The sanctions around women's sexuality and social-ization, in western culture, have made sure of that. To the world outside, two women having sex is simultaneously impossible and hugely disgust-ing; or, in the case of straight porn featuring 'lesbian' sex, a massive, unattainable turn-on. Lesbians are considered to be highly sexual, by the general population, only when they are seducing innocent straight women. Otherwise, lesbians and sex is still, in the main, seen as soft and touchy-feely rather than raunchy. But given that, out of the proliferation of lesbian images of the last few years, the ones which have had mainstream coverage have featured belts, buckles and dildos, perhaps this image is changing. Readers of the *Hackney Gazette*[2] have been treated to an almost weekly update on the legality of the women's [sic] sex shop Shhh, which most recently fell foul of some archaic law which means all the dildos have to be laid flat.

'Does it matter if they did it?' asks Sheila Jeffreys (who would herself prefer to see dildos laid entirely to rest), referring to the practice of trying to find out whether suspect women in history were actually sexually active lesbians.[3] It is a question which remains valid, and it is not only applicable to our foresisters. In the mid–1980s, Oval House in south London staged a performance of *Patience and Sarah*, based on the book of the same name, about two American women from the last century who made their home together. Against all the odds, women in the American West, very touching stuff. What would get the same numbers of women to Oval House now: Patience and Sarah mud-wrestle with Vixens in Leather? Sex is in, in a big way, in the 1990s; sex shows, sex toys, sex fiction, sex clubs, escorts, porn mags, prostitutes, are all now ours for the having, should we want them. But it has not always been so.

Strong, devoted friendships between women were probably the most widespread form of behaviour that could be called lesbian until this century. With only the slightest understanding of society's attitudes to women's sexuality and women in general comes a heavy realization of the difficulties around women articulating sexual desires at all, let alone towards each other. There has indeed been a long way to travel.

Popular wisdom – since the 1960s, anyway – insists that all intense love impulses between adults are necessarily sexual. Love between women in a post-sexologist age has become either sexual, potentially sexual or non-existent. Lillian Faderman points out[4] that, after the 1920s, women who loved other women were likely to feel compelled to consider whether there was any sexual motive, and were probably also more likely to find it. (This assumes that they were aware of current received wisdom on the subject, *pace* Freud, Ellis etc.) Although romantic friends had enough scope to be openly affectionate with each other in a way which many modern lesbians never experience, Faderman thinks it unlikely that many of them would have explored the sexual possibilities of their relationships. Whether or not this was so, it is worth pointing out that Faderman does generally take a 'lesser' view in relation to lesbian sex: 'A lesbian is a woman who makes women prime in her life, who gives her energies and her commitment to other women rather than to men.'[5] No mention of sex there. Some of *Surpassing the Love of Men* does sound tame now, as it inevitably would, almost ten years after its publication. Significantly the intervening period has seen the rise and rise of sex – as an issue, a pastime, a representation, as a backlash some would say – among lesbians.

Prior to this century, as Faderman's research shows, romantic friendship was not only acceptable but encouraged. While it was completely taboo to form friendships with other men from outside the family group, other women were a different story. As the century unfolded, changes in women's role in society gradually came about, and, with that, a (slightly) greater understanding and acceptance of women as sexual beings, so the situation changed and such friendships were looked on askance. The norm then swivelled so that other women were viewed as potential rivals. If women still did not or would not see men as sexual partners and love objects, if they clung to the view of themselves as lesbians (women who sought intense, primary, loving relationships with other women), they then had to take on the prevailing view that it was an evil thing. There was little hope for romantic friends to demand changes in the social structure, and therefore no chance for them to share their lives in the same way we understand as lesbian now. However, they certainly shared their romantic, emotional lives and sometimes, perhaps, their sexual ones. Faderman emphasizes that their behaviour and their lives should still be seen as a political act. Though far less overt than later manifestations of lesbianism, there remains a strong sense in which their choices represented a means of escape from some of the demands of femininity and heterosexuality. So in that sense maybe, no, it does not matter if they did it or not.

Noting that Kinsey's findings about the statistical normality of lesbianism were largely ignored in the 1950s and 1960s, Faderman points out how little effect statistics have in improving public opinion, using the example of studies carried out in the 1920s and 1930s which showed lesbian health in a positive light. In both cases, probably because of the contradiction posited to then dominant thinking on the subject, there was no change. Certainly in the 1950s and 1960s, with the slight opening up of attitudes to both women and sex, there were even greater reasons for keeping this kind of information from women. Again, denying lesbianism the oxygen of publicity – or at least denying it any positive press – was in motion, and it is to this that we can partly attribute the fictional, vampiric (unreclaimed variety) representations so prevalent at the time, with their depictions of out of control, predatory, parasitic sex. The attitude to active sexuality was no less ambivalent in lesbian literature, which can never exist in a vacuum from the social mores of the time. One correspondent to Arena3 wrote:

> I agree with Miss EW that a sex manual for 'lesbians' would be a useful asset to one's library, but personally I find natural instinct, love and sensible adaptation of heterosexual books such as 'Sex Manners for Men' or 'Sex and Yoga' really all that is necessary. A sex manual serialised in A3 would only attract the prurient type of reader. Let people find out for themselves. Love will always find a way.[6]

Often in these pages and during this time, active sexuality was viewed in the same light as butch/femme behaviour: 'lower-class' and generally letting the side down.

The massive upheavals in society since the 1950s brought other losses of innocence. There was an articulation of anger, about the inequalities in society, about women's narrow range of choices, which had not been so evident before. The widening of sexual boundaries in the 1960s – the 'rediscovery' of Freud, the perception of a sexual continuum as one that included, among other things, bisexuality – in liberal circles, meant that sex between women was acceptable as a possibility, provided it was not acted on as the only option. For some lesbians from the 1950s, 1960s and 1970s, unlike earlier romantic friends, there came new understanding, through feminist ideas, of the socio-political meaning of their choice. At the same time, though, there came new pressure to abandon the old bar culture, old and 'unsound' ways of relating, and embrace instead lesbian feminist sisterhood, with all its ambivalence about lesbianism. Monog-amy was considered by some to be apeing the mores of heterosexuality, proprietorial, and uncool, although many lesbians found the realities of non-monogamy a tough bullet to bite, politics notwithstanding. For a time in the 1970s and 1980s, being woman-identified meant, for some women, being a lesbian, and there was also the option of being politically a lesbian, neither of which necessarily entailed sexual behaviour.

So again, in some circles, it did not matter if they 'did it', but many lesbians balked at this desexualization and all it implied in terms of respectability and criticism. Sexual sleaze was frowned upon as a male preserve, as was what might be called the animal passion side of sex. Firmly rejecting notions of the 'natural' in relation to heterosexual sex, lesbian feminist attitudes to lesbian sex did fall, to some extent, into the same trap. Angela Carter wrote: 'We may believe we fuck stripped of social artifice. . . . Flesh comes to us out of history; so does the repression and taboo that governs our experience of flesh.'[7]

Looking back, it seems as though the 'sweetness and light' view of lesbian sex, and women in general, was offensively biologistic, and can only have contributed to the diametrical opposition of, on the one hand, uncontrollable male sexuality and, on the other, a soft and receptive female sexuality. The force with which sex has occupied the lesbian *Zeitgeist* can then, in the light of so much pressure to the contrary, start to seem an absolute necessity.

Bisexuality gained in popularity during the 1970s amidst the spacey silver suits and intergalactically heeled boots favoured by bothways-swinging Bowie and Bolan. It then hit a backlash which has never lifted, although Queer, despite its different perspective, may shift this. Faderman forecasts that, 'Women will be less and less scared off by the idea of same-sex love without examining what it entails beyond "sexual abnormality". The notion of lesbianism will be neutralized.'[12] And perhaps lesbian chic and Queer are making small steps towards this, although 'neutralizing' lesbianism may be precisely what is criticized by lesbians about both those concepts, and exactly what the Lesbian Avengers exist to counter.

Straight people are often disbelieving when told about the famous who are lesbian or gay. Even more so when faced with information about the number of so-called heterosexuals who have sex with their own gender. It may be that this also works the other way and has always done so. It is impossible to quantify any real figures of what percentage of the population is lesbian or gay or straight or anything else: there are too many reasons to lie, or at least not tell the whole truth. The interviews for this book had no pretensions towards being scientific in this way. As a sample, they were far too few to constitute anything revealing (not that this stops 'research' being published about, for instance, the gay gene theory).

But it is plain – from these interviews, from taped material at the Hall Carpenter Archive, from the interviews in *Inventing Ourselves* (which came out of the Archive's Lesbian Oral History group), and from everyday lesbian folklore – that lesbians have sex with men for all sorts of reasons. These include: the lesbian who is just having a heterosexual relationship at the moment, or who has had them previously; who falls in love with a man; who wants to get pregnant; who wants to 'keep her hand in' (as one interviewee put it), or to see whether she has missed anything; who wants to keep the family happy; who is tired of looking for girlfriends or female sexual partners.

The social and political death which could follow lesbians admitting even to thinking about sex with men during the 1970s and 1980s does not mean it was not happening. The sanctions and the fear probably stopped it being as widespread as it might have been, because the traumas which occurred when it did come out in the open are well known.

Now the cultural latitude is changing: it may be seen as an exciting option, healthy in terms of opening out sexual options, for lesbians to have sex with men, especially gay men: at the cutting edge of Queer politics. But even this idea of radical gay relationships is not a new one: again, there are several women interviewed by the Hall Carpenter Archive who had sex with gay men. Some of this may have been looking for cover, seeing if they could do it, experimenting; but if straight cover is what you are after, relationships with gay men seem an odd choice. The politics around mixed gay relationships in the 1990s are informed by the experiences and desires of their proponents, as well as having the function of 'giving leave' to people to seek such experiences and articulate these desires. These politics may take some time to filter through into how people actually behave, while others who had previously kept quiet about doing it may start talking about it.

Since the 1970s then, lesbianism has been desexed – in theory if not in practice – by some branches of feminism, and subsequently resexed. Among feminism's many shortcomings, as well as the sin that it allowed women who had never had and had no intention of having sex with women to call themselves lesbian, it was also guilty of, at the other end of the spectrum, ex-communicating women who sexed up lesbianism, bar dykes and SM dykes. The rewriting of history which has taken place in terms of dykes acting as though they never had anything to do with feminism – too cool and sex-positive to have ever been interested in it – can only be compared with women who used to rewrite their sexual histories to edit out as much heterosexuality, and certainly any enjoyment of it, as possible.

The stone butch gave but did not take sex; the political lesbian did not necessarily do either, but both were still lesbians. And while both stone butches and political lesbians are talked about as though they existed only in the 1950s and 1970s/80s respectively, that is not true, any more than the contemporary ascendant images of lesbian sex bitches and daddy dykes represent what everyone is now aspiring to or doing. Witches, marriage resisters, passionate friends can all be considered part of lesbian history, but for most lesbians in the late twentieth century, doing it does indeed matter, even (or perhaps especially) in fallow periods or times of recovery. Having sex with women means you are doing lesbian business, whether or not you decide to be A Lesbian (although not calling yourself a lesbian does not amount to anything when the homophobic chips are down). Talking about practices rather than identities, adverbs instead of nouns, in terms of lesbian definitions, can only be useful within particular contexts of time: we already know how modern is the current construct of The Lesbian. Which is not to say that women did not fuck before the twentieth century; Anne Lister, Regency Yorkshirewoman, is widely known about, and there must have been more like her, poorer and without publishable diaries.

'It seems to us that selfless love is more possible between two women than a man and a woman because sex doesn't play such a big part,'[9] said Joan and Liz in the *Sunday Times*, which was probably very comforting to its readers when it appeared in 1970. Leaving aside the questions about whether selfless love is what we want, and whether sex necessarily gets in the way, Joan and Liz may, like many other women, and many other lesbians, not be that interested in sex. Or they may just not get off on each other, or they may be in the throes of lesbian sex death, a phrase coined to describe lesbians in long-term relationships who have reached a point of boredom and lost excitement about their sex life. Faderman is doubtful that many lesbians, in an age where sexual activity is seen as basically healthy, would have no sexual life, but stresses the importance of other kinds of sexual behaviour in lesbians' lives – 'The exchanges of support in day-to-day life.'[10] Again, some people attribute what is often seen as a preference for affection and support (which in turn is viewed as leading inexorably to lesbian sex death) to the ways in which women are socialized.

The attraction of the actively sexual nature of the gay male stereotype has led to many a lesbian lamenting that we do not have the same attitudes to sex as gay men. Everybody knows the joke: What does a lesbian take on her second date? Answer: A removal van. Cosy old dykes, setting up home together and being affectionate and supportive. The two dykes in EastEnders quickly moved into a bedsit together – finding somewhere to have sex, yes (not that we will ever see that on TV), but also talking about bedspreads and putting up shelves. You cannot help wondering whether the researchers knew how accurate they were being. But some lesbians want to cruise instead of, or as well as, joint DIY, and to have anonymous sex; some wish they could go to Hampstead Heath like the boys can, although the safety angle often puts paid to that particular idea. Having said this, even a singles night at a club in north London,

Circle of One, did not last (although there could be economic reasons for this) and was reputedly full of couples.

Camille Paglia, always on hand to make an unhelpful comment, also calls lesbianism more of an emotional connection than a sexual one.[11] This claim could be based on her own experience, given her much-publicized complaint about there being no hot babes around. Confusingly, in the same programme she put forward this concept: sexually, women have a whole body response, rather than the purely genital [i.e. greater sensuality] because of their thinner skin. (I would be interested to see the physiological evidence for that.) Paglia says it is this which accounts for the obsession of male artists with producing lesbian images in their work. I would attribute it to plain old prurient jealousy.

The dominant voice now, Camille Paglia aside, is the one which was once the outlaw: the sexualized is in its ascendancy. But you cannot occupy both those spaces – dominant and outlaw – at once. The gender-fucking, man-fucking, fantasy-enacting bad girls are probably not in the majority but are occupying the cultural space, noisily. Not everybody is happy with this turn of events: 'Totally ruled by a fantastic belief in sex as the consuming passion of gays' existence, the gay press presents images of lesbians as crass as anything found in the tabloids,' says Jane Solanas.[12] And what of the rest, who remain sure about their lesbianism, who see no appeal in the public parade of their fantasies, who are left cold by the idea of blindfolds, restraints and dildos, who remain sure that lesbianism does not include sex with men, ever, at all, who want to have sex in bed with their clothes off – why should dykes be made to feel bad about that? Being an outlaw, in an age of mass communication, is no longer a lifelong stance, because outlaws are co-opted. Punk outfits on sale at Chelsea Girl, sashimi at M & S, country music and football on the *Late Show*, it is all grist to the mill of mainstream in the end. Nothing is eternally shocking any more. But, although the spotlight moves quickly on to the next outrage, each has its own impact and influence. Lesbianism is no longer transgressive in many quarters, although real live dykes may be. Exposure to anything for long enough makes the wild seem familiar, if still disagreeable or unpleasant.

All this has given rise to what some lesbians have objected to as an SM co-option of sex – a reaction to the climate, or perhaps self-publicity, which seems to be saying SM dykes are the only people who have sex at all. This is as ridiculous as saying that 'the feminists' stopped people having sex, but certainly sex was not foregrounded or visible in the way it now is. The SM ethos shouts about its own self-definition, its self-constructed pleasure – there is no wish to make a pretence of the 'natural'; quite the opposite, you have to work for it, dress up for it, devise for it. There have been many jokes about anti-SM dykes' sex lives, along the lines of non-hierarchical sex, holding hands and kissing with closed lips. The likelihood is that during the 1970s and early 1980s most women probably continued whatever they wanted to do, and may have felt guilty, but kept quiet about it. Among interviewees there were women who had been criticized or ostracized for their sexual behaviour, for being 'too much like men', and there were those who, although not interested in SM, or actually opposed to it, could see that there were some benefits from the conflicts around it, and that it had at least put sex on the agenda.

This movement in attitudes to and practices around sex has been mirrored culturally: sex is big in lesbian leisure in other ways. Now lesbians are allowed to have fixations on stars, like everyone else, and indulge in sex fantasies with the unattainable (and act them out), and we have seen posters of Madonna, k.d. fanciers' fanzines and a convention; habits which can be aired in public, in common with the rest of the world. No one would have shouted 'get yer kit off' to Cris Williamson, as they do to k.d. lang – and it was not because no one felt like it. That wholesome attitude, the non-objectification of performers or women in general, and the insistence that stars had no place in lesbian feminism, whether singers or politicos (which was never true), lies dead and buried under the weight of star-struck lesbians' poster collections.

We also had *Quim*, an independent magazine which published a high proportion of the sexual images of dykes in the UK, with a consistently high proportion of photography and illustrations to text. *Quim* wanted to keep on being outlaws. In issue 5, the editors stated:

> We want out of trendy, fashion, tabloid, images of lesbianism. Quim is about the real badgirls, beautiful outlaws of society....We are out to get their money, undermine their power, create a more caring world and fucking PARTY![13]

Anarchistic, libertarian and nothing if not ambitious, *Quim* 5, with its twin focuses on black women and fat women, continued the usual format of using lots of quotes from questionnaires, rather than concentrating on features or reports, and a vast number of contributors rather than a few of the usual journos pumping out material. Despite *Quim's* rejection of the assimilation of lesbian chic, in some ways it benefited from this: where *Quim* used to be under the counter it was later available in major bookshops, like Waterstones and Dillons. When it worked, it was a great formula; at other times it seemed as though the same answers kept coming from the questionnaires, no matter what the subject.

In film and video, we are starting to see lesbian sex on-screen, outside straight porn films, and although there is not yet enough choice, the *Well Sexy Women*, *Lesbian Lycra Shorts* and *Leather Shorts* videos constitute a beginning. The explosion in the magazine market has also played a part. The first issue of Diva offered a book club service. These are some of the titles listed: *Bad Habits* (about a dominatrix setting up a slave school); *Getting Wet*, tales of lesbian seduction; *Provincetown Summer*, 'whitehot desire between women'; *Leather Women*; *Private Lessons* – cruel headmistress ... most talented and delicious of maidens'; *Afterglow*; *Bushfire*. The Lesbian Herstory Archives in New York have a large collection of what they call survival literature, pre-gay liberation, which often features in coming-out stories: 'I found this book and knew I wasn't the only one.' These books used to be frowned upon because of their un-uplifting nature and suppos-edly pre-feminist scenarios, the butch/femme relationships and the unreconstructed attitudes to sex, compared with the classic texts which came forth from various women's presses. They were always a good read, and after all, this is our history. Titles like *Queer Affair* and *Women's Barracks* and *Whisper Their Love* give some idea of the subject matter.

These books often featured a young woman realizing her true nature, who runs away from a small town in middle America or beyond, to the urban jungle to meet her future, and she is lesbian. The future is met at a local incredibly seedy bar where she is not sure they are all women. She gets dumped and heartbroken, but if she does not meet true love by the end of the book, she has at least uncovered her true lesbian self. Unlike Patience and Sarah, who love and cuddle, sex is definitely featured, but it often ends in tears, as women having sex, of any sort, so often does.

From this to hot, wet and bad girls in less than forty years; if history is cyclical, will we be going underground again, producing more survival literature, and if so, how soon? Whether the output actually reflects what women want, rather than more peer group pressure, is another matter. There have been criticisms that the new sexual writing endlessly churns out a dreary, unimaginative 'she got wet, I got hot, and then I fucked her' scenario. Again, as more sexual writing is published, there will be more room for different outlooks, experimental writing and more or less experi-mental sex. In the introduction to *More Serious Pleasure*, the Sheba Collective note the development from work published in its precursor, *Serious Pleasure*:

Not only did lesbian writers want to write about sex, this time round they seemed eager and able to develop sustained story lines and interesting plots ... As we said in our introduction to Serious Pleasure, 'We do not expect every lesbian to like, approve of, or be driven to having sex by every story in this book.'[14]

Sarah Schulman, Pat Califia, Jane De Lynn and contributors to the High Risk books[15] have been among those who have written about lesbian sex in a cynical way. And although sometimes slightly disturbing, there is certainly an appeal to it, perhaps because of their capacity to talk about selfish sex, bad sex, uninterested and uninteresting sex, to give voice to the underbelly and also debunk the ascendant. From Sarah Schulman:

'Dolores was a cunt,' I said. 'Sex with her made me sick. She always did the same thing. Whenever she wanted it, she'd pull her shirt up and bounce around, shoving her tits in my face.'[16]

And from Jane De Lynn:

Nor was our sex particularly good. She accused me of being too passive. I didn't like her enough to touch her very much, and I guess in some way I felt that my supplying the room should in some sense compensate for my lack of activity in bed. It disturbed me a little to be thinking the way men do, but perhaps not enough.[17]

And on visiting a sex club:

The women were incredibly unattractive, overweight or unduly skinny, with pale unhealthy-looking skin – unless this was due to the lighting, which seemed designed to make everyone look like heroin addicts.... The conventionality of style and fantasy with which people into this form of sex expressed their violations of convention has always been astonishing to me.[18]

Given all of this, it is not surprising that the role of representation in forming and expressing lesbian sexual identity is being constantly discussed and reworked. Since the growth of what might loosely be called the SM canon of (largely photographic) images, this has taken precedence.

Reina Lewis examines the role of representation in forming and expressing sexual identity as one strand in her exploration of 'the changing
boundaries of internal (lesbian and gay) and external censorship' in her
essay[19] focusing on the photographic work of Della Grace, one of the best-
known lesbian photographers in the UK, who made her name through her
work on lesbian SM, although she has now moved into other fields.

The pictures which Lewis examines are about sex, but also about a
particular community and photographic representations of its practice of
sex, and so her piece casts useful light on the current scene. She sees the
response from lesbians to Della Grace's work as indicative both of the
hype around it and the continuing lack of lesbian images. *Love Bites* (the
1991 book of Grace's work, around which much of the essay is based) she
sees as 'literally re-enacting the SM dyke's favoured persona as social
outcast by being refused entry to two London feminist bookstores'. Later
work, 'Lesbian Boys', featuring 'crossdressed', androgynous lesbian
models, 'foregrounds a homoerotic reading and a Queer, rather than
lesbian or gay, identity'.

A common response to and confusion about this work, and one which is
fostered somewhat through the photographer's comments on her work, is
whether the photographs are 'authentic' or "merely" fantasy', i.e. whether
they were taken at a party or of an actual sexual encounter (documentary
of the community), or whether they were 'set up'. This blurring of the
actual and fantasy, of the 'real' and the 'unconscious', has long caused
confusion amongst anti-SM feminists and feminist-challenging SMers
alike. Lewis also brings up questions of production, which are an important consideration within such representations: Were the models paid?
Was it consensual and does that therefore mean non-exploitative? Feminism always had a troubled relationship with the sex industry and women
who worked in it, at best patronizing. For a brief moment in the late 1980s
'women who worked in the sex industry' were the vanguard, and now that
there is something of a lesbian sex industry, there is still a good deal of
ambivalence about it. The usual opinions line up in their old positions:
from the unequivocal 'this is good, exciting and radical', through the idea
that some of it could be good, 'but I don't like this and I'm worried it might
be exploitative', to 'this is offensive full stop'.

As lesbians reel under a new tyranny of fantasy enactment, pro-
censorship feminists militate against the foregrounding of sex and the
reification of fantasy in sex-play. SM dykes themselves continue to site
their position in opposition to feminism. Lewis rightly posits the question
of how far this can continue: 'The culture industry recycles images and

moods too fast for anything transgressive to be assured of its status'.[20] Strippers and go-go dancers at Eve's Revenge who first appeared in the 1980s, once shockingly innovative, are now *de rigeur*, no longer news in a world that has since seen Chain Reaction, Sadie Maisie, and the Clit Club.

Faderman believes that few lesbians were interested in exploring an SM sexuality that was so removed from their socialization, and that AIDS put people off exploration. Again, I think her prediction, coming from a book published in 1985 and so probably written two years previously, is out of touch. This is not to say that hordes of dykes are doing so, but the influence on the debate and the climate of sexualization that exist are in many ways more important and persuasive than numbers.

Safe sex continues to be discussed among lesbians, be written about, have videos and photographs made about it, but actual practice is more difficult to assess, although it has become easier during the last few years to get hold of dental dams and gloves and lube and other necessary accoutrements. London now boasts two lesbian health clinics, east and west, whose existence must be partly due to increased awareness of the importance of sexual health. Safe sex is touted as hot sex – one of the benefits from the discussions around SM has been the introduction of safe sex as a topic – but on a more everyday level there remains little certainty about what is or what is not safe, or even if that is the issue. (And similarly with SM, especially among those who do not do it, there is confusion about what it actually is: 'I'd define SM as anything from keeping your eyes open whilst making love to biting and scratching to bondage and whipping.'[21]

This apparently follows through into some of the sex writing which has been published: 'We are still interested in reading more lesbian safer sex stories and exploring the reasons, if any, why safer sex is not reflected more in the fiction lesbians write'[22] (*More Serious Pleasure*). In Jane De Lynn's writing though, safe sex is a given, if not entirely welcome:

> She got up, went over to her jacket to get something out, came back. With my eyes shut I waited for her finger, or maybe even a tongue (in those days before the Plague), but I felt something hard and unfleshy feeling press against me.[23]

The concurrent debate about virus envy – that lesbians are jealous of the attention that gay men are getting and so muscling in on an area that really has nothing to do with them – is viewed as hugely insulting by many dykes, not least those who have chosen to put their political energy into AIDS work. Sister George weigh in with a song about it:

So you think that dykes don't fuck??
Low risk = no risk: Burn your gloves?
Lesbo love is safe you think
Dental dams are just for kink!
Virus Envy Virus Envy
What do you think we do in bed?!
Dykes get sick just in our heads!!
Girl to Girl HIV transmission
is going to go on happening if we give it permission[24]

Another group of women for whom lesbian sex is attractive by virtue of its comparative 'safety' on several levels is apparently a section of *Harpers and Queen* readership. 'Their femininity is far from threatened by experiments in lesbianism; in fact, it's probably enhanced by it. Having sex with a boy without a condom is a far worse crime. And it feels safe.'[25] These are basically straight women – or dabblers or weekend lesbians, depending on how you look at it – who, concerned about HIV transmission and, conceivably, heterosexual virginity, invest in future titillation for *outré* dinner party stories and their boyfriends, by having sex with women. Lesbian chic does indeed have many downsides.

It cannot be coincidental that lesbians get to occupy the sexual stage in such a big way when the rest of the population are supposedly drawing back from it, scared of AIDS and confused about their roles. Perhaps we are headed for an explosion of lesbian sexual decadence and indulgence, similar to that in Berlin in the 1930s, to mark the end of the twentieth century and to keep the bed warm when no one else is interested or available. Will we go full circle to a post-sexualized lesbianism in another thirty or forty years? Or where else? Where else is there to go? The question, 'Does it matter if they do it?', now focuses in the other direction: towards lesbians who do it with men. For some women that means choosing to have sex with men if they want to, if the occasion and the right man arises, without confusion to their lesbian identity; or it can mean radical gay sexuality, as it has come to be known – dykes and gay men having sex together and making a politics out of their practice. So perhaps the answer has now become, yes, it is important that you do it, and how you do it, but, for some of us anyway, not with whom.

NOTES

1. Jane De Lynn, *Don Juan in the Village*, Serpent's Tail, 1990, p. 237.
2. See the *Hackney Gazette*, various issues, summer 1994.
3. Sheila Jeffreys, *The Spinster and Her Enemies: Feminism and Sexuality 1880–1930*, Pandora, 1985, p. 109.
4. Lillian Faderman, *Surpassing the Love of Men*, The Women's Press, 1985, p. 298.
5. *Ibid*. p. 380.
6. *Arena3*, vol. 17, no. 3, March 1970.
7. Angela Carter, quoted in Ros Coward, *Female Desire*, Paladin, 1984, p. 156.
8. Lillian Faderman, *Surpassing the Love of Men*, p. 414.
9. 'Me and my mate', *Sunday Times*, 25 January 1970.
10. Lillian Faderman, *Surpassing the Love of Men*.
11. *Without Walls*, Channel 4, 3 May 1994.
12. Jane Solanas, *Shebang*, no. 4, Pride 1993.
13. *Quim*, no. 5, 1994.
14. The Sheba Collective (ed), *More Serious Pleasure*, Sheba, 1990.
15. Amy Scholder and Iva Silverberg (eds), *High Risk* and *High Risk* 2, Serpent's Tail, 1991 and 1994.
16. Sarah Schulman, *After Dolores*, Sheba, 1988, p. 116.
17. Jane De Lynn, *Don Juan in the Village*, p. 63.
18. *Ibid.*, p. 143.
19. Reina Lewis, 'Dis-graceful images: Della Grace and lesbian sado-masochism', in 'Sexualities Challenge and Change', *Feminist Review*, no. 46, Spring 1994.
20. *Ibid*.
21. *Lesbian and Gay Youth Magazine*, issue 20, January 1987.
22. Introduction, *More Serious Pleasure*.
23. Jane De Lynn, *Don Juan in the Village*, p. 230.
24. Sister George, 'Virus Envy', Catcall Records.
25. *Harpers and Queen*, June 1994.

*a*ppendix

Questions for interviews

Do you want to remain anonymous or use a pseudonym in print?
Name?

Age?

What do you think it means to be a lesbian?

What does being a lesbian meant to you?

Has this been the same as long as you have seen yourself as a lesbian?

If not, how has it changed, and why do you think this is?

Do you think your attitudes about your lesbianism are shared with other lesbians, friends, or particular groups (social or political perhaps) of lesbians?

What influence does your lesbianism have on your life?

Does it have any influence on: How you look? Where you go? Where you work? What you wear? What you like doing?

Are you on the scene? What does this mean to you?

Does your lesbianism have any political meaning for you?

Do you see yourself as part of a particular group of lesbians? What does this mean to you?

Do you ever change your behaviour for particular situations? When and why?

Which names do you use to describe your lesbianism: lesbian, dyke, queer, gay, homosexual etc?

*b*ibliography

Sidney Abbott and Barbara Love, *Sappho Was a Right on Woman*. New York, Stein & Day, 1972.

Evelyn Torton Beck (ed.), *Nice Jewish Girls: A Lesbian Anthology*. Watertown, NY, Persephone Press, 1982.

Tessa Boffin and Jean Fraser (eds), *Stolen Glances: Lesbians Take Photographs*. London, Pandora, 1991.

Brighton Ourstory Project, *Daring Hearts*. Brighton, 1992.

Belinda Budge and Diane Hamer (eds), *The Good, the Bad and the Gorgeous*. London, Pandora, 1994.

Judith Butler, *Gender Trouble: Feminism and the Subversion of Identity*. London, Routledge, 1990.

Pat Califia, *Sapphistry: The Book of Lesbian Sexuality*. Tallahassee, Naiad Press, 1980.

Pat Califia, *Macho Sluts*. Boston: Allyson 1988.

Bob Cant and Susan Hemmings (eds), *Radical Records: Thirty Years of Lesbian and Gay History*. London, Routledge, 1988.

Sue Cartledge and Joanna Ryan, *Sex and Love*. London, The Women's Press, 1983.

Ros Coward, (ed.),*Female Desire*. London, Paladin, 1984.

Jane De Lynn, *Don Juan in the Village*. London, Serpents Tail, 1990.

Havelock Ellis, *Studies in the Psychology of Sex*. Philadelphia, F.A. Davis, 1924.

Lillian Faderman, *Surpassing the Love of Men*. London, The Women's Press, 1985.

Lillian Faderman, *Odd Girls and Twilight Lovers*. Harmondsworth, Penguin, 1992.

Susan Faludi, *Backlash*. London, Vintage, 1992.

Feminist Review: Sexuality, no. 11, Summer 1982; Many Voices: One Chant, Black Feminist Perspectives, no. 17, Autumn 1984; Perverse Politics: Lesbian Issues, no. 34, Spring 1990.

Sigmund Freud, *The Complete Psychological Works*. London, The Hogarth Press, 1957.

Gay Left Collective (ed.), *Homosexuality: Power and Politics*. London, Allison & Busby, 1980.

GLC/GLC Gay Working Party, *Changing the World: A London Charter for Gay and Lesbian Rights*, n.d.

GLC Women's Committee, *Tackling Heterosexism: A Handbook of Lesbian Rights*, n.d.

GLC *Women's Committee Bulletin*, Special Lesbian Issue, Issue 17, June 1984.

Shabnam Grewal *et al.* (eds), *Charting the Journey: Writings by Black and Third World Women*. London, Sheba, 1988.

Gabriele Griffin, *Outwrite: Lesbianism and Popular Culture*. London, Pluto Press, 1993.

Gabriele Griffin (ed.), *Heavenly Love? Lesbian Images in Twentieth Century Women's Writing*. Manchester, Manchester University Press, 1993.

Hall Carpenter Archive, *Inventing Ourselves*. London, Routledge, 1989.

Susan Hemmings, A *Wealth of Experience*. London, Pandora, 1985.

Shere Hite, *Women as Revolutionary Agents of Change*. London, Bloomsbury Books, 1993.

Sheila Jeffries, *The Spinster and Her Enemies*. London, Pandora, 1985.

Jill Johnston, *Lesbian Nation*. New York, Simon & Schuster, 1973.

Kinsey *et al.*, *Sexual Behaviour in the Human Female*. New York, Pocket Books, 1965.

Richard von Krafft-Ebing, *Psychopathia Sexualis*. New York, G.P. Putnam, 1965.

Leeds Radicalesbians. *Love Your Enemy? The Debate between Heterosexual Feminism and Political Lesbianism*. London, Onlywomen, 1981.

Reina Lewis, 'Dis-graceful images', *Feminist Review*, no. 46, Spring 1994.

London Strategic Policy Unit, *Lesbian and Gay Issues: Policy*

Development and Legislation 1967–1987, Briefing for the 20th Anniversary of Homosexual Law Reform. London, LSPU, 1988.

Valerie Mason-John and Ann Khambatta, *Lesbians Talk . . . Making Black Waves*. London, Scarlet Press, 1993.

Jean Baker Miller, *Psychoanalysis and Women*. Harmondsworth, Penguin, 1973.

Juliet Mitchell, *Psychoanalysis and Feminism*. Harmondsworth, Penguin, 1975.

Cherie Moraga and Gloria Anzaldua, *This Bridge Called My Back*. New York, Kitchen Table Press, 1984.

Sally Munt (ed.), *New Lesbian Criticism*. Hemel Hempstead, Harvester Wheatsheaf, 1992.

National Lesbian and Gay Survey, *What a Lesbian Looks Like*. London, Routledge, 1992.

Suzanne Neild and Rosalind Pearson, *Women Like Us*. London, The Women's Press, 1992.

Joan Nestle, *A Restricted Country*. London, Sheba, 1987.

Sue O'Sullivan and Pratibah Parmar, *Lesbians Talk . . . (Safer) Sex*. London, Scarlet Press, 1992.

Tony Parker, *May the Lord in His Mercy Be Kind to Belfast*. London, Jonathon Cape, 1993.

Barbara Ponse, *Identities in the Lesbian World: the Social Construction of Self*. London, Greenwood, 1978.

Susannah Radstone (ed.), *Sweet Dreams: Sexuality, Gender and Popular Fiction*. London, Lawrence & Wishart, 1988.

Jonathon Rutherford (ed.), *Identity: Community, Culture, Difference*. London, Lawrence & Wishart, 1990.

Jane Rule, *Lesbian Images*. New York, Crossing Press, 1975.

Vito Russo, *The Celluloid Closet*. New York, Harper and Row, 1981.

Simon Schama, *Dead Certainties*. London, Granta, 1991.

Sarah Schulman, *After Dolores*. London, Sheba, 1988.

Sheba Collective (ed.), *Serious Pleasure*. London, Sheba, 1989.

Sheba Collective (ed.), *More Serious Pleasure*. London, Sheba, 1990.

Cherry Smyth, *Lesbians Talk . . . Queer Notions*. London, Scarlet Press, 1992.

Diana Souhami, *Gertrude and Alice*. London, Pandora, 1991.

E. Spelman, *Inessential Woman: Problems of Exclusion in Feminist Thought*. London, The Women's Press, 1988.

Carolyn Steedman, *Past Tenses: Essays on Writing, Autobiography and History*. London, Rivers Oram Press, 1992.

Arlene Stein (ed.), *Sisters, Sexperts, Queers: Beyond the Lesbian Nation*. New York, Plume, 1993.

Jeffrey Weeks, *Coming Out*. London, Quartet, 1977.

Julie Wheelwright, *Amazons and Military Maids: Women Who Dressed as Men in Pursuit of Life, Liberty and Happiness*. London, Pandora, 1989.

Val Wilmer, *Mama Said There'd Be Days Like This*. London, The Women's Press, 1989.

Elizabeth Wilson, *Adorned in Dreams: Fashion and Modernity*. London, Virago, 1985.

Elizabeth Wilson, *Hallucinations: Life in the Post Modern City*. London, Radius, 1989.

Elizabeth Wilson, *The Lost Time Café*. London, Virago, 1993.

Monique Wittig and Sande Zeig, *Lesbian Peoples: Materials for a Dictionary*. London, Virago, 1980.

Charlotte Wolff, *Love Between Women*. London, Duckworth, 1971.

index